Navigating School Board Politics

SERIES | RACE AND EDUCATION

Series edited by H. Richard Milner IV

OTHER BOOKS IN THIS SERIES

Navigating School Board Politics

A Framework for Advancing Equity

CARRIE R. SAMPSON

Harvard Education Press
Cambridge, Massachusetts

Paperback ISBN 9781682539378

Library of Congress Cataloging-in-Publication Data is on file.

Published by Harvard Education Press,
an imprint of the Harvard Education Publishing Group

Harvard Education Press
8 Story Street
Cambridge, MA 02138

Cover Design: Endpaper Studio
Cover Image: David McNew via Getty Images

The typefaces in this book are Carrara and Gotham.

CONTENTS

FOREWORD

A FEW YEARS AGO, I observed heated, uncivil, and dangerous interactions between community members and school board members at meetings in response to masking policies for young people in schools. Indeed, parents, families, and community members have strong views about what policies should and should not be advanced in the interests of young people. Debates and criticisms of school board members are pervasive, and some have even threated the lives and health of school board members when views collide over issues such as race, gender, and sexual preference.[1] School board meetings have been described as "ground zero of the nation's political and cultural debates."[2] School board members have always played an important role in educational matters; however, increasingly as polarizing political views amplify, the role, salience, and importance of school board members must be studied as an essential element of public education in the United States. Indeed, although the work and people of school boards have always been important to public schools and education, a major "difference is that many of these debates now appear to be increasingly common, increasingly political, and less clearly centered on the specific needs of students."[3]

Carrie Sampson has produced an important book about navigational processes and politics of school boards. With equity placed front and center, this book showcases an understudied area during a time when we need to know more about the work of school boards in an increasingly changing democracy. Drawing on her years of experience and research as well as extant literature, Sampson has written an important book that powerfully addresses the intersections of school boards, school board members, politics, equity, and possibility. Too rarely do we (those inside and outside of education) hear and learn from perspectives of school board members themselves—many of whom are committed to eradicating and reversing inequities and harm. Sampson has rehumanized what it means to be a school board member and how broader contexts shape their work and espoused commitments to improve schooling and educational experiences for all—including families, educators, and especially young people.

Sampson guides readers through a scholarly journey about aspects of school board policies related to important issues such as governance and educational equity. Indeed, as research, policy, and practice communities, we need frameworks to better capture the work of school boards, and Sampson is to be applauded for her essential efforts. Moreover, the vivid cases she explores—from Tucson to Clark County to Salt Lake City—shed light on complex and nuanced issues that deserve continued study in pursuit of equitable policies and practices. In short, through illustrative, compelling, and complex stories, Sampson guides readers through what it takes (and should involve) for school boards and others to develop robust and meaningful opportunities for young people often placed on the margins. In my view, this book offers an important heuristic—a framework—to advance justice in school board politics, which can make a real difference in education. Our young people, our educators, our field, our families, our communities, and our politicians need this book. Bravo to Carrie Sampson!

H. Richard Milner IV
Cornelius Vanderbilt Professor of Education
Vanderbilt University

PREFACE

WHEN I WAS a high school student, I knew nothing about school boards, including the one in the school district I grew up in. I was among only 30 percent of my senior class to graduate from what was considered one of the lowest performing high schools in Las Vegas, Nevada. Nearly all of us students were low income, and over 90 percent of us identified as Black or Latinx. Many of our parents worked in casinos and other service industry jobs, surviving paycheck to paycheck.

My father, a Black man with a college degree that turned out to be not very useful to him because he was also an ex-felon, worked in construction. During the construction boom of the late 1990s, this unionized work moved us from our trailer park home in a small town in Arizona to an apartment complex in an urban area in Las Vegas. My mother, a Mexican American woman, was the first in her family to graduate from high school. She worked in factories, retail, child care, and later as a receptionist for the Culinary Union.

My schooling experience varied. I had some great teachers and some not-so-great teachers. Starting in tenth grade and throughout the remaining years of high school, I worked almost forty hours a week to help my family pay bills and save for college. I was suspended in high school for violating the dress code because my shorts were above my fingertips and deemed "too short"—an absurd rule, especially when you live in the desert. Many of my friends were pushed out of high school because they violated these types of rules. Some did not receive a high school diploma after becoming teen parents, while others only received a "certificate of attendance" because they did not pass the high school proficiency exam.

The stakes were high. The struggle was real. And while education became a way out of poverty for me, that was not the case for many around me.

I was lucky to have access to critical educational opportunities. I was not part of any special program, such as honors, gifted and talented, or Advanced Placement courses. However, I did complete an application that my science teacher handed me and other students about participating in a program for minority students interested in medical school. I got accepted. This affirmative action program paid for about fifty high school minority students to travel to University of Nevada, Reno that summer to learn about medical school. For a week, we stayed in the dorms, ate in the dining hall, and experienced what a college campus was like for the first time. I never went to medical school, but that opportunity paved the way for me to leave Las Vegas and start my college career away from the difficulties that were embedded in my community. By the time I returned home to Las Vegas after earning a master's degree at Syracuse University, I was able to support my parents, who were struggling both financially and with their health.

Throughout my time in high school, I did not know how my school board affected my educational experience. All I knew was that, while my schooling experience did not sufficiently prepare me for college, I used the navigational skills that I learned through my struggles and successes in my personal family life to earn my college degree. I do recall a sophisticated-looking Latino school board member handing me a scholarship check at an event before I left for college. Nearly twenty years later, I interviewed him for my dissertation research. That scholarship check, along with all the other financial support and educational opportunities I received, helped me to get through college successfully.

I mentioned these few personal experiences because I understand the struggle that many of our most vulnerable students are going through. Educational opportunities through targeted policies, practices, resources, and services can make a powerful difference in the life trajectories of not only our students, but also their families and communities. They made a difference in my life.

When I began researching school desegregation in Las Vegas with my research advisor, I learned that an all-white school board in the 1970s approved a plan that imposed most of the burden of busing to desegregate schools on Black families. The plan was in place for twenty years until Black mothers pushed the district to change it. From this, I learned three significant facts. First, I learned how powerful the school board was. Second, I learned how the school board was not reflective or responsive of *all* the communities they were serving. Third, I learned that local community involvement and advocacy can successfully push the school board to change their policies. This led me to wonder: (1) Would this busing plan have been different if there were Black members of the school board? (2) How do school boards affect educational equity in this current environment? (3) How responsive are school boards to community advocacy in this current environment? As a PhD student, I set out to find the answers, which led me to more questions and answers throughout the past several years.

THIS BOOK

For this book, I relied on the research studies that I have conducted over the last decade. I also relied on the research and deep thinking of other scholars. Collectively, I have conducted research interviews with nearly one hundred school board members, superintendents, district administrators, and community leaders throughout the United States, all with a focus on school board governance and educational equity. In these interviews, I have been able to hear the beautiful, and sometimes heart-wrenching and tear-filled, stories that have made it clear to me that many school board members care deeply about educational equity for our youth, and how that matters to our communities. I have collected and examined hundreds of videos and documents from school board meetings, state-level meetings, media sources, and other archives focused on school board governance and equity. Within these texts and videos, I have come to understand how policies and practices are developed and implemented in school districts, as well as how they shape the educational opportunities for minoritized youth for both good and ill. These stories, perspectives, policies, and discourses inform the content of this book.

My own experiences have also shaped this book. This includes growing up in a working-class family as a mixed-race Black and Chicana woman who attended the Head Start program, a private Catholic school in kindergarten and first grade, and my neighborhood public schools after that, in both a small town and an urban area; and then as a student activist in college, where I attended public and private universities in Nevada and New York. Now, as a mother of two school-aged children enrolled in public schools, I have advocated against racism, gender inequality, and other forms of violence that I have witnessed in their schools. As a tenured professor at Arizona State University, I teach students about educational laws and policies and the sociopolitical contexts that influence education. I have gotten involved, spoken up, organized, and shed tears in my push for educational equity. This book reflects my deep desire and commitment to eradicate and reverse injustices that show up in our classrooms and harm our babies, their families, and ultimately our communities.

As David Stovall, a professor of education and Black studies, once said to my class, among minoritized communities, "We're engaged in a struggle in perpetuity . . . and many of us were educated, not because of, but despite the school system." As you will see throughout this book, schools are not often set up to adequately serve those who have the least. Instead, we must fight for that. And I strongly believe that this democratic project of elected school board governance is a vital part of the fight to advance equity for those among the most vulnerable in our society.

This book is organized into four major sections. Through the lens of educational equity, I set the stage in chapter 1 with a brief history of school boards, key educational policies, and the current politization of school boards and public schools in the United States. In chapters 2 and 3, I describe the School Board Governance for Equity (SBGE) framework, which highlights four principles—knowledge, understanding, skills, and strategies—that current and prospective school board members can adopt to advance equity in their school districts.

In chapters 4, 5, and 6, I bring the SBGE framework to life by sharing research-based case studies of three elected school boards and their roles in advancing and hindering educational equity. The sites of these cases were Tucson Unified School District (TUSD), in Tucson, Arizona; Clark County School District (CCDS), in Las Vegas, Nevada's metropolitan area; and Salt Lake City School District (SLCSD), in Salt Lake City, Utah. These cases are all located in metropolitical areas of the Mountain West region. I selected this region because it reflects the shifting demographics of overall trends in student enrollment in K–12 public schools in the United States. Nationally, white student enrollment has decreased dramatically, from almost 90 percent in the 1950s to 46 percent in 2020, whereas enrollment among students of color increased during this time, with a recent rise in Latinx student enrollment from 12 percent in 1990 to 28 percent by 2020. Similarly, the Mountain West region is an area that used to be characterized as politically conservative and libertarian, largely white and working class, and relatively older. However, this area has shifted and is still shifting toward being more liberal, racially diverse, educated, and young.[1]

These demographic shifts are important to understand because they contribute to critical sociopolitical changes that emerge at the school board level. As legal scholar Cheryl Harris notes in her *Reflections on Whiteness as Property* amid the COVID-19 pandemic: "Zip codes do more than encode maps; they tell stories. Black geographies; Latinx spaces, 'ghettos,' 'barrios,'—all places where 'others' live—are structurally deprived of the means or the opportunity to protect, to provide shelter (in place), their occupants always in fraught relation to place, to property, to rights. The places are erased, renamed, redeveloped, improved. Sometimes there are traces."[2] These places help define communities.

School board members represent these communities that embodied the histories, herstories, and theirstories of places and spaces, and of key moments in time that have shaped and continue to shape communities. In these three case studies, and through the principles of knowledge and understanding in the SBGE framework, you will understand how the demographic shifts over time and these (his/her/their)stories played an important role in the policies and practices that influenced educational equity. You will also learn how the principles of skills and strategies among school board members and other district and community leaders in these case studies played a vital role in advancing equity.

In the final chapter, chapter 7, I discuss the connections among these three cases and explain how school board members can apply the lessons learned from these cases in their own school districts. Then I spend time identifying what types of future research are needed to support the work of school boards and their role in fostering educational equity. Finally, I end the book by sharing my heartfelt thoughts on the future of school boards and their journey toward advancing equity.

My hope is that this book will inform, inspire, and guide school board members, those interested in becoming school board members, and those working with school board members to join or continue the struggle to advance educational equity.

1

The Politics of School Boards in the United States

SCHOOL BOARDS IN the United States represent the core of democratic governance in education. They come in all shapes and sizes: some boards are appointed, but most are elected. Elected school boards, more than appointed ones, are at the heart of local governance in education. This level of governance urges local communities to invest in and oversee what is arguably the nation's most important common good—public schooling. School boards can be a powerful force for (or against) equity in education. They are at the center of ongoing issues such as student learning, school desegregation, school choice, and shifting demographics. In recent years, many school boards have had to navigate divisions in local communities over more recent and highly contentious issues, including the debates about removing school resource officers (SROs), safety precautions during the COVID-19 pandemic, and anti–critical race theory (CRT) and anti-LGBTQIA+ sentiments. As attention to the politics over education grows in numerous districts, elected school boards often become the vehicle through which local communities democratically engage in advocacy and push for policy changes. Tasked with representing their local community's concerns and desires, elected school board members are also responsible for ensuring that all students have humanizing and equitable opportunities to learn. Yet the question is: Can elected school boards accomplish this lofty undertaking, and do they even want to?

In a democratic society, the public should have a stake in the public education paid for by tax dollars. Public education is one of our most precious public goods, one that not only offers families opportunities for upward mobility, but also provides children the experiences that can make them feel valued and excited to be a lifelong learner, as well as the skills and knowledge to contribute positively to our world. Publicly elected school boards are not only the link between local communities and school districts, but they also often operate as political conduits between school districts and policymakers at the state and federal levels on issues of education. Board members are the checks and balances who oversee the millions of dollars that the public invests in schools, who ask important questions and voice critical concerns, and who monitor the pulse of what is happening locally so schools can be responsive to all the communities they serve. At least, that is the ideal.

The reality, however, is messier. Community leaders, families, and youth have grappled with school boards, calling into question whether these entities are an effective form of governance for public education. In late 2021, the media called this phenomenon the "School Board Wars."[1] And critiques of school boards are warranted. Many school board members commit to a job that is often unpaid and requires a great deal of time, knowledge, energy, and skills where they receive inadequate training and support.[2] Yet school boards are supposed to reflect the local community: they are composed of local community members, representing constituents in shaping what happens and does not happen in public schools.

Still, there is another problem. The lack of financial compensation, training, and support makes becoming and remaining a school board member unattainable for many, especially those who are among the most marginalized. In many communities, school boards are not representative of the community that they are elected to serve. For instance, even though nearly 52 percent of K–12 students were nonwhite in 2018, approximately 78 percent of school board members identified as white.[3] While the lack of racial representation might be problematic for racially marginalized communities, school boards are also often not representative of their local communities in terms of other demographics, such as gender, sexuality, socioeconomic status, and religion. It is difficult to forge a strong link between the community and the district without having school board members who represent and have similar lived experiences to *all* the communities that their school district serves. The inability to speak to community issues sufficiently and accurately, coupled with inadequate training and support, can contribute to school district governance that does not reflect the community's interests or values. Consequently, such school boards run the risk of developing and supporting inequitable policies and practices.

Throughout this book, I will emphasize three propositions. First, school boards are responsible for representing *all* communities. Second, school boards are responsible for governing to advance equitable educational opportunities for *all* youth and their families. And third, the first and second principles sometimes conflict, contributing to many challenges that school board members face in their journey toward educational equity. This intersection is central to this book. I demonstrate through research how school board members who are fairly elected, are reflective of the communities they represent, maintain positive perceptions of minoritized communities,[4] and are adequately trained and supported are the best tool for achieving a governing system that will contribute to an equitable public education for *all* youth.

In a nation whose history is scarred by the legacy of oppression, including slavery, racism, settler colonialism, and genocide, this democratic project must be led by individuals with the commitment, knowledge, and skills to dismantle inequities. These inequities are deeply entrenched. Not only must they be addressed within a school board member's local district, but also within individual board members, their community, and within the interlocking systems that districts operate in at the state and national levels. Through my research as a scholar of educational policy via school boards and my personal experience as a woman of color and mother of school-aged children, I know that racism and other forms of oppression in our educational system are pervasive and will not be reversed in my lifetime. Still, I contend that the work of school board members is critical to combating inequities so that we can incrementally improve educational opportunities for many more youth. Grounded in my research drawn from interviews, school board meetings, and archives that span from the past decade, this book sets out to demonstrate the role of school board members in this work and how they can begin the journey in moving their districts toward equity.

HISTORICAL OVERVIEW OF THE ROLE OF SCHOOL BOARDS AND EDUCATIONAL EQUITY

What Is Equity in Education?

Many people are familiar with the concept of the achievement gap, which is the perceived difference between groups' ability to "achieve" as measured by specific educational outcomes (e.g., test scores and graduation rates). But this concept falls short when it comes to defining equity in education. An achievement gap reflects what scholars call a "deficit view."[5] In other words, it defines groups—often minoritized groups—by what they are perceived to lack.

I prefer to use the term "opportunity gap" as a more accurate and useful lens into educational equity.[6] The idea of the opportunity gap builds on the concept of the education debt, which recognizes the legacy of injustices that minoritized communities have suffered historically, economically, politically, socially, and morally. The education debt recognizes the inequitable opportunities that minoritized communities experience as a major contributor to disparate outcomes in education.[7] Rather than fixating so narrowly on outcomes, the opportunity gap focuses on inputs as a measure to remedy the education debt. For instance, studies emphasize how adequate funding supports the hiring of more teachers, which can reduce class sizes (inputs) and contribute to the outcomes of more effective teaching and learning.[8]

To be clear, this is not a zero-sum game. We are one, and therefore, expanding opportunities for each child is a win-win situation for everyone involved. To bridge the opportunity gap, we must ensure that *all* children, and their families, receive the inputs (or opportunities) that they need, both in and out of school, to achieve success in education and beyond. School boards are one of the key actors that play an important role in providing equitable opportunities.

School Board Responsibilities

One of the unique qualities of elected school boards in comparison to other elected bodies is their sole focus on one issue: education. Other policymakers, like state legislatures or city councils, govern an array of issues including housing, health care, and emergency services. While school boards are limited to one area, their responsibility is nevertheless vast.

School board officials are expected to provide leadership on a variety of matters. As governing bodies, one of school boards' main responsibilities is to develop policies for their districts. Some school boards create policy in conjunction with school administration (namely, the superintendent), but ultimately, school boards determine whether policies are instituted.[9] Such policies include those related to funding and budget distribution, facilities, and personnel. Another task that school boards take on is to develop academic goals for the school district that drive policy and funding decisions.[10] Finally, school boards determine school districts' managerial leadership by hiring and firing superintendents, which is arguably one of the most vital positions in school districts.[11]

These responsibilities tend to "set the political tone" for districts.[12] Acknowledging the heightened existence of school reforms, Michael Usdan, scholar and former board president, notes that school boards are frequently "the only entities that provide continuous institutional leadership through times of constant change and administrative churn."[13]

Early History of School Boards

Following the American Revolution, the US government supported schooling as a way to shape citizens' morality and protect the nation from anarchy and dictatorship. The first step toward locally controlled schools occurred in 1647 in Massachusetts, when towns were legally required to build and sustain schools (not for free, and not for anyone).[14] Nearly two hundred years later, in 1837, Horace Mann was elected to the first state-level board of education in Massachusetts. He pushed forward and expanded these previous ideas into the "common schools" movement. *Common schools* were public schools funded by local tax dollars, common in teaching literacy and civic education, and open to all children.[15] They spread quickly throughout the North. Meanwhile, although Horace Mann took an antislavery stance, many states in the South made it illegal to teach slaves to read or write.[16]

Education Following Emancipation

After the Civil War, free ex-slaves embraced universal schooling, only to experience extreme resistance from many white landowners who sought to maintain illiteracy among Black people—thereby continuing to exploit their labor via unfair contracts and blocking them from participating in civic activities such as voting. Despite the resistance, Black Southerners fought to establish their own forms of local schooling, often financing this endeavor themselves because local school boards offered drastically unequal funding to Black schools compared to their white counterparts. While Black children were allowed to attend school, they often experienced inequitable educational conditions.

They had access to significantly fewer resources and services than their white counterparts.[17]

Around 1880, white landowners realized that their continued resistance to universal schooling would only be met with increased political conflict. Instead, many of them worked to shape schools in ways that would maintain a subservient Black population and to codify oppression via Jim Crow laws that legalized segregation and inequity.[18] Meanwhile, state and local leaders continued to inequitably and inadequately fund and support Black schools.[19]

The Role of School Boards in School Desegregation Efforts

Fast-forward to *Brown v. Board of Education* in 1954. While this is the case that often first comes to mind when we think of desegregation, this was not the first time that the question of segregation in schools came before the courts. Prior to *Brown*, a Latinx family in California won the *Mendez v. Westminster* (1947) case in federal court. In this case, the attorney representing the Latinx family did not argue that they were unlawfully discriminated against due to race, but rather that they were unlawfully discriminated against due to the Mexican children's ancestry and language.[20] While this case overlooked racial discrimination, it nevertheless set the stage for *Brown v. Board* by outlawing segregation by language and ancestry.

In 1954, plaintiffs, supported by the National Association for the Advancement of Colored People (NAACP), sued the school board in Topeka, Kansas. The US Supreme Court then combined four local court cases on segregation and issued the famous *Brown v. Board* decision, which outlawed racially segregated schools. However, the Court did not provide details on *how* desegregation should unfold. In *Brown II* (1955), the Court issued a second decision giving local school boards the ultimate authority to decide how they would racially desegregate schools, and ordering that it must be done with "all deliberate speed."[21] The contradictory call for both deliberation and speed allowed some districts to avoid making any or all changes to achieve desegregation. Consequently, most districts took years to desegregate schools, and many ended up under Court supervision and federal enforcement to implement school desegregation plans. In fact, nearly 722 districts and charter schools are still operating under a Court-issued desegregation order or voluntary agreement.[22]

When it came time to decide on the plan to desegregate schools, local school boards made the final call—even if they had to be forced through court intervention. This demonstrated the extent and latitude of their decision-making power. They either desegregated schools by deliberating with all the affected parties, or inequitably, by deliberating only with those who had more power and resources. Many school boards failed tremendously at advancing equity. Instead, most boards wielded their power to appease and support white communities at the expense of Black communities. Prince Edward County in Virginia, for example, closed all schools in 1959 for five years to avoid desegregation altogether, while providing white families with funding toward private school tuition until the court forced the district to reopen its schools.[23] In another example, in Clark County School District in Las Vegas, Nevada, the all-white school board voted on a plan that placed the burden of busing on Black children and their families, which had immensely negative impacts on the Black community.[24]

Legacy of Inequities

This brief history of the development of school boards in the context of the "common schools" movement, slavery, emancipation, and segregation barely touches the surface of these key moments related to equity. It also fails to mention many other important histories. These include the US government's role in forcing Indigenous children to leave their families and attend Indian Boarding Schools, providing inadequate and inequitable education to English learners (*Lau v. Nichols* [1974]) and students with disabilities (*Hendrick Hudson School District v. Rowley* [1982]), the exclusion of undocumented children from public schooling (*Plyler v. Doe* [1982]), and much more.

It's important to remember that school board members inherit a legacy of inequities that were brought forth and instituted, in part, by their predecessors. This is not something to shy away from. Rather, it is our responsibility to contend with and grapple with these histories to right the wrongs that many minoritized communities have endured and to advance equity. It is not only our responsibility, but our obligation to do so.

From *Brown* Until Now

But making good on this obligation is not easy; it requires a clear understanding of the history of school boards, how they have served—or ignored—the needs of their communities, and the many factors that affect their ability to govern. The impact of events during the Civil Rights Movement in the 1960s and 1970s resulted in increased bureaucracy in education, particularly at the federal level. Eleven years after *Brown v. Board of Education* and one year after the Civil Rights Act of 1964, the federal government passed the Elementary and Secondary Education Act (ESEA) of 1965. ESEA allocated supplemental funding to schools through Title I funds to serve low-income children, and soon afterward, it added grant funding for students with disabilities and English learners. Through court rulings and legislative avenues, the federal government increased its role in education and used the incentive of federal funds to legally mandate local school boards to help ensure that *all* children received an equal education. Even though many school boards complied only after lengthy legal, political, and social battles,[25] school districts eventually evolved to meet these legal mandates. In this evolution, districts became more bureaucratic, requiring administrative leadership such as superintendents to take larger decision-making roles.

Meanwhile, school board demographics shifted in many school districts as some states and localities changed their electoral structure from at-large elections to single-member district (or ward) elections. Allowing voters to select school board candidates from a pool of only their neighbors often contributed to more racially diverse school boards because most neighborhoods were (and still are) segregated by race and income.[26]

The 1980s marked a new context in which school boards were operating. This era was filled with increased standards and accountability, as opposed to productivity and opportunity.[27] The role of the state in education became more profound as funding sources shifted from localities to states. In 1920, localities funded about 80 percent of education. By 1970, this dropped to approximately 40 percent, while states increased their funding to almost 50 percent. States began to require that school districts comply with what was known as standards-based reform, prompted largely by the 1983 federal *Nation at Risk* report.[28]

The *Nation at Risk* report used test score data to highlight two narratives: (1) the perception that US students were less proficient than their non-US counterparts, and (2) significant differences existed in students' test scores based on race and socioeconomic background. The authors of this report linked these data to a potential threat to the nation's prosperity and advocated for states to adopt two goals: "equity and high-quality schooling."[29] After the *Nation at Risk* report, in 1989, President George H. W. Bush invited governors to attend a national education summit to urge increased state and federal intervention in local schools.[30] Evidence of such state intervention is reflected in the fact that twenty states assumed control of more than fifty-five school districts during the 1980s and 1990s.[31]

This national scrutiny of schools, coupled with a higher level of state and federal funding, ushered in new systems of accountability based on new standards for school boards to follow.[32] What was once a very locally controlled system was now threatened. In his book *The Future of School Board Governance*, Thomas Alsbury echoed this concern, stating, "For better or worse, there is less attention now to the need for democracy (either on school boards or in schools) due to our obsession with the threats on globalization, international competition, accountability, and high-stakes testing."[33]

In 2001, under the George W. Bush administration, the federal government reauthorized ESEA, signing into law the No Child Left Behind Act (NCLB).[34] The NCLB era was known to many educators and scholars as the emergence of "high-stakes testing."[35] NCLB required states to (1) develop standards and accountability systems based largely on data from student test scores; (2) disaggregate and publicly share these scores at the school level by race, income, ability status, and language; and (3) intervene if schools continuously failed to meet the state standards.[36] Intervention options included state takeover, which moved authority from the elected school board to a state-appointed entity. In addition, families could enroll their children in a school outside their school zone if their local school failed to meet these standards. NCLB also instituted a new type of federal funding (Title III), targeting English learners, but with a much narrower aim toward supporting English proficiency rather than bilingual or multilingual proficiency.[37]

NCLB further increased both federal and state involvement in local school districts, for the most part bypassing school boards. Academically, the law had various impacts. On the one hand, the law's requirement to disaggregate data revealed concerning disparities among some specific student outcomes at the school level. Yet it also provoked fear and stress among educators (even contributing to cheating on tests),[38] narrowed curricula to align with testing (teaching to the test), and increased disengagement in learning among students. And overall, NCLB fell short of its goal of not leaving any child behind in terms of student achievement as measured by test scores.[39]

In 2009, President Barack Obama's administration allowed states to opt out of NCLB; instead, it promoted a Race to the Top (RTTT) initiative which began in 2012. Under RTTT, states could apply and were granted funding for reforming state-level policies that focused on adopting Common Core standards and assessments, improving academic gains, and closing the achievement gap, allowing the expansion of charter schools, and improving the teacher and school leader workforce. Over the five-year span of RTTT, over $4 billion in funds were awarded to eighteen states and the District of Columbia.[40] For two of these years, an RTTT competition also occurred at the district level, including charter schools, with twenty-one awardees.[41] Interestingly, among school district applicants, RTTT required school boards to create an evaluation system to measure their own performance, the first federal requirement of its kind.[42]

During Obama's second term in 2015, and with bipartisan support, Congress replaced NCLB with the Every Student Succeeds Act (ESSA). Like the RTTT initiative, under ESSA, states were given more authority to develop standards and accountability. Still, ESSA required state standards to align with "college and career readiness," maintained testing mandates in reading, math, and science, and included one nontest measure identified by the state. Unlike NCLB's sidelining of school districts and boards, ESSA shifted more authority to districts and required states to invite and consider the input of local partners (e.g., community leaders, parents, educators) in shaping new standards and accountability measures. While this requirement created more opportunities for public input in developing these systems, the level and extent of public deliberation varied based on each state's willingness and capacity to invite and institute this input.[43]

During President Donald Trump's term, from 2017 to 2020, ESSA remained. However, Trump appointed Betsy DeVos as secretary of education, who was a heavy proponent of school choice, including the expansion of charter schools and voucher programs.[44] Although ESSA was not changed through reauthorization, ESSA-related requirements and equity-oriented provisions decreased, and DeVos dismantled various policies within the Office of Civil Rights (OCR). For example, districts were no longer required to submit data on certain student-level factors and there was less commitment to investigate OCR complaints.[45] In addition, voucher programs expanded tremendously, with twenty-nine states instituting sixty-two programs in 2019.[46]

When President Joe Biden entered office in 2021, more than half of K–12 schools were operating virtually due to the COVID-19 pandemic.

Much of the first few years of Biden's administration focused on getting schools safely back to in-person learning and addressing the impact of COVID-19 on students' academic and social-emotional learning.[47] Aligned with these goals, Congress issued nearly $190 billion in Elementary and Secondary School Emergency Relief (ESSER) funds to educational entities, including over 16,000 school districts and charters, to spend on services and resources to support COVID-19 relief.[48] These federal funds have been used to support social-emotional learning, academic interventions, and the hiring of staff. However, with these funds discontinued in fall 2024, many districts were left to sustain these supports without the additional funding.[49]

These last several decades of major policy and political maneuvers at the national level has made a significant impact on schools. As school board members, it's important to understand how federal-level interventions have shaped their respective school districts and their ability to govern. While many school boards find themselves on the losing end in terms of power and authority, the push and pull between federal, state, and local governance in education is always shifting. What's critical, as I will discuss later in this book, is knowing how to leverage each level of government to advance educational equity in our schools.

Changing Nature of School Boards in the United States

Focusing on the local level, let's discuss how school boards and school districts have shifted. Throughout much of the 1800s, schools remained in the hands of local boards. These boards had an average of 21.5 members and included mostly untrained laypeople.[50] Although states had legal jurisdiction over education, their resources were limited. Similarly, staffs at the federal level were small and lacked authority.[51] Ultimately, local control of schools reflected an American value that embraced a so-called democratic process built to meet the needs of each and every unique community deemed valuable enough to educate (which excluded many groups, as highlighted previously).[52]

Toward the end of the 1800s, some school boards engaged in political patronage and corruption. These school boards became associated with local political machines and were less accountable to the community. Compounding matters, the state and federal governments lacked capacity to intervene at the local level.[53] By around 1900, progressive reformers grew tired of political corruption and demanded a change in government bureaucracy.[54] They embraced Frederick Winslow Taylor's scientific methods, grounded in goals of efficiency and accountability, with the ultimate desire to reshape management. This, in part, altered school board governance toward reaching these goals and contributed to decreased corruption.[55] For the next few decades throughout the 1930s, the development of state, and later federal, bureaucratic structures focused on accountability, with standardization soon replacing community-run schools. In addition to confronting existing corruption, reformers developed curricula that reflected white, Anglo-Saxon Protestant values aimed at assimilating immigrants and those who were considered poor through education.[56]

The long-term effects of the reformer movement resulted in a more centralized education system. States consolidated and hired experts to oversee school districts. Soon, there were fewer school boards with fewer members.[57] The size of school boards shrank dramatically, going from an average of 21.5 members in 1893 to around 7 in 1913.[58] As shown in table 1.1,

TABLE 1.1   Changes in school district composition and student population

		STUDENT ENROLLMENT	
	TOTAL PUBLIC SCHOOL DISTRICTS	AVERAGE PER SCHOOL DISTRICT	ENROLLMENT IN TRADITIONAL PUBLIC SCHOOLS
1937	119,001	218	25,975,108
1957	47,594	704	33,528,591
1987	15,577	2,568	40,007,022
2007	13,838	3,562	49,292,507
2021	13,373	3,494	46,724,794

Source: Berry, 2005; Howell, 2005; NCES, 1993; NCES, 2011; NCES, 2023.[59]

there were 119,001 school districts serving an average of 218 students in 1937.[60] By 1957, there were fewer than 50,000 school districts. By 1987, this number dropped to around 15,600 school districts serving an average of approximately 2,600 students apiece.[61] The average size of schools increased from 87 students in 1936 to 440 per school in the 1970s.[62]

The increase in the size of schools and districts has generally resulted in lower costs, more centralized power from entities such as school boards and teacher unions, less engagement from communities, and increased racial and socioeconomic diversity in schools. The operation of larger school districts with smaller schools is the most optimal in terms of academic and economic benefits. Yet the trend shows that this is not usually the case. Instead, many school districts consolidated and have closed schools with smaller enrollments. The result is the opposite of optimal—larger schools operating in larger districts.[63]

While the total number of districts continued to decrease, enrollment in these districts also shifted downward by more than 2.5 million students from 2007 to 2021 (see table 1.1). This is likely due to the expansion of charter schools. Since 2010 to 2021, enrollment in charter schools nearly doubled from 1.8 million to 3.7 million students.[64] As of 2021, there are 7,800 charter schools and 4,140 charter school districts, most of which are governed by appointed boards and led by charter management companies.[65] Still, elected school boards currently govern nearly 13,000 school districts.

Importantly, these numbers illustrate the shifting trends of the districts that elected and appointed school boards are expected to govern. Governing a district with an average of 218 students—likely located in a relatively small and homogenous community—is much different from a geographically expansive and diverse school district that serves thousands of students. While larger school districts tend to experience less community engagement, they are often relatively more racially and socioeconomically diverse. This diversity likely contributes to a broader commitment to public schools by a more diverse set of families and community members across cultural and political differences.[66] This also may lead to more conflict over what these differing communities value. When it comes to issues of equity, district factors like size and geographic areas will likely shape how school boards approach governance, requiring a different way to navigate changing student populations and various types of conflicting views.

THE ROLE OF SCHOOLS IN THE CURRENT POLITICAL CLIMATE

David Tyack, a well-known professor of education history, observed that "no amount of wishful thinking could have transformed the politics of education into neutral administration, for schooling is and has always been intrinsically political. The question is not whether politics but whose politics."[67] This statement sums up the previous sections, highlighting the federal government's role in education. It also, however, reflects the extreme politization that arose during the years of the COVID-19 pandemic, with school boards in the center. As COVID-19 swept the United States and most public schools closed their doors around March 2020, families and local community members watched and listened, and many eventually took a stance on key issues related to equity and schooling. These stances, often associated with political ideologies, evolved into at least three major political conflicts that unfolded at the realm of local school boards—police and safety officers in schools, COVID-19 safety precautions, and anti-CRT/anti-LGBTQIA+ sentiment.

First, the murder of George Floyd at the hands of the police on May 25, 2020, followed by other police killings of Black people in the United States, elicited racial protests nationwide. Youth activists called for school boards to defund school police, and at least forty boards did.[68] Equity-minded board members, like Gloria Reyes, the Madison Metropolitan School Board president and first Latina elected to the board, called on institutions to "take a hard look at . . . how they feed into the racist practices."[69] Many other school boards followed her call to defund school police. More importantly, boards used this moment to reckon with racism in schools.

The second conflict, COVID-19 safety precautions, came in two stages. The first began around the fall of 2020, when school districts experienced local and state pressure to transition back to in-person learning and many school boards pushed back. For instance, in July 2020, school board members in Arizona led a press conference at the state capitol urging the governor to maintain school closures. Many school board members grappled with COVID-19's disproportionate impact on minoritized communities, and as one board member, Devin Del Palacio pointedly stated: "This pandemic has highlighted many inequities that have been around for decades. Our Black, Brown, and Indigenous communities are getting hit the hardest."[70]

The second stage of this conflict had multiple levels and occurred after many districts made plans to reopen, which lasted through the 2021–2022 school year. This time, the issue was about mandating COVID-19 safety measures in schools, particularly vaccines and masks.

On one level, school boards engaged in a political conflict against statewide leaders. In as many as eight states, conservative state leaders banned school districts from mandating masks.[71] Some school boards, particularly those in urban communities, pushed back against these state bans despite threats from governors to remove funding from their districts. In Texas, for instance, as many as seventy-one districts and their governing school boards defied Governor Greg Abbott's orders and instituted mask mandates.[72] In many states, these conflicts evolved into legal battles, including on behalf of children with disabilities, whose families believed that mask mandates allowed their children to attend school safely.[73] These conflicts are an example of how school boards have resisted and navigated state power and authority.

On another level, school boards engaged in conflict with parents and community members. Parents, local community members, and even residents from outside school districts showed up at school board meetings in droves to protest mask mandates. Sometimes this conflict went beyond protests. For example, in April 2021, the school board of the Unified School District in Vail, Arizona, canceled the meeting because attendees, some armed with guns, refused to wear masks. Outside of the school board meeting venue, protesters falsely proclaimed that the school board resigned and then staged a school board election. Using Robert's Rules of Order via Facebook Live, people nominated and "elected" an entirely new school board, whose first order of business was to lift the district's mask mandate. Interestingly, many of the attendees were admittedly not residents of the district.[74] Moreover, between May 2021 and November 2022, police arrested or charged at least fifty-nine people because of disorderly conduct and violence at school board meetings over mask mandates and anti-CRT or LGBTQIA+ sentiment.[75]

The third conflict, around anti-CRT or anti-LGBTQIA+ sentiment, is often conflated with the second conflict about COVID-19 safety measures.[76] In the wake of the Black Lives Matter (BLM) protests in September 2020, conservative advocate Christopher Rufo made several media appearances denouncing CRT. After a discussion with Rufo, former president Trump banned all federal-level training focused on "critical race theory," "white privilege," or any training that implied that the United States or any racial or ethnic group is "inherently racist or evil."[77] This caused tension for the many school boards who put forth resolutions stating their commitment to antiracism and equity after the BLM protests. Soon after the Trump ban, school boards became the target of anti-CRT efforts. People attended school board meetings to call for the removal of anything equity-related, including curricula about race. They called for banning books that mention sexuality, and they pushed back against accommodations and restroom facilities for transgender students. Between 2021 and 2022, officials launched 563 attempts (351 at the state level, 177 at the local level, and 35 at the federal level) to dismantle anything supposedly CRT related. Of these, 226 laws were adopted and instituted at the K–12 school level.[78]

These conflicts affected the daily function of school boards and increased the pressure that they face. First, local board members experienced what was likely the highest number of attempts to recall individual board members. At its height, in 2021, there were 237 recall attempts, which is 73 percent more than in 2020.[79] Around 85 percent of these recall attempts were for school board members who supported implementing COVID-19 safety measures.[80]

The second impact was a rise in local and national organizations that focused on anti-equity efforts in education. At the local level, many groups formed to recall school board members, some with their very purpose in the name, such as "Recall San Francisco Board" and "Recall Scottsdale."[81] At the national level, politically conservative groups like Moms for Liberty and Parents Defending Education, both founded in 2021, emerged and grew quickly. For instance, after only two years in operation, Moms for Liberty has 278 chapters in forty-five states with more than 100,000 members. Some of the Moms for Liberty members have ties to the Proud Boys, a far-right militant group that led the insurrection at the US Capitol on January 6, 2021.[82] In fact, after the January 6 attack, many Proud Boy members shifted their focus from the national scene to schools as an attempt to "think local, act local." They attended school board meetings as "muscle," to evoke fear and coerce school boards into adopting a largely anti-equity agenda.[83]

Along with advocating at school board meetings, these organizations also targeted school boards in elections with the goal of "flipping" boards. In other words, they worked to get a majority vote on the school board to support a politically conservative agenda. In 2022 and 2023, Moms for Liberty endorsed at least 372 school board candidates throughout eighty-eight districts. Almost half won.[84] In some places, however, progressives responded by organizing groups such as "Save Our School Boards" and supported candidates to flip the school boards back.[85] In Pennsylvania, voters flipped three school boards toward a politically democratic leaning.[86] Here, one democratic school board candidate and parent recalled that when Moms for Liberty candidates took over the school board, "they came in, they caused chaos, they caused fear, and brought a political agenda that should never be in a classroom or in our schools or districts."[87] This political agenda included actions like banning diverse books and the use of gender-affirming pronouns, creating an environment that students described as violent. These actions, she explained, sparked pushback from parents who disagreed. This included parents organizing to center their local communities, support public schools, and eventually revert to a school board that represented them.

Still, as some school boards flipped, conservative board members worked to push out their superintendents and reverse the equity-related work in their respective districts.[88] School districts across the country, even those that had not been flipped, became increasingly hesitant and fearful of being targeted by conservative watchdogs for using terms like "equity."[89] Note that these concerns are not unwarranted; pursuing equity is not risk-free.

Groups have launched efforts to target school boards and district leaders who support equity work. For instance, Turning Point USA created School Board Watchlist, a website that "exposes school board leadership that supports anti-American, radical, hateful, immoral, and racist teachings in their districts, such as Critical Race Theory, the 1619 Project, sexual/gender ideology, and more."[90] Parents Defending Education developed an "IndoctriNation Map," which identifies equity-related policies, events, and practices in school districts throughout the United States and connects individuals with the local groups advocating against issues related to equity.[91] In suburban districts with shifting demographics and increasing numbers of minoritized students, these conflicts were particularly heightened.[92] When relatively white and more affluent communities face demographic and political changes, they often perceive these changes as threats to what they think of as their "normal" way of life, and sometimes they react in what Carol Anderson refers to as "white rage."[93]

As these recent examples illustrate, even as school boards move policies and practices toward equity, their advances sometimes meet resistance.

All this is to say that if you are on a school board working to advance equity, you should be prepared for explicit pushback. As these past and ongoing conflicts have shown, some anti-equity efforts are also antidemocratic strategies that can undermine the democratic project of school boards. Advancing equity also requires protecting our democracy.

The Attempts to Dismantle Public Schools

A centerpiece of democracy in the United States is a public education system that is equitable and accessible to all children. As school boards tackle explicit anti-equity efforts, they are also governing under intense political and economic efforts to dismantle public schools in favor of privatizing education. These efforts, while related to the series of conflicts laid out in the previous section, are different in an important way: they are often disguised as equity-oriented but are usually the opposite. They come in the form of expanding charter schools, portfolio districts, school voucher programs, state and mayoral takeovers of school districts, open enrollment policies, and high-stakes testing and accountability, to name a few.

Rooted in the logic of capitalism, a free-market worldview, and (sometimes) racist ideologies, advances to privatize education are not new. As the United States grapples with desegregating schools by race, responses like "white flight," increasing enrollment in private schools, and even the country's first pseudo-voucher program instituted in Prince Edward County in 1959 (only provided for white families as mentioned earlier in this chapter) had one thing in common: they created a pathway for white families to circumvent having their children mix with the "Other."

Milton Friedman, a Nobel Prize–winning economist, was an early proponent of school choice. A year after the *Brown* decision, he published an article entitled "The Role of Government in Education," and in 1962, he published *Capitalism and Freedom*, a book that addressed school segregation, among other topics. In both, he argues that government is too involved in schools and that parents should be able to choose their children's schools. He called this "the appropriate solution" to "the problems of segregation and integration."[94] Supporting the Prince Edward County pseudo-voucher program that granted tuition to white students to attend whites-only private schools, Freidman argued that most families would choose integrated schools if given the freedom to do so.[95] But we know this belief to be false.

We must avoid the pitfalls of equity-like narratives and fancy language that obscures the broader reality of what has been happening for decades. Even though school choice seems innocent on the surface, we know that at least so far, it has led to increased segregation and inequitable opportunities. As school choice expands via charter schools, open enrollment policies, and voucher programs, so does school segregation by race, income, language, and ability status.[96] Factors such as families' preferences for homogenous schools, families' varying abilities to navigate school choice programs (e.g., information and transportation), selectiveness of admissions, and often relatively fewer services for students with the most needs (e.g., English learners, students with disabilities) in nontraditional public schools and private schools contribute to segregation in a school choice environment. What's more (and what's most relevant to school boards), choice is often unregulated and undemocratic.[97]

Segregation is not inherently unjust on its face. But research shows that racial and economic integration in schools contributes to more positive societal and relational impacts—that is, less prejudice and stereotyping.[98] This is a bonus of meaningful integration. What is inherently unjust, however, is the variability of opportunities that comes with segregation.

If we think about the definition of equity as an "opportunity gap," school choice is a vehicle that perpetuates that gap. Not only do "choice" schools vary in terms of quality, and consequently, those children who have access to these schools vary by factors such as race and income, but the expansion of choice also drains funding and resources from public schools. As students leave traditional public schools for the promise of something better, they take with them the funding needed to maintain quality learning opportunities and to keep neighborhood schools open. Sometimes they return to their neighborhood schools after the funding followed them to the previous school, which often means that the neighborhood school enrolls that student without the per pupil funding to support them. States require public school districts to find a way to serve these students, along with any other students who nontraditional schools have denied because of lack of services (e.g., language and disabilities) or discrimination (e.g., religion, sexual orientation, and disabilities).

In addition, with expanded enrollment policies, families can enroll their children in schools outside their districts, both charter and non-charter. Under these policies, many districts have designated resources often needed for student programs and resources toward marketing or opening exclusive "choice" schools to compete for students outside their districts. They do this to combat declining enrollment, and ultimately school closures.[99] This leads to a host of concerns, including the impact on school board governance when not all families enrolled have the legal right to vote or even run for the school board in the district where their children attend school.

Finally, recent waves of new district systems and frameworks center their efforts on outputs and accountability rather than inputs and support. These often overlook the legacy of inequities that seep into schools, such as housing inequality, environmental injustices, and mass incarceration. These include portfolio models that relinquish so-called underperforming schools to different entities (i.e., charter management companies), and "innovation" schools, which utilize school district resources but operate autonomously and are governed by an appointed rather than an elected board.[100]

These also include emerging frameworks like the Student Outcomes Focused Governance (SOFG) framework, which requires school boards to identify three to five goals. These goals are framed as "student outcomes" that SOFG defines as "a measure of what students know or are able to do."[101] These goals are almost always narrowly focused on statewide standardized test scores. The governing board then holds the superintendent accountable to meeting these goals. This kind of framework mimics the high-stakes accountability policies of NCLB. But at the district level, such a framework often coincides with efforts to keep school board members "in their lane" by training them to focus intently on these narrow goals.

To be clear, and as I illustrate in the School Board Governance for Equity (SBGE) framework in chapter 3's section on strategic planning, school boards should have specific goals, including ones focused on academics. However, these are not the only goals of a school board. Schools are often the center of our communities. While youth in our schools are the priority, school boards also represent the ecosystem that schools emerge from, including the families of our youth, the communities that surround and shape our schools, and those who work within and for our schools. In addition, standardized tests are not the only way to assess student learning. Other measures, such as student presentations and performance portfolios, can assess student learning in less prescriptive ways. Finally, along with understanding "what students know and can do" (student outcomes as defined by SOFG), we should be equally, if not more, concerned about how students feel. To do this, school districts can administer surveys and conduct focus groups with students and their families to measure students' socioemotional learning and levels of engagement.

One of the biggest problems with frameworks that centers their goals and accountability system on standardized testing is that the efforts required to achieve these goals often come at the expense of higher learning. Since educators experience immense pressure to meet these goals, they will often "teach to the test," reduce learning opportunities that are not related to the test, and incorporate perverse incentives for teachers and students to perform well on the test. In her book *Leaving Children Behind*, Angela Valenzuela, a professor of educational policy, emphasizes these concerns, noting that "the very notion of a mainstream, standardized educational experience implies a systemic disregard of children's personal, cultural, and community-based identities. Rather than providing children with an empowering sense of how their lives can connect productively to the world that they inhabit, a test-centric curriculum compelled by the long arm of the state [or district] through standardized, high-stakes testing reduces children's worth to their test scores."[102]

As Valenzuela describes in this excerpt, the dehumanizing, prescriptive, and reductionist consequences of a test-centered framework constitute a huge equity issue. Similarly, in *This Is Not a Test*, José Vilson, a former math teacher, details the grueling experience of administering the statewide standardized test in his class. He reflects, "By teaching students of color that the best way to succeed is to respond to tests the way the state demands, determine the validity of an argument under the state's rule, and examine essays only if they follow the state's standards, we are creating education via deculturation, or stripping a culture; instead of transculturation, the merging of cultures. We didn't land on education reform. Education reform landed on us."[103] It is important that school board members understand that the consequences of high-stakes accountability testing, even if it is unintended, can be detrimental to a culturally responsive and sustaining education, particularly for minoritized students.

Moreover, in schools that are underfunded and lack appropriate and adequate inputs (opportunities), test-centered goals are often unachievable, unsustainable, or both. When these goals are not met or sustained, school districts are often deemed as "failing." Failing districts have sometimes resulted in states and mayors taking them over, which has happened in districts such as Chicago in 1995, and more recently in Houston in 2023. Overall, the efforts to undermine and underfund public schools in favor of privatized systems that seemingly promote choice and freedom are usually undemocratic and inequitable.

It is not enough for elected school boards to champion public schools. They must also understand the history of education reform, the political ideologies that drive conflicts over education policy, the complexities of school choice, and the "new" wave of ideas (which are often just old reforms that have been recycled and repackaged). School board members need to learn to navigate this system effectively. While school districts are local operations, they are also very much influenced by political, economic, and social forces outside school districts. This means building the knowledge and understanding of the social and political contexts and then enacting the skills and strategies to protect democracy, identify possibilities, and commit the necessary inputs to advance equity in education. In the following chapters, I present a framework that is centered on these principles.

Who Is This Book Intended to Help?

The rest of the book will offer a SBGE framework, followed by three case studies that informed the creation of this framework. As you move through this book, if you are a school board member, remember that governing toward educational equity requires a critical eye. History and context matter. You must critique current and emerging policies and practices within the context of our nation's history and the broader political landscape that schools are operating in. Do your homework. Ask deeper questions. Finally, use a lens of equity ensuring that *all* children have access to equal opportunities for educational success, which is measured beyond just the surface metrics of test scores.

If you are an educator, parent, youth, or community member, you have an equally important role in governing our schools. You can likely vote for school board members who commit to equity. And you can support equity efforts through an opportunity gap lens by speaking up at school board meetings, building coalitions with school board members, and advocating for more equitable opportunities via policies and practices at all levels of government.

If you are a researcher, you can make high-quality research accessible to school boards and school districts to help them make evidence-based decisions. There is an overwhelming amount of information about education, but so much of it is not supported by both quality research and an equity lens. You can ensure that what gets in the hands of school board members is legitimate so they can make the best moves.

School board governance that advances equity requires a collective effort. We can either put in the hard work to make this democratic project equitable for all our communities or give up and allow everyone to fend for themselves. I hope you choose the former, and that together, we will work hard to the benefit of your children, my children, our children, and the future generations of children to come.

2

The School Board Governance for
Equity Framework Principles 1 and 2:
Knowledge and Understanding

A FRAMEWORK AS A RECIPE FOR SUCCESS

Most potential and current school board members come to the position
with a desire to make a positive difference. But each school board member is one person wearing many hats while often juggling their family,
day jobs, and other commitments. In this chapter and in chapter 3, I present the School Board Governance for Equity (SBGE) framework, which
offers school board members guidance on how they might spend their
precious time and energy to advance equity in their local context. The
purpose of this framework is to help potential and current school board
members to identify specific areas of influence, build strategies to disrupt inequities, and develop ideas to push an equity agenda forward.

A framework is a cornerstone to success. It is like a recipe for a special
meal. And like a recipe, the SBGE framework can be assessed, adjusted,
and/or combined with other frameworks to meet the needs of each

board member and each collective school board. Also, since many school boards are divided over equity-related issues, this framework can be used by individual school board members and/or a full school board. No matter what, school boards need a framework to guide their work. Without a framework, school boards will flounder, and the possibility of advancing equity will be left to luck. Our children cannot afford to rely on luck; they all deserve the opportunity to learn and grow in schooling environments that embrace and love them.

School Board Governance for Equity: An Overview

The SBGE framework has several moving parts and might appear abstract at first glance. However, these parts are grounded in a significant amount of research and have concrete uses when it comes to advancing equity. The framework will take you on a journey from the individual to the systems level. As with a recipe, you must read through all the ingredients and the step-by-step directions before starting to make the most of it. Similarly, this framework requires that you take what you learn, reflect on it, and think about where you are, what you need, and how you can utilize it for your work as a school board member.

The SBGE framework has four major principles, as outlined in figure 2.1:

1. Knowledge
2. Understanding
3. Skills
4. Strategies to address equity

These principles operate within five areas over which school boards have influence—the district, the school board, the community, and state and federal governments. The first three areas—the district, the school board, and the community—are directly linked because school board members should be the link between a school district and its community. The other two areas—state and federal governments—are more distant from school boards depending on the political context.

FIGURE 2.1   School Board Governance for Equity framework

In this chapter, I discuss the principles of *knowledge* and *understanding*. These are woven together. Knowing is gathering information; understanding is becoming consciously aware of things that are more abstract and fluid (e.g., ideas, experiences, or processes). Under these two principles, the first area of focus begins with knowing and understanding oneself as a board member, including one's (1) identity, (2) experiences, (3) relationship to the community, and (4) beliefs. The second area of focus encompasses knowing and understanding the district, including one's respective (1) school board and (2) school district and local community.

In chapter 3, you will learn about the principles of *skills* and *strategies*. Skills are needed to accomplish a task or goal, whereas strategies map out how to accomplish a particular goal or task. Within these principles, the first area of focus is school board members learning to build momentum and support through (1) engaging in coalition building and coalition politics and (2) leveraging state and federal politics in that effort. The other area of focus is school board members working toward material outcomes in the form of policies and practices. These include (1) preparing to be proactively responsive to the complexities aligned with equity work and (2) imagining the possibilities of a future where equity is achieved for each and every child through strategic planning.

While this work begins with oneself as a potential and current school board member, the combination of knowledge, understanding, skills, and strategies should be approached as a cyclical process. Thus, school board members should revisit each principle on a regular basis to flow with the constant shifts in the three Ps: people, policies, and practices.

Developing Deep Knowledge and Understanding of Oneself as a Board Member

The first two principles of *knowing* and *understanding* are critical starting points in the SBGE framework. Without knowing and understanding yourself in your role as a school board member and the context and people around you, moving forward toward action is futile at best and harmful at worst. With these principles, you will learn the questions to ask, the information to seek out, and the areas to reflect on to deepen your knowledge and understanding.

These principles begin with the self (the school board member), discussed here. This includes an overview of how social constructions of others contribute to one's beliefs and actions. The next section describes *knowing* and *understanding* the district community—the board; superintendent; district administration; those in schools, including teachers, staff, family, and youth; and those outside of schools in the local community.

As a board member committing to advancing educational equity, it is critical to start with yourself. There are at least four levels in this individual effort, including being clear about (1) how you identify your-self, (2) how your experiences have shaped you, (3) who you are in rela-tionship to your community, and (4) the beliefs that drive your decisions. Ideally, the work of positioning oneself should begin as you contemplate your decision to run or apply for a school board position. The simple and broadest questions are "Who am I?" and "What is my positionality in my local context?"

Identifying yourself

Let us start at the most basic level. Whether you are a current school board member or thinking about becoming a school board member, you should be transparent, at least with yourself, about how you iden-tify within a realm of demographic factors, including race, ethnicity, gender, sexuality, socioeconomic status, age, ability, religious affilia-tion, educational background, professional background, and any other areas of identification that might matter within a district or community. Although these demographics do not define your character, they do inform how you have experienced the world. These factors can also be fluid. For instance, you might have grown up in a low-income family but are now middle or upper class, which offers you a unique perspective on socioeconomic differences.

Experiences

The next level is to map your professional and personal experiences on which you might rely. These experiences should draw from both your professional and personal life. Are you a parent with children in the school district, are you a former teacher or current teacher, or are you a first-generation college student? It is also important to examine your schooling experiences. Did you have a positive experience in school, or did you encounter barriers because of your race, language, or gender? No matter how objective you try to be, these experiences, and others, are the lenses through which you will understand the education related issues that arise.

Relationship to the community
The third level is to be clear about how you, as an individual (or potential) board member identify with your surrounding community. Although all school board members reside within the same school district boundaries, each member's connection will vary depending on their physical, social, and economic position in that community. Questions to consider include: Were you born and raised in this community? Do you own or rent your home? Did you freely choose or were you forced to relocate to this community for economic reasons, or because you wanted your children to go to the schools in this neighborhood? What parts of the community are you physically and socially closest to and furthest from? This level explores what brought respective board members to this community, what keeps them there, and with what aspects of that community are they deeply embedded and far removed from. These are factors that not only inform how a board member might make decisions but also act as a guide to welcoming community voices and building community support for advancing equity in a school district.

Beliefs and social constructions of populations around you
After being clear about how you, as a board member, identify and position yourself in relationship to your district and community, then it is essential to explore beliefs that you and your community have about the various groups within your community. In research, we often refer to beliefs as social constructions because we recognize that our beliefs are not inherently our own. Instead, society helps to construct the beliefs that we adopt. Race and gender, for example, are social constructions built on the societal beliefs about various groups using cultural and historical markers, stereotypes, and identifiers.[1] The social constructions that we use to identify groups of people shape how we develop and implement policies and practices that affect these groups. In addition, these groups often internalize the policies and practices in ways that shape how they interact within society.[2] If those who operate and work inside of schools

socially construct a racialized group of children (white or Latinx children for example) as less smart than another racialized group, practices in schools might include separating (or tracking) these children into "high performing" and "low performing" groups. Children in the low performing groups might internalize such social constructions and the practice of being separated (or tracked) in ways that make them feel less motivated to engage in learning, a phenomenon that psychologists refer to as "stereotype threat" or "imposter syndrome."[3]

Social constructions shift over time and space and are instituted through legal, political, and social venues. For instance, the US Census questionnaire changed the racial category of "Negro" in 1960 to "Black, American, or Negro" in 2010.[4] Also, the Navajo tribe has traditionally and formally recognized four genders, whereas many areas in the United States acknowledge only two genders.[5] When we understand how social constructions operate, we can "unmask" assumptions that reinforce inequities. And "the point of unmasking is to liberate the oppressed, to show how categories of knowledge are used in power relationships."[6]

In education, we use the terms "deficit-based" and "asset-based" beliefs to categorize negative or positive social constructions about children and their families. Like the term suggests, deficit-based beliefs imply that certain people are deficient and lack qualities, skills, values, knowledge, and other positive characteristics. Asset-based beliefs imply that we believe that certain people have value and strength. These beliefs often coincide with policies and practices in schools. A deficit-based belief of English learners (ELs), for example, would assume that ELs cannot learn in school until they speak fluent English, and therefore, it would support the policy and practice of requiring ELs to take only English immersion courses. On the other hand, an asset-based belief would assume that ELs are capable of learning before they are fluent in English, and therefore, it would support teaching ELs in their home language, in English, and using alternative tools such as pictures, cultural symbols/artifacts, and numbers. Furthermore, an asset-based belief would recognize ELs as emerging bilingual and multilingual youth (rather than just ELs) who are attaining incredible skills, such as navigating a new culture and learning to translate for their families and community.

As this example illustrates, school board members' social constructions of groups as deficit- or asset-based can influence how they make policy decisions that affect children and their families. Not surprisingly, different decisions often contribute to different educational outcomes (or disparities) by demographics such as race, language, socioeconomic status, and ability. When it comes to education, researchers have linked various policy decisions to educational disparities, such as policies related to educational tracking (e.g., gifted and talented programs), funding inequities, school segregation, disciplinary measures, and school choice.[7]

Many school boards govern school districts that are experiencing negative disparities in educational outcomes among groups of students such as ELs, students of color, and students who live in poverty. Not only this, but many groups of students and their families (e.g., LGBTQIA+, students of color, undocumented youth, and others) also feel that their school environment is not welcoming to them, which is likely to contribute to academic disengagement and even negative mental health experiences. When considering ways to achieve educational equity for minoritized populations and improve schools' climates, school boards need to wrestle with many of the existing social constructions that reflect various populations within their school districts. And they might need to either reconstruct or disregard social constructions that are deficit oriented.

One way to do this is to approach student populations from a humanizing and asset-based position. School board members must ask themselves: What does it look like to understand that every student comes from a community that has valuable knowledge and wealth based on their social contexts, culture, and experiences, and deserves a school that teaches them in a way that promotes connection to what they are learning and their community around them?[8] When school boards govern from asset-based beliefs and social constructions, not only will they see students differently, but they will also make different decisions. For example, they might see ELs as emerging bilingual or multilingual youth and allocate resources toward cultivating their linguistic abilities through dual-language and bilingual programs rather than resources that strip their native language from them through English immersion programs. As Tyrone Howard, a professor of education, pointedly explains in his book *Why Race and Culture Matters in Schools*, there are "countless numbers of students who are classified as 'low achievers' by traditional standards," and yet they "are often some of the most talented, intellectually gifted, creative, and critical thinkers on school campuses." But, as he further describes, "the manner in which schools are structured frequently inhibits the students' ability to express these skills and show their intellectual prowess."[9] School boards must govern in a way that affirms their community's cultures and lived experiences so students can show up in school as their authentic selves and thrive. School boards also must remember that all students and their families contribute to their respective district communities.

Knowing and Understanding the School District

Advancing equity without knowing the context of the district or community is nearly impossible at best, and reckless at worst. School board members are both policy makers and educational leaders. They engage in the policy-making process, and they also provide district leadership. More than that, they are part of a team of leaders within their respective districts and communities. Because school board members are leaders within these broader entities, it is crucial for them to make the effort and take the time to deeply understand these establishments.

The internal system of a school district includes several layers. There is the districtwide leadership, who include school board members, the superintendent, and other central office leaders (also known as "district administrators"). There is also school-level leadership, who often include principals, assistant principals, deans, instructional coaches, counselors, and parent-teacher organizations and associations. Then there are classroom-level leaders, such as teachers, teaching assistants, students, and families.

Ultimately, as we see, these establishments are made up of people. When we prioritize equity, we must also prioritize the stories and experiences of people who have been treated inequitably. In her article "Whose Vision Will Guide Racial Equity in Schools?" Sonya Douglass reminds us:

> To truly transform education, we must first deepen our understanding of the great battle that we are in. This begins with actually asking people of color what they want and need and then listening to what they say. The voices, concerns, ideas, and vision for what students, parents, and educators of color want and need is the evidentiary basis upon which any agenda for educational equity must be developed, if that is, in fact, what we truly seek to do.[10]

As you increase your knowledge and understanding of your community, remember that the voices of those who have historically been and are currently most marginalized must be elevated during your journey to advance equity.

The school board

In this section, I present a series of questions for school board members. These questions are not exhaustive. Instead, they can be used as a starting point to get school board members thinking about what they might need to know to build contextual knowledge and understanding of their school boards. Getting answers to these types of questions will require identifying and asking longtime community leaders and district employees about their experiences and opinions on the boards and in their districts and communities. Some of these questions can also be answered by researching archived board meeting agendas and minutes, as well as in the media.

Every school board member should begin by knowing every other individual school board member. These are the people with whom each board member will be working directly to make district decisions. To move forward any changes in the district, every decision and action that the board pursues requires a majority vote. Every vote counts, but you also do not need *every* vote to move a decision forward—just more than half the votes. And, more importantly, knowing the school board president is crucial. The president is often the individual who usually sets the agenda for board meetings. The research clearly supports the notion that if an item is not on the agenda, the school board may not even have the opportunity to discuss it, which can stop equity efforts from even surfacing.

Here are some questions to ask of each board member:

- How long have you been serving in your position?
- Were you elected or appointed?
- What part(s) of the community do you represent?
- How do you identify and position yourself (e.g., racial background, gender, profession)?
- What are your beliefs about the different people within the district and community?
- Do you think students from minoritized backgrounds are being adequately served by the district? If so, how? If not, why, and what do you think needs to change to make this happen?

Then it is important to understand how these individual board members operate as a collective board. *The following include questions related to the board as a whole:*

- Which school board members collaborate the most? Which school board members are at odds with each other?
- What issues are board members collaborating about? What issues are board members experiencing conflict over?

- What is the relationship between the board and the superintendent?
- How has the board addressed equity issues?
- Is the board divided over any issues pertaining to equity? If so, who is/are the target population(s) (racially, economically, etc.) of these issues?

Board members should also explore the history of their school board. This not only helps to contextualize the current board's efforts around equity issues, but also offers insight into what the community (particularly its voters) has favored over time. In my research, I noticed stark differences in both school board demographics and issues that school boards have devoted attention to over the last few decades. *Questions that explore the historical context of the board include the following*:

- Who have been the individual school board members serving on the board over the last couple of decades?
- What work have the various members done related to equity?
- Were their efforts in support of equity or not?
- Were their decisions about this work unanimous or split, and if split, why?

The district community
Superintendent

One of the most vital relationships for school board members is with the district superintendent. A school board member should be intentional about understanding the positionality of the superintendent. *Questions to answer about the superintendent might include the following*:

- How long has the superintendent been in this position?
- What other positions and districts have they worked in?
- What is the background of the superintendent in terms of their credentials, experience (personal and professional), and associations with organizations (personal and professional)?

- Are they well received by school leaders, teachers, parents, and community members? Why or why not?
- How do they identify, and what are their beliefs about the community, particularly those from minoritized backgrounds?
- Do they talk about communities in deficit- or asset-based ways?
- Do they suggest or develop policies and practices that align with their stance on equity?

While many superintendents will champion equity, others might not. More often, they will support advancing equity, but only to the extent that equitable policies and practices directly result in outcomes that increase a district's rankings. One superintendent of a district that I studied spent a significant effort achieving what he termed a "return on investment." He said that this was "being accountable for the money that we put into programs and the success of the students we get out of it" and "looking at that through everything we do." This sounds smart. Yet success is often defined through narrow metrics, such as test scores or graduation rates. These metrics fail to account for a holistic perspective of equity. Other important measures, like the number of times that racist incidents occur or students or staff are harassed based on their sexual or gender identity, are not reported via test scores. The question of how a district superintendent measures district effectiveness and success is vital. In other words, will the superintendent champion equity issues for the long haul, regardless of these issues' connection to rankings or community support? And if not, school board members should plan to hire an equity-focused superintendent, and in the meantime, find ways to direct and work around the current superintendent to advance equity (e.g., using voting power and coalition building, which I discuss further in chapter 3).

Other district administrators

School board members should also have a deep understanding of the second level of leadership in school districts. These are the administrators (sometimes called "central office administrators") whose responsibility is to lead district-level work in specialized areas. While the terminology might vary by district, their job titles are often directors of "XYZ," such as special education, ELs, human resources, technology, or family and community engagement. In addition, in the past couple of decades, there has been an emergence of directors of equity and inclusion (DEI) in many districts.[11] The institution of equity directors in districts is usually a response to some sort of racist or similarly based incident that sparked a community uproar. Consequently, like most DEI positions, these are vulnerable positions that require a great deal of support to be effective and maintained.

The administrators at this second level of leadership often know how inequities exist and function throughout their district. They are also key actors in helping to create and implement policies and practices that aim to address equity. Knowing who they are and how they themselves are in terms of identity, in relationship to the community, their professional expertise, and the social constructions and beliefs of the different populations in the district is important.

One district that I observed created an equity office in response to an Office of Civil Rights (OCR) investigation concerning ELs. The district hired a Black woman for a DEI position. She was well respected in the community and had extensive experience as a teacher and school leader in two places—a more progressive city and the city where she accepted the DEI position, which was known to be less progressive. She also was pursuing a graduate degree through a program well known for its equity and inclusion focus on education.

This woman and her team had a deep understanding of equity. She demonstrated her expertise to the school board by effectively using data and theory. Notably, this equity team felt confident enough to push back on school board members' beliefs about certain students. For instance, during one meeting, a board member shared a concern about how "those refugee students who are coming in and don't have prior knowledge" were unprepared for coursework. In response, a team member said, "It's worth noting too that some of our students who are immigrant students have been educated in their country." Soon after, the equity team member also noted, "I really challenge us to rethink how we talk about kids." The board received this pushback favorably. The board's close working relationship with the equity team created a level of trust that allowed discussions that could shift social constructions and beliefs. Together, the team and the board were able to make some significant changes to policies and practices in schools, including a requirement for all teachers to earn an EL-endorsement, which was needed in the context of the OCR complaint and investigation.

Despite this successful example, research on equity directors finds that these positions are vulnerable in both structural and political ways.[12] Structurally, they are often vague and insufficiently resourced. Politically, they lack the power to advance equity. It is not enough for school board members to simply understand and engage with administrators in positions related to equity. They should also consider how they can clarify and enhance the role of these positions, as well as share power with those in these positions with the aim of advancing equity.

Inside schools

It is not only important to know people at the district level; it is also important to become familiar with and connected to those in schools and classrooms. Individuals at this level will probably be more difficult for school board members to know personally. They are often most distant from board-level work, especially in larger school districts. Still, school board members should make the effort to develop at least a broad understanding of *all* the schools and classrooms, aiming to get connected with every school leader and at least two to three teachers. By "connected," I mean to make sure that they know you and feel comfortable reaching out to you with questions or concerns, and vice versa. You might connect with them via social media or give them your card with a phone number and email that they can use to reach you, and in return, ask for their contact information. These spaces inside schools are where policy and practice unfold into teaching and learning.

School board representation varies. Sometimes board members are elected "at ward" to represent a specific neighborhood and a specific set of schools. Other times, board members are elected "at large," which means that they are tasked with representing the full district. Either way, school board members should always remember their responsibility for governing all schools in the district, regardless of who elected them. Not all schools are equal. Each school and each classroom has a different set of advantages and challenges. It is important for school board members to have a clear idea of what these challenges and advantages are so that they know what initiatives, resources, and services to support to advance equity at the school and classroom levels.

School community

School board members should have a working knowledge of each school community. This includes the school's demographics of its students, teachers, and staff, as well as classroom sizes, staff retention, and the dynamics of its respective school zone. As a board member, you should also learn what these student demographics are in a disaggregated manner and in association with academic and socioemotional measures. For instance, this means knowing the percentage of students by common identifiers (e.g., race, gender, language, income, and disability status), and who showed proficiency on academic tests (e.g., state and federal tests). Digging deeper, it's important to know how students are doing on performance assessments beyond test scores, such as portfolio assessments, creative literacy, and reading assessments that measure factors such as students' excitement about reading (e.g., Gholdy Muhammad's *Cultivating Genius*) and whether districts are even encouraging and acknowledging non-test performance assessments (hopefully they are).[13] Other key indicators include graduation rates, participation of students in special programs (e.g., gifted and talented services and advanced placement courses), and the types of students who are being disciplined (e.g., with suspension, expulsion, and detention).

This type of data can often be found on district websites, state education board websites, and other national websites such as those of the National Center for Education Statistics (nces.ed.gov) and OCR (ocrdata.ed.gov). If important data are not reported, school board members can request them from the superintendent and other district leaders and even ask that they present this information in more depth and with more explanation at school board meetings. Sometimes, especially in large school districts, there is a data/research department that collects and stores data, and board members can make specific data requests. Finally, districts can partner with consulting firms (e.g., American Institutes for Research and WestEd are notable ones) and university faculty to help them with data collection and analyses.

It is also important to know what questions to ask about the data when it is presented. For instance, school board members might want to understand what the cut off scores are that define the various levels of "proficiency." They also might want to ask for numbers alongside percentages because, while percentages are useful for comparative purposes, percentages sometimes obscure the numerical impact. In addition, data on individual students to measure such factors as growth of student assessments are often more useful than cohort data.

Data go beyond numbers. Qualitative data that measure school climate and culture are equally important as quantitative data, if not more so. This type of data might be more difficult to collect, but school boards can allocate funding used to conduct regular (e.g., annual or biannual) surveys, interviews, focus groups, and observations that can measure key factors that impact students and contribute to healthy (or unhealthy) schools. Using these data, board members can develop questions that will allow a greater understanding of what is going on in schools related to equity over time.

For instance, if the data indicates that only 5 percent of students in gifted and talented programs are Latinx, but Latinx students represent

25 percent of the district, board members should ask why Latinx students are underrepresented in this program. Many schools identify students for these special programs based on parent and teacher recommendations, and sometimes through tests. Yet teachers might have racial biases based on their social constructions that keep them from recommending Latinx students, for instance, at the same rate as other students. In addition, parents of Latinx descent might not have adequate knowledge to navigate a system that requires them to recommend their children to access this program. They might not even know that they *can* request that their children be tested. And tests, as they are developed by people, also can have inherent biases based on cultural nuances of the questions asked. Moreover, if the students are also ELs, they might be able to pass a test in their first language, but not in English. That should not be a reason to exclude them from these services. In fact, there is a whole debate about whether these "special" programs should be offered only to specific students rather than the whole school community, which is another important question that board members should explore.[14]

Another way to learn about the school community is to invite school community members to present at school board meetings. If not already instituted, the board should consider making this a regular practice by inviting one or more schools to present highlights and lowlights on a rotating basis at every meeting, or at least at every other meeting. This is an opportunity for board members to ask critical questions at the school and classroom levels.

Board members should also visit schools with a purpose beyond showing up and showing their faces. Board members can use this time to ask questions and talk with school leaders, teachers, and students, as well as observe various dynamics in schools and classrooms. Observations can reveal inequitable practices that might be normalized in schools, as well as practices that advance equity. In one district that I studied, a board member shared that he found that ELs were being segregated from English speakers while visiting a school. When he asked the principal about this practice, the principal noted, "Those are the Mexicans . . . they don't speak English." This observation and conversation with the principal prompted the board member to call for further investigation. These practices were soon deemed inequitable and reversed to offer a better learning environment for ELs throughout the whole district. His willingness to critically observe, ask questions, and speak up mattered.

School board members should also engage in conversation with teachers, students, and families as much as possible. It is important to recognize that many students are being raised and cared for by several people whom they consider their family, including parents, grandparents, siblings, aunts and uncles, cousins, and even close family friends. Board members' engagement with families should coincide with their engagement with the community. That starts with taking advantage of opportunities to attend sessions like parent-teacher organization (PTO) or parent-teacher association (PTA) meetings to get a sense of what is going on within the district's schools. Still, school board members must go beyond the PTO/PTA to reach families.

Family community

There is a lot of research demonstrating the power of family engagement and how this contributes to more equitable learning environments. Yet deficit perspectives of families from minoritized backgrounds are very common.[15] Many of these families cannot or will not participate in the normalized practices that schools use to engage parents, including PTO or PTA meetings, because they feel unwelcomed or because those creating these activities do not think about how to engage *all* parents. Knowing this, school board members must move beyond these typical practices to reach families whose voices are often unsolicited. Some ways to do this include inviting families to join committees, asking those family members to invite members of other families, and asking teachers and principals for connections to families. Another way is for school board members to be present in school neighborhoods.

My colleague and I recently spent a few hours on a Saturday afternoon knocking on doors and talking to families in a neighborhood surrounding a school. The Black and Latinx families we spoke with were eager to answer our questions, and these conversations revealed deep inequities in this school's admissions policies. All of them shared that they wanted their children to attend the stellar Montessori school that was within walking distance from their homes, but they could not get their children enrolled despite multiple efforts. We also asked about their school board. Most of them had never engaged with a board member, but they said that they often vote in the school board elections. Interestingly, one person said they voted by looking for a Spanish-sounding last name among the candidates. These are the families that school board members are unlikely to engage with at a PTO or school board meeting. But they live in these schools' neighborhood and can shed light on various inequities related to their neighboring schools.

Teacher community

Teachers are at the ground level with our children. Not surprisingly, evidence supports that teachers are one of the most impactful factors in students' learning and schooling experiences.[16] In addition, teachers with more years of experience are often better equipped to support student learning.[17] Also, teachers of color are often more keenly aware of schoolwide inequities.[18] For instance, as Garcia, Muñiz, and Garza found in their research, "Because Latinx teachers are sometimes the product of the same unjust educational pipeline as their students, they are critically conscious about policies and practices that perpetuate inequality and are more willing to act as agents of change."[19] Observing teachers in a supportive (not a disruptive) manner, coupled with connecting to experienced teachers and teachers of color, will offer school board members important insights into classroom experiences and issues of (in)equity that they might be able to influence at the governance level.

Youth community

Students are highly sensitized to and conscious of everyday inequities that they and their peers experience.[20] Sadly, however, these experiences are often disregarded in governance-level decisions. For instance, in one study, many of the educational decision-makers, including school board members, failed to listen, reflect, and implement youth suggestions authentically. When youth spoke out about the need to address racism, the board members responded by discrediting these youth, acting surprised at their articulation of problems, and praising their presentation skills rather than the content that aimed to address racism.[21] Melanie Bertrand, a professor and scholar of youth participatory action research, envisions a "Third Space"—a space that "could become sites where Students of Color and educational decision makers co-create hybrid and dynamic solutions to address inequalities."[22] School boards can adopt this concept to think about ways to not just solicit input from youth and their families, but to work with them to cocreate solutions to injustices that they experience in schools.

The local community

Although the center of my research has focused on school boards and district governance, the cornerstone of this work is the community. When I first started conducting research, the umbrella question I sought to answer was "How can communities disrupt educational inequities?" At first, I examined this question through a policy lens, asking what local policies can advance equity in education and who makes these policies. This led me to examine the role of official policy makers at the local level—school boards. I soon realized that I could not disentangle school boards from the community. These two entities are intertwined, especially when it comes to the work of moving equity forward.

Who is the community? For school board members, the community includes a range of populations. There is the *school community*, which I highlighted in the previous section. This includes youth, families, and people who work and volunteer in the school district. Overlapping the school community is the *district community*—those who reside, work, and play in the neighborhoods that surround the schools of each respective school district. These are often the voters who decide the fate of an elected school board. To be clear, not everyone who resides in the community can vote (e.g., undocumented residents in most, but not all, states). Moreover, not every family whose children attend the district school or every employee of the district lives within the school district boundaries, making them unable to vote for board members or propositions that affect that respective school district.[23] Yet these people are still district constituents because they are part of the community that the school board governs. There are also *community leaders*, who often transcend multiple communities. Community leaders tend to be situated within a community-based organization, a different local or state political system (e.g., city council, county commissioner, state legislature), or a business that has a stake in that community and whose mission and purpose is to provide services and/or resources to residents within a school district.

To emphasize the importance of school boards knowing the community, I draw from an educational leadership and policy professor, Terrance Green, and his *Community Equity Literacy (CEL)* framework.[24] Using this lens, CEL argues that educational leaders, such as school board members, should be literate about their community in ways that disrupt the inequuities that transcend schools. CEL urges educational leaders to learn the community's history, identify and utilize the community's assets, and know how to work around barriers to advance equity in schools and the community. Some school board members embody CEL because of how embedded in and committed to their communities they are; others are literate in only parts of their community. Still, some might be literate but do not have the desire or courage to advocate for equity. Nonetheless, board members cannot do the work of advancing equity alone. As one community advocate put it:

Community involvement over the past seven years has changed the district and, in my opinion, it has made it better. . . . It has challenged the district and the system—the public school system—to be better, and the public has done that. Now we've had good talented people in positions to drive that change, but we got a long way to go. But if it wasn't for the engagement of the public, and holding them account-able, and pushing them and challenging them, then you wouldn't see what's going on now.

As reflected in this comment, working with the community requires commitment over the long haul. It also requires school board members to gain a deep understanding of that community's history so they can identify the root causes of inequities. School board members can utilize this knowledge to use existing community assets (e.g., community lead-ers, businesses, nonprofits, public spaces) and to build new community assets that penetrate the district system and lead to real and sustain-able change.

In the three districts that I studied, inequities were addressed only when community advocates got involved. They either gained or used existing knowledge and then acted on this knowledge to address ineq-uities. This unfolded differently in each district. For example, in one district, community advocates representing their organizations found out about academic disparities by serving on districtwide committees. They leveraged this knowledge to advocate for more racially and cul-turally diverse district leadership, including new board members. In a different district, when one community advocate learned that the dis-trict had adopted discriminatory practices for ELs, they filed an official complaint with the OCR, which led to major policy changes. This same community member later became a board member. In the third district, after state policies prompted several inequities, community advocates who deeply understood the community's history ran for school board. When elected, they had an equity-driven majority vote that they used to hire an equity-focused superintendent and allocate resources to support the district's most minoritized communities. All these community leaders used their knowledge of inequities to advocate for changes in their districts.[25]

CONCLUSION

Educational inequities are institutionally and systemically entrenched in districts, schools, and classrooms. These inequities are not easily recognizable, nor will they go away overnight. The principles of *knowledge* and *understanding* will lay the foundation that school board members need to recognize inequities and to identify the necessary resources and practices to disrupt them. Key aspects of this critical work for board members are to know who they are in relation to their community, acknowledging how they socially construct the various facets of their community, and building an understanding of both the district and the community that it serves. In chapter 3, I will lay out the last two principles, *skills* and *strategies*, which, when connected to *knowledge* and *understanding*, will spur the actions needed to advance equity.

3

The School Board Governance for Equity Framework Principles 3 and 4: Skills and Strategies

THIS CHAPTER DESCRIBES principles 3 and 4 within the School Board Governance for Equity (SBGE) framework: skills and strategies. As mentioned earlier, *skills* are the actions needed to accomplish a task or goal, whereas *strategies* map out the steps to achieve this task or goal. I detail four areas within these principles: (1) coalition-building and coalition politics, (2) leveraging state and federal policies, (3) being proactively responsive, and (4) imagining the possibilities. To begin, I explain why and how to engage in coalition building as a school board member. Then I describe the importance of using state and federal policies and ways that a school board member might do this. Next, I outline why school board members should be proactively responsive to equity issues that arise. Finally, I wrap up this discussion by urging school board members to imagine what is possible, how they might achieve these possibilities through strategic planning, and what questions related to equity they might pose during their planning process.

COALITION BUILDING AND COALITION POLITICS

School board members cannot advance educational equity in meaningful ways alone. Building coalitions among fellow board members, district administration, families, community leaders, and other state and local policy makers is a prerequisite to moving equity forward. Coalition building happens when two or more individuals or groups work together toward a shared goal. Coalition politics involves coalition building at a political level that is focused on changing policies, systems, and institutions. As discussed in the previous section, getting to know yourself and the world that surrounds you is only the first part. Building coalitions and engaging in coalition politics make up the second part.

For instance, to get issues on the agenda, school board members must work with the school board president, who typically decides what is on each meeting agenda. Further, the board also must gain a majority vote on these issues to support or create a districtwide policy, implement a practice, or integrate a resource or service. Suppose that the board president or the majority of the board does not support a particular issue. In that case, the alternative is to use school board members' coalitions with families, district administrators, and the community to push for the issue to be heard and prioritized.

These coalitions can advocate for issues in board meetings during public comments and reports from the superintendent or other district leaders. Coalitions also can lobby board members by sharing their support of issues via email, in individual meetings with board members, or during districtwide meetings, such as town halls or community councils. Moreover, these coalitions are often positioned to use their voting power to campaign against or elect board members who support moving equity forward, and vice versa. Developing coalitions with school board colleagues and advocates supporting similar issues is critical to moving anything forward at the governing level.[1]

What Are Coalition Politics?

Shirley Chisholm, elected in 1968 as the first Black woman to the US Congress and later the first Black candidate to run for US president under a major political party, was also one of the first people to use the term "coalition politics." In her 1972 article, "The Politics of Coalition," she explained that "there is hope for oppressed groups if we unite and challenge the forces which now hold the power in our country." Having "long spoken out in favor of coalition politics," Chisholm described that "Black women surely know the value of such action" because they have been "involved in both black and women's liberation."[2] To engage successfully in coalition politics, individuals or groups must come together across boundaries of race, class, gender, and other differences to advance shared goals and support each other's goals.

In my work, I explored coalition politics between Black/African American and Latinx communities. One of the school districts I studied experienced a considerable shift in student demographics. Over twenty years, from 1990 to 2010, the Latinx student population increased 250 percent districtwide, and the statewide population of English learners (ELs) increased 255 percent. Meanwhile, the Black student population remained steady at around 12 percent. After these demographic shifts, the two communities experienced tensions over the limited resources that they both needed to serve their respective communities adequately. I also happened to grow up in this community, where I lived for nearly fifteen years and straddled the boundaries of this racialized space as a mixed-race, Black and Chicana person. I knew firsthand that the tensions between Black and Latinx people in this community ran high. These tensions often resemble competition over political, social, and economic power and resources.

In this district, we found that Black and Latinx community leaders, including board members, were often too distracted, divided, and distrusting of each other to engage in coalition politics. Many considered building a coalition long after they began advocating for policy changes. Still, by that time, it was too late to identify a shared goal that would honor each community's needs in terms of equity. Because they advocated for their issues separately, district officials tried to appease both communities with one watered-down policy that failed to meet each community's unique needs adequately. Between both communities, they would have had the power and influence to push for substantial changes if they had worked together. But unfortunately, this was a missed opportunity.[3]

Although the idea of coalitions is broadly understood, I draw from feminist scholars to define coalition politics. Engaging in coalition politics requires a few steps. First, people do not need to share skin color or even ideologies to coalesce.[4] Angela Davis, an activist and Black feminist scholar, explains, "We need to be more reflective, more critical and more explicit about our concepts of community." After pointing to the heterogeneity within groups, Davis urges that "we need to move away from such arguments as 'Well, she's not really Black.' 'She comes from such-and-such a place.' 'Her hair is . . .' 'She doesn't listen to "our" music,' and so forth. What counts as Black is not so important as our political coalition building commitment to engage in anti-racist, anti-sexist, and anti-homophobic work."[5] Often, boundaries, such as race, gender, or sexuality, inhibit connections. But it's these connections across boundaries that can be powerful enough to reverse injustices.

Second, coalescing requires groups to build solidarity. Chandra Mohanty (2003), a transnational feminist scholar, defines solidarity as "mutuality, accountability, and the recognition of common interests as the basis for relationships among diverse communities. Rather than assuming an enforced commonality of oppression, the practice of solidarity foregrounds communities of people who have chosen to work and fight together. Diversity and difference are central values here–to be acknowledged and respected, not erased in the building of alliances."[6]

Once groups recognize and value the attributes that both connect them and differentiate them from each other, they can understand and advocate for each other's needs. As Audre Lorde (1979) puts it, "divide and conquer, in our world, must become *define and empower*."[7] To define and empower is to identify a shared goal and support each other's efforts in moving toward that goal.

Third, groups must move from coalition building to coalition politics. Coalition politics are not easy. Bernice Reagon, a Black feminist activist, points out that communities of color use coalitions as a strategy "to ensure their immediate survival and that of future generations."[8] She says that this "is some of the most dangerous work you can do. And you shouldn't look for comfort."[9] It is a commitment over the long haul that requires working through disagreements to advance a common goal, even though people (in this case, school board members) might not achieve the goal of educational equity in their lifetime.

BOARD MEMBERS AND COALITION BUILDING

As I have argued previously, school board members are the link between the district and the community. Board members who embody Community Equity Literacy (CEL) are positioned to be the builders of coalitions, and advancing equity in education often requires coalitions.

Equity is broad; it is an umbrella concept encompassing multiple issues of injustice. The work of equity includes identifying systemic and institutional injustices across communities. Then it requires people in leadership to invest, redistribute, and normalize resources, services, policies, and practices in ways that provide equal opportunities for all children and their families. It is an uphill battle against white supremacy, patriarchy, capitalism, and other forms of oppression that create a power imbalance. To do this work, board members must identify whom they can coalesce with within and beyond the school board.

Identifying the Who

You cannot coalesce with everyone and anyone. This is especially true when it comes to advancing equity. This, and the fact that coalition-building is hard work, mean that school board members should strategically identify with whom they can build coalitions.

Shared positionalities

Coalitions are concentric circles. Begin with your inner circles. These people usually share similar positionalities (e.g., demographics, geographic connections, social understandings, and commitment to racial and social justice) as you. If you are a minoritized person, this might mean identifying other people who are also minoritized (in similar or different ways from you). You are likely to share everyday experiences when it comes to systemic and institutional oppression, and perhaps even similar cultural practices. These shared experiences often result in common beliefs and commitments to equity issues.

Still, as the saying goes, "Not all skin folk are kinfolk." Just because people share similar backgrounds, whether that be race, gender, sexuality, or some other demographic, does not mean that they automatically have similar beliefs. White supremacy, patriarchy, colonization, and other forms of oppressive systems are powerful, and those who experience this can certainly internalize and reify oppression.[10] Although many Black, Indigenous, and other people of color (BIPOC) school board members whom I have interviewed and observed were champions for equity, you cannot assume anything about their worldviews, beliefs, or actions based on their backgrounds. I have witnessed some people who act in harmful ways toward minoritized communities, including their own. Sometimes they operate with a very different set of morals and ethics that do not align with equity work. More often, though, they do not clearly understand how oppressive systems operate. Instead, they have bought into the myth of meritocracy, as discussed next.

Myth of meritocracy

The myth of meritocracy is the false idea that anyone can achieve anything if they work hard enough.[11] This myth negates systemic barriers that exist because of racism and other forms of oppression. It often points to a few successful people, like Oprah Winfrey (a famous and wealthy Black woman), and declares, "She is successful despite her background and demographics. Why can't you be?" In education, this myth assumes that all students receive the same instruction, but it fails to acknowledge that all students do not start from the same place and do not receive the same opportunities along the way.

This myth is further perpetuated by a myopic focus on student metrics, such as test scores, arguing that outcomes are reflective of student achievement and learning. Therefore, students and their families are credited or blamed for their "achievement" level on tests, which are presumably connected to student outcomes. The myth of meritocracy favors equality over equity. For instance, people who subscribe to this ideology will likely believe that the government should allocate the same per-pupil expenditures for each student, regardless of differences. Meanwhile, those who understand meritocracy to be a myth would support the redistribution of wealth and thus support the allocation of more funding for students with higher needs, such as ELs and low-income students. But again, this requires an understanding of why and how inequities are so deeply embedded, including historical legacies of oppression, and a commitment to rectifying these injustices.

The utilitarian injustice

Unlike the myth of meritocracy, some people subscribe to utilitarian actions that might support equity or provide different resources to different populations, but only to the extent that this does not threaten the majoritarian population. If this threat exists, those in power will easily dismiss the needs of those living on the margins.[12] For instance, in one study, a state threatened to remove funding from one of its districts if the district continued its ethnic studies program. This program provided targeted support for students who showed signs of academic struggles (they were primarily Latinx). One Latino board member was the swing vote, voting with two other white board members to eliminate the program. Meanwhile, the only other Latinx board member voted against the elimination and wanted to challenge the state based on racial discrimination. The school board eliminated the program by a 4–1 vote.

In his comments, the Latinx board member who was the swing vote said that he had "sworn to abide by [the law]." Concerned about the district losing state funding, he also explained, "My first responsibility as a governing board member is to provide a quality education to all students in this district." In a later interview, reflecting on his vote, he said that he "took a utilitarian approach . . . for the greater good." His support of this program, in other words, was only to the extent that it would not affect the larger population.

After the board eliminated the program, it took nearly ten years of litigation to reverse the law after the court declared that this law was racially discriminatory. Imagine if there had been a coalition on the board and three members had voted against the elimination. Perhaps the school board could have forced the state to reckon with its state-sanctioned injustice much earlier, thereby saving the program, as well as time and resources. More important, the district could have better served those minoritized children who live on the margins. This example reflects a board member operating without a clear understanding of how inequitable systems function and how they can be dismantled with coalitions and by leveraging state and federal policies, which I will discuss later.[13]

Color-evasive racism

I have also seen board members act in color-evasive ways, making it hard to coalesce over equity.[14] For instance, in one district that my colleague and I studied, the lone BIPOC board member, a Black man, disregarded Black families' concerns about racist acts in the schools.[15] He said that he "just doesn't think it [racism] is going to go away. We can't control that. We definitely can't control that in schools." Then he tried to shift the focus to the racial achievement gap, which highlights the difference in test scores between BIPOC students and their white counterparts. Yet Black families were not concerned about test scores. They were concerned that the students and educators were treating their children in racist ways. This type of treatment, in fact, is often a significant contributing factor to achievement gaps. In other words, racism, along with economic and other types of oppression, are often the root problem of disparities in student outcomes. And achievement gaps are simply a symptom of these problems.

Many parents expressed their distaste for this board member's comments, with one parent noting, "We all know that you're not going to end that [racism]. But we don't tolerate it. We don't allow it to go unprosecuted." These parents pointed out what this board member should have been able to identify—that racism should not go unchecked. When it does, the district sends the message that it does not believe that racism is a big problem and it will condone or overlook racism, which increases the chances of increased explicit racist acts in schools. It is nearly impossible to build meaningful coalitions with individuals who ignore or tolerate racism or any other type of systemic and institutional oppression unless they can shift their perspective.

Allies and coconspirators

Coalitions often require allies and coconspirators. Allies are people with privileges who align their interests and commitments with those who do not share those privileges.[16] Their alignment supports minoritized communities' efforts to advance an agenda that is either shared or similar. Sometimes the agenda differs, but they are willing to support it in return for support on their own agenda.

Coconspirators go beyond allyship

As Bettina Love, a scholar of education and abolitionist teaching, explains, "coconspirator functions as a verb, not a noun." Coconspirators operate with both courage and a deep understanding of systemic injustice. They listen to those who experience oppression and are willing to forgo their privileges in exchange for others being able to experience freedom and justice.[17]

Allies share responsibilities

Allyship is more common than coconspiratorship. Allies invite minoritized people to the decision-making table and step in to do their share of the work. Yet because minoritized representatives are often needed in these spaces, such as school boards, it is easy to tokenize them and expect them to do all the equity-related work. These expectations can be depleting for minoritized people, so they fail to put forth all their energy and effort toward advancing equity. For instance, in one district that I studied, several white school board members expressed their support of the lone Latinx school board member. They declared him the leader on issues affecting Latinx students, low-income students, and ELs. By doing this, they could move this responsibility from their plate to his. In other words, they supported him, but their support simply meant more work for him and less for them.

In an interview, this Latinx board member recalled feeling like "I'm not your token Brown person. I can speak on everything. Don't just ask me to speak on [English-language learners]. Don't just ask me to speak on poverty." His comments reflect the position of many BIPOC board members who serve as the only or one of the few BIPOC individuals in these spaces. Often, others will pigeonhole these folks to represent only issues of equity. And while this is important, they should not be the *only* ones speaking on these issues.

He later explained that "as a Latino board member," he is "trying always [to] identify allies to speak on issues and offering [his]self to be an ally on other issues so that there's diversity of representation for an issue." Building on this, he said, "When we have allies that don't look like me talk about this, for whatever reason in our society, they have more credibility. Because I just look like I'm self-serving, and I'm only talking about my kids, you know?"

Although it was not his experience, this board member highlighted the power of allyship in offering a broader level of support that legitimizes equity issues. He argued that their shared agenda is grounded in the idea that every board member should be committed to *all* students, not just those who look like you.

Coconspirators take risks

Conversely, coconspirators are willing to put themselves on the line for others with fewer privileges. In February 2023, a school board voted to terminate a Black female superintendent who served in a small, rural school district in Arizona. While the reasons for the board's termination of her were not made clear in the school board meeting, many people agreed that racism and sexism were the culprits. The school board was all-white and nearly all-male (there was only one female member). Two board members, including the woman, voted against the termination. The white male board member who opposed the termination stated during the board meeting, "I want to say this very clearly. I think if Dr. Battle looked a little more like me and a little less like a woman of color, we would not be sitting here." When asked for his vote, he said, "Fuck no!" This is the action of a coconspirator.[18]

That said, it is important to tread these waters carefully. School boards advancing equity should take their time observing and being in conversation with people before deciding to build coalitions. And they should be able to identify whether people will act as allies or coconspirators, or even when their support might waver depending on the circumstances. The school board member who said "Fuck no!" when voting to terminate Dr. Battle is an example of someone who should have carefully considered his actions beforehand (which he likely did). His actions might provoke a backlash from his school board peers or others in the community who are anti-equity (even though, as a white man, the back-lash would likely be less significant compared to a minoritized person). Yet his actions signaled his unwavering support of this leader and his willingness to speak out against racism and patriarchy. They might have also indicated to fellow school board members committed to equity that he was someone to consider coalition building with.

Within the Board
Building trust and attentiveness

Over the years, many board members have described to me how they built coalitions with each other. Some began with developing relation-ships in informal settings. One Latinx board member called this work "ally building." This board included five white women, one Latinx man, and one Black woman. The work of ally building, in this case, was with the white female board members. He explained that his goal was to build "relationships, camaraderie, and emotional intelligence" as a group to contribute to a "high-functioning" school board. He was also intentional about connecting with board members during conferences and other informal events.

He shared a story of inviting the school board to a holiday party that he hosted at his home. The party had a mariachi band. He reflected on how much "they loved it," even though "they didn't know what the hell they were singing." These moments created a level of trust needed to coalesce as a group.

This same board member also shared the importance of his coalition between him and the only other board member of color, a Black woman. They often supported each other by voting together. Sometimes it was tricky to collaborate because open meeting laws limited discussion of board business outside of public meetings. He described their collabo-ration as a game: "If you know the game, you can go 'Well, I know what she likes. She wants this. I'll give her support and she'll see the vote.' And next time I do something, she'll be 'OK, I can do that.'" These board members were committed to equity, but in different ways. Because of their positionalities and connections with the community, one of these board members represented the Latinx community and the other represented the Black community on issues that directly affected them. Their coalescing, as illustrated, required attentiveness to each other's efforts and direction.

As these examples show, you can expect that the type and depth of the coalitions that you build will likely change over time. You might coalesce with some people on more of a surface level (e.g., votes over small items, gestures of support) until you can trust them at a deeper level. This will require conversations, observations, and maybe even a little research on the background of individuals to learn about their histories and alliances. Once you trust individuals, you will be able to coalesce over an array of issues and initiatives. This requires knowing and being willing to support each other's agendas.

Either way, it's important to identify people who are committed to equity, understand what type of equity they care the most about, and know the extent of their commitment. For instance, some board members might care only about issues related to gender inequities or socioeconomic inequities. Others might care only about issues of race. By knowing this, you can identify the issues that you will be able to coalesce over relatively easily. And once you build trust, you can work toward encouraging them to support issues of inequities that are beyond their scope of commitment. This might require deeper discussions, sharing your stories or other people's stories, and urging training and professional development on relevant topics.

Beyond the board

Equity work is often messy and complicated. A school board will likely not always agree on issues related to equity. In fact, board members who are not committed to equity might also coalesce, and then it turns out that there are two coalitions working in two very different directions. If this is the case, or even if a board is unanimous about an issue, the board will likely need outside support to move matters forward. This might mean urging district administration to develop, support, or implement a policy, resolution, or practice. Either way, as I will discuss below, building coalitions with individuals who work at the district level is essential.

Board/superintendent coalitions

Coalescing with the district superintendent is key at this level. This relationship can speed up, slow down, or break equity work. Many people have written about the relationship between superintendents and the school board regarding effective district governance. Some scholars examine school board motives and the various ways that they understand, or even misunderstand, their roles and how this influences their approach to working with the superintendent. For instance, Meredith Mountford, a scholar of district leaders and governance, classified these differing board approaches as either "micromanagers" or "collaborators." She highlighted similar research that classified board members as perceiving themselves to have "power over" or "power with" others.[19] On the other hand, this research also points out that board members might perceive and experience superintendents who wield a lot of power (indeed, perhaps too much) over the school board.

Collaborating and sharing power and authority are the most effective ways to approach a coalition with the superintendent. However, if the superintendent is not supportive of equity work, board members are responsible for enforcing equity advancement by supporting issues despite the lack of superintendent support. Advancing equity work without superintendent support is not easy; it may require micromanaging for a short period. A board might need to vote to override the superintendent's decisions to shift the district's direction toward equity.

Simultaneously, board members can identify, recruit, and hire new district leadership with whom they can collaborate and share power.

A coalition with the superintendent often will be more effective when it involves three to five major players. For instance, a coalition might include one to two board members, the superintendent, one or two key community leaders, and another central office administrator.

Board/other administrator coalitions

Other district-level administrators serve essential roles in promoting and supporting equity, particularly in the implementation phase of this work. As mentioned previously, these administrators oversee work focused on particular areas (e.g., ELs, special education, low-income, gifted, and talented students, family and community engagement, and human resources). They typically lead to the implementation of the systems and practices that reflect district-level policies and goals. They are regularly connected with all the schools in the district and build relationships with principals and teachers to support them in addressing various areas of equity.

School board members should select carefully those individual administrators whose work aligns with the areas of equity that the district plans to address. Likewise, engaging key teachers, community leaders, and maybe even youth in coalitions that align with these individuals' work is equally important.

Private and public coalitions

These coalitions do not need to be prominent and publicized. In fact, sometimes the less public this equity work is, the less opportunity there is for these issues to become politicized and for naysayers to push back. When consulting with a district, Carl Cohn, a former superintendent, wrote, "I suggested the rhetoric and resolutions around equity be toned down in favor of simply implementing programs that reduce inequality without a lot of fanfare and moral posturing."[20] The rationale, he said, was to avoid "trigger[ing] the forces of the right to start mobilizing resistance and fielding school board candidates of their own, perhaps with outside financing."[21] Cohn argued that the "fanfare" may very well end up dismantling equity efforts that could have supported some of our most vulnerable students and their families.

In an interview, one Latino board member shared how the district's superintendent did not fund EL services publicly. He believed that if he did, the media and the community would "crucify us." Yet, because this board member developed a small coalition of community leaders that urged the superintendent to support ELs, he quietly and occasionally allocated three to four million dollars at a time to EL support. This funding helped to boost these specific programs without public pushback.

Although school boards should normally not promote and publicize their coalitions that advance equity work because this will likely prompt disruption and resistance, sometimes this work should be made public. Many school districts are confronted with students or even educators who commit blatant acts of injustice against other students, their families, or their colleagues.

A few years ago, high school students in Arizona posted a video on social media of themselves singing "Fuck all N-word," which made its way throughout the school district. Outraged and hurt, Black youth and their families in the community came to the school board, shared this video, and brought up several other racist incidents that they had experienced, asking the board to reprimand the students responsible for the video and address the other incidents. The school board took a hands-off approach, saying that they could do nothing. Yet after Black leaders organized, protested, and intensely critiqued the district at board meetings and in the media, the board passed an equity-oriented resolution and instituted an equity office.[22]

Sweeping injustice under the rug does nothing to advance equity work. Instead, it further burdens those who have already been harmed and sends the message that injustice is tolerated, and perhaps even welcomed. When incidents like these come to light at the school board level, school boards must communicate their values on equity in both words and actions regardless of any pushback. They must take these allegations seriously, investigate, and find ways to coalesce with community leaders, including youth. Coalitions will offer support and leadership to develop appropriate and sustainable solutions that can lay a foundation for a district to grow a healthier environment.

LEVERAGING STATE AND FEDERAL LAWS

School board members should understand state and federal laws that affect education, use these laws to advance equity, and push back against laws that undermine equity.

States are responsible for public education. They legally institute and guide school boards; thus, boards operate under state power. While they vary in the amount of power and authority that they give to local school boards, states are in charge for the most part. Sometimes states are heavily involved in education but do not give districts the necessary resources to implement directives, leaving them with unfunded mandates. Even when states are less involved, school districts often need more state-level resources to advance equity.

Meanwhile, under the US Constitution, the federal government wields some power over the states. Specifically, the federal government requires that states offer public education without discriminating against any federally protected group. Also, the Elementary and Secondary Education Act (ESEA) of 1965 and its reauthorizations were designed to improve educational equality. Under this law, the federal government provides funding to states and school districts to supplement (not supplant) the resources and services allocated to students with unique needs (e.g., low-income students, students with disabilities, and ELs). This federal funding carries with it various federal-level standards, accountability, and oversight over local districts.

Since school boards are explicitly accountable to states and the federal government to some degree, leveraging these entities is essential to advancing equity efforts. Without a solid understanding of how state and federal law can shift a school board's ability to support equitable policies and practices, districts could be significantly disadvantaged despite their desire to enhance equity.

The Example of COVID-19 and Anti-CRT Laws

As I mentioned in chapter 1, the events of COVID-19 and the efforts against critical race theory (CRT) and diversity, equity, and inclusion (DEI) are recent examples of state laws affecting educational equity at the district level.

As districts grappled with instituting COVID precautions to open and maintain healthy schools, some state governors, like those in Arizona and Texas, adamantly opposed these precautions. For instance, they issued statewide laws to ban mask requirements despite official health guidelines or the high numbers of COVID cases in specific districts or schools. Yet some districts maintained their stance on health and safety. For example, in the summer of 2021, Arizona's governor signed a budget that banned local school boards from mandating masks. Disregarding the governor's ban, the Phoenix Union High School District's governing board supported a districtwide mask mandate in alignment with health officials' recommendations. A teacher sued the superintendent and governing board over what he believed was a violation of state law. The judge held that the state law was not enforceable until September 29, 2021. Soon after that ruling, numerous school districts across the state followed Phoenix Union's lead to institute a mask mandate. Then a coalition of educators and advocates, including two school board members from Phoenix Union, filed a lawsuit against the state. The plaintiffs argued that the state legislature violated the state constitution, which requires each bill to clearly reflect its content in the title and include only one law per bill. The state legislature passed four laws, including a ban against mask mandates and prohibiting educators from teaching CRT, under one bill and then called it a "budget bill." Consequently, the judge found that the state was, in fact, in violation of the state constitution's stipulation of single-subject law.[23]

In this case, the school board in Phoenix Union demonstrated their leadership by maintaining a commitment to their local community despite the state law. Phoenix Union is in the urban core of Phoenix, Arizona. This district serves almost 4,300 students, of whom nearly 96 percent identify as students of color and 77 percent qualify for free and reduced lunches. As with many other low-income communities of color, the Phoenix Union community experienced the impact of COVID-19 in detrimental and disproportionate ways. When the district first implemented mask mandates, the superintendent explained, "We spent a lot of time in our system as a governing board, as an executive team talking about the implications. But at the same time, we go back to our core values. We go back to our core mission which is, it's our job to not only educate our broader community but to protect our broader community." He followed this by stating, "It's not just about our students and it's not just about our staff. They go home to siblings, spouses, aunts, uncles, grandparents. It's our job to protect them as well."[24]

After this district took its stance, other governing boards felt more comfortable doing the same. Prepared to stand in their core values and deal with the ramifications of a potentially complex legal battle and possible community reactions, Phoenix Union built a strong coalition of community leaders. It also utilized its legal team to fight back against the state law. This legal battle successfully pushed back against the ban on mask mandates and halted the anti-CRT law that had previously passed.

This example illustrates how district leaders can coalesce and strategize to dismantle inequitable policies at other levels of government. It requires courage to stand up against state and federal laws. It also requires capacity and strategy, including a solid legal team, to help district leaders navigate state and federal laws.

Current State of State Involvement in Education

Although public education was always a state-level responsibility, it began as a locally driven entity. However, over the past century, state and federal involvement increased substantially.

Funding and reforms

As the percentage of school funding shifted from the local to the state level, school districts have become more reliant on states for funding and under more pressure to comply with state law if the ramifications of noncompliance are the state withholding its funding. Especially in states with more control, school boards should have a deep understanding of state law, participate in efforts to lobby state policy makers, and have a solid legal team to help them navigate anti-equity efforts and push equity-focused policies and funding forward.

In addition, as discussed in chapter 1, key moments, such as legal battles (e.g., *Brown v. Board of Education* [1954] and *Lau v. Nichols* [1974]), social activism (e.g., civil rights movements), and federal-level reports (e.g., the *Moynihan Report* in 1965 and *A Nation at Risk* in 1983) mark apparent increases in federal involvement. Although many federal laws have pushed districts toward more equitable practices, this also shifts power away from local districts and the boards that govern them. Increased funding, coupled with these spotlight moments, has prompted national awareness about educational outcomes and related disparities. As a result, states and federal governments have instituted several education reforms that often positioned local districts on the receiving end and, in some cases, stripped local boards of power or authority altogether.

For instance, the No Child Left Behind (NCLB) Act of 2001, a reauthorization of the ESEA, disregarded district-level governance. NCLB required that states hold schools accountable, essentially leaving districts out of the equation. Specifically, the law made states responsible for developing school-level standards, reporting outcomes, and taking over so-called failing schools. In 2015, Congress reauthorized ESEA and replaced NCLB with the Every Student Succeeds Act (ESSA). This reform offered to return some power to local districts by requiring states to include local stakeholders in offering input toward developing standards and reporting measures. Still, states (not districts) had discretion in how they would engage with and use the input of these stakeholders.[25]

School district takeovers

Meanwhile, states have taken over nearly 110 local districts.[26] In most cases, states replace elected school boards with state-appointed ones. These takeovers are often political and racialized.

For instance, in the controversial 2023 takeover of Houston Independent School District (HISD), the eighth-largest school district in the country, Texas replaced nine elected trustees with appointed ones. Notably, HISD serves nearly 90 percent students of color (62 percent Latinx, 22 percent African American), and 60 percent low-income students. The state cited continuous poor academic performance as the main reason for the takeover despite the district showing increased academic outcomes in recent years. It also pointed to "chaotic board meetings marred by infighting" and that the board "routinely exceeded their authority, directing staff in violation of the school laws of Texas."[27] Soon after the state announced this takeover, local community members opposed it. One parent stated, "I am protesting the hostile takeover of Houston ISD to empower other parents to fight for their rights and for the rights of our children." Another parent proclaimed, "Education is a right, not a privilege, and taxpayers like me would like to see more equity, school funding tied to enrollment and inflation, and the end to using [state testing] to shame our communities, instead of hijacking the largest ISD by the state for political reasons."[28] As these parents' comments reflect, equity is often the centerpiece of the tension between states and localities.

Similarly, the mayoral takeover of districts in large and racially minoritized cities, including Chicago and New York City, was a trend in the early 1990s.[29] States usually initiate mayoral takeovers. State takeovers are more frequent among school districts serving the majority of students of color and low-income students, with recent takeovers occurring in nearly 33 percent of majority-Black school districts, compared to 4 percent of majority-white school districts.[30] Although the reasons for takeovers often cite poor academic performance, studies suggest that state and mayoral takeovers decrease local control and fail to sustain higher educational performance outcomes.[31]

Instead, state-level policy makers often can and do engage in takeovers to flex their political authority over local districts. And even though most school boards are nonpartisan, these takeovers are often tied to political divisions in the state. One Houston teacher noted, "It's partisan politics playing with [the] education of 196,000 students." She then explained, "We're a democratic city that constantly has pushed back against the governor [Republican Greg Abbott]. During the pandemic, HISD was one of the school districts that instituted a mask mandate with the state saying that we cannot institute a mask mandate. So we have done some things that have pushed back on the political atmosphere."[32] Her comments highlight the push and pull between the state and local districts.

The Plot of Urban Districts Against the State

I conducted a study focusing on three districts in three states that primarily served students from urban communities. By "urban," I mean these communities were densely populated. In addition, demographics in these districts reflected a majority of students of color, mainly Latinx students (42 percent, 44 percent, and 62 percent, respectively). Two of these states had a Republican majority in state leadership and government, and in these states, participants continuously pointed to the districts' struggles with the state legislature.

One school board member said, "We are not a favored district in the state, and so if there's gonna be any imposition, any enforcement of any law, they're happy to do it in [this district]." In a different district, one board member explained the difficulty of getting state resources, noting that "at the state legislative level, it's not a high priority because it only impacts a few school districts," which served most ELs in that state. This board member also explained that "the legislature really dislikes [this city] in general because we're this liberal pocket in a conservative state. And so our legislature loves to stick it [to us]. Anytime they can, they do." These shared experiences illustrate the closely tied political and racialized dynamics that often lead to tensions between the state and district.[33]

Strategies to Leverage

Not all states are interested in getting involved in local governance. In fact, most states do not have the administrative capacity or funding to improve equity. Yet, as Kevin Brady, a researcher and author of the book chapter, "State Power and Equity," argues, coalitions among state-level policy makers and local boards show "the greatest potential for advancing equitable educational policies," primarily since local governance "provides a check on uncontrolled state activism."[34]

Symbolic, exclusionary, and restrictive state policies

In the study about the three school boards mentioned earlier, state-level policies did little to advance equity for ELs in the districts that needed the most support. These policies were *symbolic, exclusionary,* and *restrictive,* which are three characteristics that often show up in policies promoted or masked as equity-oriented. In one state, state-level policies and funding were largely *symbolic* because they supported only about 18 percent of this district's growing EL population, rather than all ELs. In the second state, state-level policies were *exclusionary* because they supported only programs designed to promote multilingualism and targeted mainly non-ELs rather than ELs. The third state passed policies that restricted ELs to an English immersion program for four hours a day, despite research suggesting that doing so further disadvantaged ELs.[35] As board members, it's important to understand which students are being served by state policies and how they are being served (or not served).

Advocate, engage, resist, and navigate

Based on my research, school board members should consider four strategies when thinking about advancing equity in education at the state-level: *advocate*, *engage*, *resist*, and *navigate*. School board members can *advocate* for state policies and resources. For instance, if you are on a school board, you can work to commission research to identify evidence-based needs and solutions in your district. With fellow board members, you can testify at legislative meetings and work with legislators to create state policies, funding streams, and equitable funding formulas designed to serve minoritized students adequately.

As school board members, you can *engage* with existing state policies and funding streams to provide resources and services to students who need them. For example, some states have funding to support programs like dual immersion programs. These are often designed for English speakers to learn another language. However, the school board can engage this policy and direct these resources to support ELs through a dual-language program in their district.

School board members might need to *resist* state policies that harm equity. As the previously discussed example demonstrates, some school boards resisted governors' laws to oppose mask mandates based on health and safety issues in mostly minoritized communities, which COVID-19 disproportionately affected.

Finally, school boards are constantly tasked with *navigating* state laws. State laws that oppose curricula and teaching about race and racism, for example, often stop teachers from offering culturally relevant curricula, which research shows enhances educational equity.[36] Some school boards might need to resist these laws directly because of their harmful impact. However, depending on how laws are written, school boards can solicit legal opinions to help the district navigate laws to protect teachers and still offer culturally relevant curricula and pedagogies. For instance, this might use different language in classrooms but continue to have critical and honest dialogue about differences and history (e.g., avoiding terms like "racism" and instead using "different treatment" or allowing students to lead parts of the dialogue on controversial topics and speak from their own experiences).

PROACTIVELY RESPONSIVE: PREPARING FOR THE FIRES

During several interviews that I conducted, board members critiqued school boards and other district leaders for reacting to everything around them. Using the analogy of putting out fires, one board member proclaimed "They're [school boards] like firemen. They just put out fires. They're not preventive. Board members are not preventing a lot of things. They are encouraging what's currently going because they like to get reelected." Similarly, another board member said to me:

> The majority of our work, Carrie, is dealing with adult problems. Very much the energy that we put into, and even the superintendent, is all about putting out fires between adults to where at some point it's like, "Come on, adults. Get it together so we can focus on these babies that shouldn't have to wait for us to get along or decide what works while we're losing them. They're going to jail. They're being impoverished."

These sobering comments reflect the reality that some school boards are steeped in political battles and their members forgo their responsibilities as district trustees. Instead, they react to everything around them and lose sight of their goals. Without a plan, school board members will likely fail to advance equity.

It's Not If, It's When

School boards will always have fires to which they must respond. There will always be a community coalition or an individual who attends a school board meeting upset at something that the board might or might not have control over. There will always be a disgruntled employee who pushes the board to address their concerns. There will always be insufficient funds, ineffective policies, a shortage of teachers and staff to address students' needs adequately, and many other unlisted challenges. New school board members must remember this. Problems will arise. When they do, are school boards ready to respond to these problems?

School board members can use the previously discussed areas of the SBGE framework to be proactively responsive. As a school board member, you can prepare to respond by building knowledge, understanding, and skills. You should be able to foresee issues that will land on your plate because you will know and understand your communities' concerns and desires. By understanding your own capacity as a board member, you should be able to know which problems can be solved without much support. If you need support, you can rely on your carefully built coalitions. Knowing and understanding state and federal policies and building coalitions will help board members leverage policies to respond to the district's needs. Creating a plan to respond proactively is vital, which I discuss more toward the end of this chapter.

The foghorn metaphor

Although only focused on six school boards in the state of Georgia, "The Lighthouse Study" is among the most comprehensive studies to date conducted on school boards and their impact on student achievement.[37] This research was supposed to be a "lighthouse" or guide for boards. The findings suggested that school boards' higher level of confidence in their staff and more positive perceptions of students positively influenced student achievement. While these findings are helpful, the study did not highlight educational equity. The journey of equity is often complex, messy, and requires boards to be proactively responsive.

In a previously written article, I built on this lighthouse metaphor and described school boards' journey of advancing educational equity as a "foghorn."[38] A lighthouse is a tall building near the shore with a bright light on top that guides ships docking at night. On the other hand, the sound from a foghorn guides ships when storms make it difficult to see the lighthouse because of heavy fog. Educational inequities are often like storms that school boards must navigate through. By proactively responding to these storms, school board members can use the lessons from the foghorn.

School board members must be able to gauge the conditions of the district to understand when these conditions change and when it is difficult to navigate toward equity. When that happens, school boards should take a step back and listen for the foghorn, which often comes in the form of people (either within or beyond the district) who point to inequities that are happening. Often, they also point to potential solutions. Using these sounds, school board members can sometimes shift their perspectives and change their directions to move safely toward equity-oriented solutions. Moving and docking safely requires the patience to stop and listen. It requires the humility to admit if you are going in the wrong direction and the willingness to change course. Listening for the foghorn is about being proactive, and changing course is about being responsive to what's happening around you.

Keeping Their Eyes on the Prize

Another critical component of being proactively responsive is that school boards should always keep their eyes on the prize. Recently, I was part of a group discussion about the increasing political tensions that superintendents were experiencing. This group was interested in offering better support and preparation for incoming superintendents to navigate the politics of this role. I urged the group to be more specific by asking, "To what end are they navigating politics?"

What is the goal of navigating through, or even engaging in, politics? Like the board member I interviewed said, some school boards are devoting a ton of energy toward putting out fires rather than focusing on our babies. Unfortunately, school boards cannot choose between fires and babies. The fires will come. And the babies will be here. It is the school board's job to solve problems *and* remember why they are solving those problems. Ultimately, knowing and preparing for what lies ahead—being proactively responsive—will give you the best chance to put out fires and still advance educational equity so each baby has the opportunity to learn at their fullest potential.

IMAGINING THE POSSIBILITIES

In his book *Freedom Dreams*, Robin Kelley reminds us, "Love and imagination may be the most revolutionary impulses available to us, and yet we have failed to understand their political importance and respect them as powerful social forces." He urges us to "tap the well of our own collective imaginations, that we do what earlier generations have done: dream."[39]

If, as many of us do, they believe that education is a door that can help lead us toward a collective liberation, school board members must dream and cultivate the dreams of those around them. They must be able to imagine how we will disrupt a system full of inequities and build a system that breathes life into our youth, their families, and our communities.

Because school boards are positioned within both the system and the community, their purview is grand. It is easy to get stuck in the weeds of inequity. But school board members must keep their eyes on the horizon. They must imagine what seeds they can plant that will turn into a beautiful garden of liberatory opportunities for all our children. These seeds start with a plan.

Strategic Planning

One way that school boards can imagine the possibilities is by developing a strategic plan. Most school boards approve a planning document for the district. These documents are often entitled "Strategic Plan" and are usually five-year plans. These plans can be a helpful tool for identifying where the district is at when it comes to equity and where the district needs to grow in the areas of equity. Plans typically center around the primary focuses of a district, such as curricula, instruction, learning, family/community engagement, evaluation/assessment, technology, and facilities.

Although most districts have plans, many do not develop and use these plans as effectively as they could. In my research comparing school boards in a number of districts, each school board adopted a strategic plan at some point. Yet one stood out. I will describe the two that did *not* stand out first.

The first district's plan that did *not* stand out was sixty-six pages long, with twenty-five goals within five areas over five years. Using the "Specific, Measurable, Attainable, Realistic, Time-bound (SMART)" framework and then an additional task of "Describe Possible Evidence," they broke down each goal by year. In each year, the "SMART" and "D" elements included several points given in small font and divided by letters and bullets. It was detailed, but it was also long and difficult to digest, and much of it remained broad regarding metrics.

The second district's plan that did *not* stand out was sixteen pages long and aesthetically beautiful, with colorful, full-length pictures of a child, the superintendent, and the school board on the first three pages. A breakdown of the district demographics and a brief description with figures followed these three pages of photos. Another three pages of the plan included full-length images of students and an additional one of the superintendents with students. They identified five imperatives, seven focus areas that included thirty-three vague targets, and fifty-two strategies—none of which were numbered but instead were presented in bullet points. The plan lacked years and deadlines. While the plan was mainly nice on the eyes, it lacked any sense of time, specificity, and explicit measures.

The third district's plan, which *did* stand out, was twenty-seven pages long and available online in Spanish and English. The plan covered five years, with the first few pages offering an overview of six major goals, with associated action steps numbered and broken down by year. The following three pages presented a committee of approximately ten people (some who were school board members) for each of the six goals, including each person's name and title and an indication of the committee chair, whose name was bolded. After this, the plan described each goal. The final pages included an outline of each goal, broken down by year, action step, the person responsible, and metrics. Interviewees confirmed that they relied on this plan, which was tied closely to each person's vision and how they operated. Each school board member referred to the plan as central to their operations. In fact, every other school board meeting highlighted one goal and included people from that goal's committee to present an update of their status of achieving that goal as outlined in the strategic plan. Interestingly, while the board composition was pretty similar in each district, this third district's superintendent had been in their position for nearly ten years at the time of the study, which was much longer than the other two districts' superintendents. Also, while there was not a high commitment to equity among all the board members, no one was adamantly against equity efforts in this third district, which was similar to the second district.

In terms of content, the third district's plan also emphasized equity relatively more. For instance, it mentioned equity forty-four times, ELs forty-eight times, and diversity (e.g., "diverse student needs") five times. The first district's plan mentioned equity zero times, ELs six times, and diversity (e.g., "diverse student learners") six times. The second district's plan mentioned equity five times, ELs zero times, and diversity (e.g., "diverse groups") thirteen times. Unfortunately, none of these plans hardly mentioned race or ethnicity in general, nor anything specific to race.

Although not perfect, the third district's plan had a clear vision of equity, presented specific goals, and included a detailed road map. Along the road map and at every stopping point, the plan had metrics, deadlines, and people associated with the actions required to achieve their respective goals. School board members were part of building this plan and took responsibility for supporting and following up on these goals regularly in their meetings. Not surprisingly, in this comparative study, the third district was able to advance the most substantial policies and practices regarding equity for ELs. The plan allowed space and time for the district to imagine the possibilities collectively and specify how they could be turned into realities.

Considerations in planning

The principles in the SBGE framework can help spur the development of a strategic plan. Next, I describe how school board members can rely on these SBGE principles when developing a plan:

1. Starting with knowing and understanding the context of the board, district, and community, school boards can identify who should be involved and invited to contribute to the plan. This information will also give them a starting point in terms of equity to identify and address the most apparent and discreet inequities.

2. The plan can and should provide the opportunity to invite district partners to contribute and coalesce around the plan. Partners should include youth, families, district and school-level staff, and community members. Boards should ensure that the invitation for district partners to contribute is actual, not symbolic.

    As an example of a symbolic gesture, my children's school sent home a flyer with a one-day notice that stated, "Parent Voice in Need . . . Please Join Us in Our Strategic Planning Steering Committee." Under this statement, they listed the meeting date/time/location, which was at 9 a.m. on a Wednesday at the school. We received this flyer on Tuesday after school. Then it concluded with "See you there!" This school primarily serves working-class, low-income, and Latinx students; many of their families speak mostly Spanish. I knew immediately that the attendance would be low because most of these families work during the day, probably do not know the purpose of a strategic planning committee, and some may not have been able to understand the flyer, which was only in English. I attended. And guess what? I was right. Three parents showed up, including myself, and the other two parents worked at the school as staff members. This invitation to contribute was inauthentic and careless. Do not make that mistake. School boards should ask and confirm how the district invites people to contribute and ensure that this happens carefully and equitably throughout the district.

3. By understanding state and federal politics, school boards can identify how to use this as part of the plan. For instance, state and federal entities could allocate specific grant funding to support districts in implementing programs that aim to reverse disparities in student discipline. Often, when applying for grant funding, a plan is needed. A strategic plan is a great place to identify the who, what, when, where, and how to pursue these funding opportunities.

4. Building coalitions and engaging in coalition politics can help invite critical players to contribute to both the development and execution of a strategic plan.

5. Finally, as part of being proactively responsive, school boards can include ways to consistently gauge the pulse of the district. This might mean identifying when and how to survey or host meetings with partners (e.g., families, youth, and staff) regularly and then decide how to use what they learn from this information.

Like the foghorn metaphor mentioned previously, a strategic plan should be a solid document that will help districts stay the course despite any storms that might arise. But it is also a working document. State and federal policies might change, budgets might vary, and community demographics might transform. School boards should allow space to shift the plan, especially to ensure that equity is always front and center.

In one district that my colleague and I studied, school board members were on the receiving end of community advocacy after a racist, anti-Black incident that harmed many of the district's Black students. At first, the school board did not respond well. They made excuses and dismissed the community's concerns. Finally, after months of community advocacy, they made some changes to address inequities districtwide. Although school boards might have a plan in place, they sometimes must shift the plan to advance equity after listening to and understanding their communities.

Questions to Center Equity

I urge school boards and district leaders to place equity central to the development of the strategic plan and recenter equity when they revisit and execute the strategic plan. Next, I have outlined questions that school boards can aim to address in their centering of equity within their plan. These questions, which I developed based on past research about and interactions with school board members and districts, are not easy to answer. It will require time, research, and effort to answer them. Yes, these questions and the subsequent answers will help school boards understand where the district is in terms of equity and then be able to envision and plan what they need to do to advance equity:

1. How do *school district leaders* define educational equity and inequity for minoritized youth, families, and educators in the school district?
2. How do *school and classroom leaders* define educational equity and inequity for minoritized youth, families, and educators in the school district?
3. How are educational equity and inequity for minoritized youth, families, and educators defined within the realm of high-quality research and best practices?
4. What groups of minoritized youth, families, and educators (e.g., BIPOC, LGBTQIA+, low-income, linguistic minorities, undocumented people, and people with disabilities) experience inequities in the school district?

5. How do these respective groups define and envision an equitable and quality education? Their vision might be different than the school board or others who work in the district.

6. What are the inequities that these respective groups experience?

7. In what ways do these respective groups experience equitable educational opportunities?

8. What current policies, practices, financial decisions, staffing, curricula/instruction, and programmatic/services in the district contribute to the educational *inequities* that these respective groups experience?

9. What current policies, practices, financial decisions, staffing, curricula/instruction, and programmatic/services in the district contribute to the *equitable* educational opportunities that these respective groups experience?

10. What state and federal policies and practices contribute to educational inequities and equities in the school district?

11. What partnerships does the school district have that contribute to educational inequities and equities in the school district?

Using these questions, you can identify what areas of equity to prioritize in the given timeframe (most strategic plans are five years), specific goals focused on these areas, and ways to measure these goals. And remember, at the foundation of this area within the principle of *strategy* is the need to use our collective imaginations to dream about what is possible. Possibilities can and should be beyond simply having bodies in a classroom or test scores that seemingly tell us what children are capable of. Instead, this is about what our children should feel about themselves and those around them, what excites them, what keeps them motivated, and the types of healthy and joyful environments we can create for them to learn, grow, and flourish as community.

4

The Case of Tucson Unified School District: "The Perfect Storm"

IN THE NEXT three chapters, I share the stories that emerged from a study of three elected school boards in school districts located in Arizona (Tuscon), Nevada (Las Vegas metro-area), and Utah (Salt Lake City) within the US Mountain West region.[1] In this study, I focused on the role of these school boards in policies and practices related to Emerging Bilinguals (EBs) (more commonly known as English learners) in the post–No Child Left Behind era. However, additional findings surfaced that highlight how various policies and practices impacted other demographic groups of students (e.g., Black, Latinx, low-income) as well, which I also discuss throughout this book.

This chapter's case tells the story of a district facing extremely restrictive state laws that affected equity. These laws constrained many services, resources, and programs for the district's most vulnerable students. To use the words of several district leaders, the Tucson Unified School District (TUSD) experienced a "perfect storm." This "storm" included its school desegregation case, the dismantling of the Mexican American

Studies (MAS) program, statewide changes to laws for English learners (ELs), the Great Recession, and hypercompetitive school choice policies, as well as the sudden death of their longest-serving school board member, a staunch supporter of equity.

This story emphasizes how the school board navigated, resisted, and complied with state laws and consequential events. It serves as a cautionary tale of how bad actors can manipulate a system and the difficulties of pushing back and being civilly disobedient. You will learn how key events and actors can change state and federal laws, but also how compliance and compromise among board members can dismantle decades of equity work. You also will see how the pendulum of equity can swing back and forth over time with the power of democracy through legal cases and elections. From this, you will learn helpful strategies to successfully push back and work around inequitable state policies. Importantly, this case shows why it is critical for school boards to understand, engage, leverage, and mobilize at all levels of government. Even if school boards are small fish in a big ocean compared to other larger forces (e.g., state and federal governments), school board members' ability to navigate these forces in coalitions is vital for moving equity forward.

I begin this story by briefly describing the state and local contexts. Then I share how the context of state policy and unexpected events contributed to major changes in TUSD for ELs and other minoritized students. Finally, I discuss the social constructions of ELs in the TUSD community and how these beliefs may have informed EL policies and practices.

KNOWING AND UNDERSTANDING TUSD

The School Board and Superintendency

The TUSD school board includes five members who represent the whole district. Members are elected, in a staggered fashion, to four-year terms and are unpaid.[2] During the four years that I monitored the school board, there were nine school board members. Of these members, three were women and six were men. Racially, the majority of this board was white, with five members, and the rest were Latinx (three members) and Asian American (one member).

The school board hired two superintendents during the four-year period that I observed the board: one white man and one Latino man. The first superintendent was John Pedicone, who was hired unanimously by the board and served in TUSD for nearly three years. He resigned in 2012, explaining that he felt the newly elected board should hire a new and fully supported superintendent.[3] In 2013, the board voted four to one to hire Dr. H. T. Sánchez as TUSD's thirty-third superintendent. Bilingual in English and Spanish, Superintendent Sánchez had more than fifteen years of educational experience but had not been a superintendent before.[4]

District Context and History

Arizona followed Nevada as the second-fastest-growing state in the United States. In ten years, from 2000–2010, Arizona's population increased by 25 percent. Unlike the rapid student growth experienced in the Clark County School District (CCSD) (discussed in chapter 5), TUSD's population declined 26 percent from 1997 to 2018.[5] Although TUSD served nearly 53,000 students in 2010 and was the second-largest of Arizona's 230 districts, the state's open-enrollment school choice policies and friendly charter school laws contributed to TUSD's decreasing student population.

Arizona ranked the lowest in per-pupil funding in the United States, at approximately $6,448 annually.[6] After the 2010 Great Recession, Tucson also ranked near the bottom in recovery compared to other Arizona cities, recovering only 32 percent of employment by 2015 compared to the state's 79 percent.[7] In 2013, TUSD closed ten schools due partially to decreases in the budget, which amounted to around $17 million.[8] And from 2010 to 2015, TUSD experienced more than $78 million in cuts in capital funding.[9] These enrollment decreases, along with statewide budget cuts and school closures, situated TUSD in a precarious position.

In addition, student demographics changed relatively dramatically.[10] In 2013, Latinx students made up the majority of TUSD, at 62 percent. The white student population was 22 percent, down from 45 percent in 1997. The EL population was about 6 percent in 2013, a 19 percent decline from six years prior. State policy changes that prompted ELs to be reclassified (and misclassified) more rapidly to non-EL status contributed to the sharp decline of ELs, which I expand on later in this chapter.

Federal Lawsuits and State Legislation in TUSD

Lawsuits and state legislative actions have the power to shift educational equity significantly, affecting school board decisions in positive and negative ways. What local districts, like TUSD in Arizona, experienced offer a prime example of how this happens. A major contributor to these changes in TUSD came from laws and court cases on two subjects: education for ELs and instruction that reflected Mexican histories. Legal cases and state laws, such as desegregation efforts and those related to immigration, can ultimately have huge impacts on schools decades later. School board members need to understand their school districts' histories, the complexities inherent in these histories, and how these histories show up in contemporary efforts to support or dismantle equity practices and policies. In TUSD, these areas collided, contributing to the "perfect storm" that several district leaders described.

TUSD school desegregation lawsuit

In May 1974, the National Association for the Advancement of Colored People (NAACP) filed a lawsuit against TUSD on behalf of African American students, claiming that the district had unlawfully segregated them. About five months later, Latinx families, represented by the Mexican American Legal Defense and Educational Fund, filed a similar lawsuit against the district. The plaintiffs combined the two cases, which became known as *Fisher and Mendoza v. Tucson*. The plaintiffs settled with TUSD in exchange for the district's agreement to eliminate discrimination in twenty-one schools through desegregation efforts.

As a result of this case, TUSD remained under court supervision for more than twenty years to maintain compliance with the court order. In 2009, the court gave the district post-unitary status, which ended the court supervision. However, in 2012, the court ruled that TUSD was no longer compliant and returned it to court supervision. Under a court-appointed special master, TUSD implemented a plan in 2015–2016 "to eliminate the vestiges of segregation, provide every student with the opportunity to attend a racially and ethnically integrated school, increase the number of TUSD schools that are integrated, and enhance the learning *opportunities and outcomes* of all students, especially African American and Latino students who are the plaintiffs in this case."[11]

As required by the court, Arizona allocated nearly $64 million annually to TUSD. TUSD could use this funding to implement the plan, which included services to support EL education, such as dual-language programs.[12] Once the courts would find TUSD in compliance again, the court would no longer require the state to allocate these dollars. Many district leaders expressed that this "desegregation funding" was critical for maintaining TUSD's equity-oriented programs, and thus feared that if they lost this funding, many of these programs would diminish.

Navigating: The Roots of Arizona's EL Policies

In the 1970s and 1980s, TUSD emerged as a national leader in EL practices.[13] However, outside of the district, in 1992, EL families filed *Flores v. Arizona*, a class action lawsuit against the state of Arizona, claiming that it provided inadequate resources to educate ELs.[14] Miriam Flores was the named plaintiff in this case, which included families throughout fifteen counties in Arizona. Miriam was a quiet elementary student enrolled at a Nogales Unified School District school, located an hour south of Tucson, near the Mexico border. She received bilingual education from bilingual teachers in both Spanish and English, at which she excelled. Then, in third grade when her monolingual teacher offered instruction only in English, Miriam started to struggle. After receiving a call from the teacher about Miriam's inattention and talking, which was unlike her, her mother asked her, "Why are you talking in class? Why aren't you listening to your teacher?" Miriam replied, "I talk to the other kids because I have to ask them what she [the teacher] is saying." After the district failed to offer support, Miriam's mother joined the class action lawsuit.[15] Many Arizona policymakers fought this lawsuit, resulting in over twenty years of litigation and costing millions of taxpayer dollars.

There were a few key moments related to this case. The first was in January 2000, when the US District Court sided with the plaintiffs, calling Arizona's EL funding mechanism "arbitrary and capricious," or otherwise inadequate. This lack of funding, the court claimed, contributed to unequal access to education for ELs. The court decision was a win for EL families and advocates.

The Emergence of Structured English Immersion

Only months later, in November 2000, 63 percent of Arizona voters passed Proposition 203, entitled "English Language Education for Children in Public Schools." It included the requirement to use an English-only approach through a Structured English Immersion (SEI) program for ELs, with some caveats. By the terms of the proposition, parents or guardians could request a waiver to opt out of SEI if their child is over ten years old, speaks English, or has "special needs best suited for a different educational approach."[16] During the first few years after Proposition 203 passed, the Arizona Department of Education (ADE) left much of the interpretation of the law up to school districts, resulting in a wide array of practices, including the continuation of some bilingual programs.[17]

It is important to note that Proposition 203 was part of a larger national movement by English-only advocates in the 1990s. Ron Unz, an entrepreneur from California with no children and no background

in education, largely financed Arizona's proposition and similar measures in California, Massachusetts, and Colorado.[18] Then, in 2002, voters
elected State Superintendent Tom Horne, whose campaign was supported by Unz. Under Horne's direction, the ADE developed stringent
implementation standards to discontinue bilingual education in Arizona. Horne led the successful elimination of most of Arizona's bilingual
and dual-language programs, particularly those that served ELs. These
new standards also made it difficult for even Native American students
to access dual-language programs in their heritage language.[19]

Meanwhile, the court's decision required the state to use a cost study,
relying on research evidence, to determine how much it would cost to
provide ELs with an adequate education. Three studies were conducted
between 2001 and 2004. The results varied: one study suggested that it
would cost $1,200 per year per student to educate ELs adequately; and
another suggested that it would cost $2,500. The third study did not
provide specific funding amounts. Given these cost estimates, Arizona's
relatively low allocation of only $179 per EL student was especially con-
cerning at the time. Although the state legislature rejected these studies, it passed House Bill 2001, which increased their per-pupil allocation
for ELs to $340. Arguing that this increase was insufficient, the plaintiffs
appealed to the court in 2002.

After an ongoing battle, State Superintendent Horne appealed to
the US Supreme Court on Arizona's behalf. In 2009, the Supreme Court
decided in a 5–4 ruling that the violation found in one school district
(Nogales) did not apply to the entire state. Before this decision was issued,
the state developed an EL Task Force that included researchers, educators, and policymakers, but it did not take seriously the voices of experts
and scholars, including those on the taskforce, who were pushing back
against English immersion practices. Instead, the EL Task Force embraced
the recommendations from a consultant from California named Kevin
Clark, an outsider who became a key player in pushing policy in Arizona
as well as California. His recommendations led to Arizona's prescriptive

model of English immersion, in spite of what research-based evidence had made clear about the benefits of bilingual education for EL.[20]

As a result of the court case and statewide legislative decisions, two major changes to EL education occurred: (1) the state agreed to provide school districts $432 per EL, and (2) a statewide requirement aligned with Proposition 203 to enact a stringent SEI program in 2008–2009. This SEI program required ELs to be pulled out of mainstream classes to receive a minimum of four hours per day of English-language development, with an exception that parents and guardians could opt out if their children were over ten years old.[21]

To be clear, research on SEI models in Arizona has demonstrated their harmful consequences for ELs. These include segregation from their non-EL peers, lower performance on academic tests compared to ELs in other states, and lack of access to both core and high-quality curricula, which has contributed to one of the country's lowest graduation rates among ELs. Further, these students have experienced negative social-emotional impacts, such as depression and anxiety related to school.[22]

Many district leaders in TUSD echoed the opinion that SEI negatively affected ELs. They described the program as "not humane," "not good for students," "horrible," and "modern-day segregation." One school board member stated the following: "Anyone who is an educator, I think, is really saddened by the state—the requirements that we have to isolate these children, it's discriminatory. I have not spoken to one educator that is in favor of isolating these students in the room."

Another district leader shared a story of a group of Navajo teachers in a different area of Arizona who were deeply committed to language revitalization. They used dual-language programs to teach Navajo children their native language, Diné Bizaad, in order to strengthen their culture. Yet the home language survey, which asks parents and guardians about languages spoken at home and by the student, prompted many Navajo children to be tested and disqualified for the dual-language program and required to participate in the SEI program. As described by this district leader, these teachers "were very clever and found a really interesting way to circumvent the law." They explained to parents that if they only put English on these surveys, their kids would qualify for the dual-language program. They also noted that for students in these programs, "their reading and math scores were through the roof . . . and [those] results parallel forty years of data on strong bilingual programs." As shown by this group of Navajo teachers, some communities in Arizona made quiet and strategic efforts to resist SEI. Quiet and strategic resistance can be a useful way to advance equity, at least in the short term.

What is important as a school board member to understand is how deeply outside influences can affect educational equity at the district level. It took one person, Ron Unz, with an explicit agenda and no professional experience in education, to bankroll and push a political campaign that significantly changed state laws and the lives of millions of children. Similarly, Kevin Clark designed the program that Tom Horne effectively implemented. And although leveraging the courts is often one way to push back against unfair policies and practices, in this case, the legal system fell short of offering justice for Arizona ELs, despite courts having previously determined that ELs were underfunded in education. In spite of—or because of—the potential harm of such wide-ranging impacts, school board members should know how state policies affect their districts. Board members must work to coalesce with community leaders, other district leaders, and national leaders to navigate these types of terrain in the short term and develop a plan to overhaul these policies in the long term.

Navigating the terrain for ELs in TUSD

TUSD was the state's target when it came to its EL education programs. According to one account soon after Proposition 203 passed, "Unz claimed that 'school districts, including Tucson Unified and Sunnyside, are ignoring the mandate of Arizona voters last year to dump most bilingual-education programs' and charged that these districts were 'committing outrageous educational fraud' in interpreting the waiver provisions.[23] Unz and his colleagues threatened lawsuits; however, none were ever filed."[24]

Many district leaders echoed the state's disdain for TUSD. One TUSD administrator called TUSD "ground zero" and shared, "our [TUSD's] relationship with the state is not very good" because "the state sees us as 'There they go. TUSD again. Wanting to do their own thing." Although he believed that "their own thing" was simply "do[ing] things as we see are right for our kids."

Regarding the school board, this administrator said that although "the board has been very supportive . . ., it has come with a lot of public scrutiny," and "it requires them to have some pretty thick skin and be a little bit of a fighter." One such fight that most of the school board got behind was when district leaders challenged the state because of a newly established statewide test used to classify ELs, called the Arizona English Language Learner Assessment (AZELLA).

During a school board meeting on December 13, 2011, TUSD's Language Acquisition Department informed the board that ELs were being reclassified to non-EL status at an alarming rate. In six years (from 2004–2005 to 2010–2011), the percentage of ELs dropped drastically, from 19 percent to 6 percent of the student population.[25] This change came after the state implemented the AZELLA to assess ELs' English fluency. TUSD leaders speculated that the standards of this assessment were lower than the previous one. They were concerned that many of the reclassified ELs were not adequately proficient in English and were being misclassified. In addition, the state incentivized schools by adding "points" to the school's annual letter grades (a state-level accountability grading system) for reclassifying ELs at higher rates.

Meanwhile state leaders boasted of positive results and the corresponding decreases in state-level EL funding. The court decision in *Flores v. Arizona* (1992) mandated that the state allocate targeted funding for ELs until they are reclassified as non-ELs. In other words, the faster ELs were reclassified, the less money the state would be legally required to spend on ELs.

In this same December 13, 2011, meeting, one school board member, Adelita Grijalva, showed the most interest and concern. Aside from the introduction of AZELLA as the new assessment to evaluate ELs' English proficiency, Grijalva explained that she was unaware that TUSD had implemented the four-hour SEI model and thought that the district was working with a hybrid model. Grijalva's concerns were that different grade levels of ELs were being combined during the four-hour blocks and no research suggested that the four-hour model was effective.

One of the more conservative board members, Mark Stegeman, also showed concern, but in the other direction. He said he was "struggling" with what the district staff noted about it taking nearly three years for 80 percent of ELs to be reclassified. He believed that Spanish was an easy language to transition from, so in his opinion, it did not make sense that it took even three years to reclassify the majority of ELs. However, Stegeman also noted that "the state policy is the state policy." He further explained "that the AZELLA, which is our test, is commonly acknowledged to be too weak. And so, in other words, students can pass the AZELLA before they are meaningly proficient." Then he noted, "I'm not an expert on this. I've never even looked at the AZELLA, but this is what basically seems to be a consensus among the teachers."

Like many school board members throughout the United States, most TUSD board members were not experts in EL education. Yet many of them understood the research, and they understood that this new set of policies and practices did not benefit ELs. It is critical for school board members to have at least a basic understanding of evidence-based practices and policies that are both helpful and harmful to all groups of students so they can support good policies and push back against or mitigate bad policies, which is what some TUSD board members supported.

TUSD staff kept close track of the data by assessing ELs who were getting reclassified using the AZELLA. Almost a year later, at a school board meeting on October 23, 2012, department staff stated that 2,450 ELs in TUSD had been misclassified. The department shared the data with the

US Office of Civil Rights (OCR) staff, who found that the ADE violated Title VI of the Civil Rights Act, as well as the Equal Educational Opportunities Act. Specifically, OCR found that because ADE relied on only one test and lowered cutoff score criteria for proficiency, "approximately 28,000 ELLs were prematurely exited and under-identified between 2006 and 2012" throughout Arizona.[26] The OCR mandated that ADE provide additional services for the identified ELs who were misclassified; however, the state and federal leaders refused to provide funding to the district for these services. This became an unfunded mandate to right the wrong of a statewide required test. One board member noted of this unfunded mandate: "The state pulled a fast one on us and instead of providing additional funding . . . superintendent Tom Horne . . . gave the directive that we could fund that through our desegregation dollars."

When the government passes a law or institutes a new regulation, they decide whether to provide funding to the entity who is mandated to implement that law or regulation. For instance, if it is within state and federal legal requirements, a locally elected school board can mandate that schools in their district provide specific services for students with special needs. In most cases, it is reasonable for school boards to fund this mandate adequately. Otherwise, they need to understand the consequences of not funding the mandate, and that schools will likely sacrifice current resources and services, such as cutting a teaching position, front desk staff, or something similar, to make room in their budgets for the new mandate. Similarly, when state or federal governments give school districts unfunded mandates, the districts can either appeal these decisions or get the funding by moving resources from one area to another. Nonetheless, it is important to leverage other forms of government to remedy injustices, such as the one that occurred in TUSD with ELs and the AZELLA testing criteria. If it is a losing fight within your realm of influence, it might also be useful to publicize these injustices by inviting media sources to report on the situation, and community leaders to advocate for justice.

In the meeting, board responses varied. Again, Grijavla posed several questions that reflected concern about the logistics for these ELs. The newly appointed board member, Sugiyama, asked about translation services to communicate the changes to parents. The superintendent praised the department for identifying and reporting the issue and referred to TUSD as a leader in the state for EL services. Following this comment, Stegeman asked, "Am I understanding you, that we were the snitches on this?" Later, one board member noted that the four-hour model was not a "reasonable pedagogical approach" and explained that "it's a bit of a strange regime we are in now."

From this situation, we can see that not only were thousands of ELs forced to enroll in a program that did not support their native language, but also pulling them from their subject-matter courses left many behind academically. Consequently, thousands of ELs were also misclassified and left without adequate services. Although the school board showed concern and supported the OCR complaint, their fight was limited in advancing equity. Reflecting on the *Flores* case, and upset about the SEI requirement for ELs, one community leader stated, "I wish the board would more strongly say, 'That's no way to teach kids. We got to find out what is it we can do against that.'" She further explained, "I know that those are the state rules. I think that they're horrendous ... it's a huge part of the achievement gap and our graduation gap." Then she noted, "That's where the Mexican-American Studies [program] came in ..., [it] basically said, 'You kids count. You really matter. You need to know it and you need to work from that baseline. We count and we're proud of who we are.'" In the next section, I share what happened with Mexican American Studies (MAS) in TUSD.

Compliance: The Quest to Dismantle Mexican American Studies in TUSD

As if sweeping changes to EL education were not enough, state leaders (particularly Tom Horne) went after TUSD again. Still, this time it was to destroy the MAS program that this community leader praised.

In 1998, under its desegregation plan, TUSD had implemented MAS to increase student achievement, particularly among their largest population—Latinx students.[27] MAS not only became a premier program in the district, but served as a model program throughout the country. Students enrolled in MAS experienced significant increases in student achievement across course subjects and graduation rates.[28] Nonetheless, in 2006, State Superintendent Tom Horne began his quest to eliminate MAS after he learned that Dolores Huerta, a Chicana civil rights activist, stated that "Republicans hate Latinos" during a MAS-invited speech.[29]

Arizona was already becoming an anti-immigrant environment when, in 2010, Governor Jan Brewer signed into law House Bill 2281, otherwise known as the "ethnic studies ban." This law was passed only a few weeks after Senate Bill 1070, which required people in Arizona to carry documentation of their citizenship status and gave police officers the right to arrest anyone they suspected was undocumented. With the help of Kris Kobach, a politician from Kansas, Arizona senator Russell Pearce ushered in SB 1070, which was perhaps one of the most controversial anti-immigration laws in the US since the federal government's "Operation Wetback" in the 1950s.[30] Although the Supreme Court later ruled that most of SB 1070 was unconstitutional, it and HB 2281 had profound effects in Arizona, including increasing hostility toward immigrants. During this period, Arizona experienced a huge decline of undocumented immigrants, calculated at about 40 percent, and a surge in fear and mistrust among many families—with all these effects spilling over into schools.[31]

Tom Horne and Russell Pearce were key figures behind the ethnic studies ban, which aimed to ban curricula that taught students "to resent or hate other races or classes of people."[32] This law directly targeted TUSD's successful MAS program and garnered widespread attention among the media and activists, putting the district into the national spotlight.

During this time frame, the TUSD school board consisted of two conservative members (Mark Stegeman and Michael Hicks, white males) and two progressive school board members (Adelita Grijalva, a Latinx female and Judy Burns, a white female), along with a fifth board member who was considered a swing vote (Miguel Cuevas, a Latinx male). The progressive board members were MAS supporters and vocal about their stance against HB 2281. Initially, the majority of the TUSD school board maintained that the MAS program did not violate HB 2281. Yet the school board president, Mark Stegeman, put a proposal on the agenda to dissolve MAS.

On April 27, fifteen students ran to the dais and chained themselves to the school board members' chairs before the meeting began. The students chanted, "Our education is under attack, what do we do? Fight back." This was just one of many protests against the proposal to dissolve the program. The superintendent and three of the board members (Hicks, Grijalva, and Burns) stepped into the boardroom to acknowledge what was happening, while two others (Cuevas and Stegeman) remained behind closed doors. The school board canceled the meeting, but the superintendent stated that the proposal would remain on the agenda.[33]

Days later, on May 2, the ADE commissioned an independent audit to determine whether TUSD's MAS program had violated HB 2281. The audit showed that MAS did not violate HB 2281; instead, MAS students experienced "positive measurable differences" compared to those not in the program.[34] Yet state leaders rejected the report's findings and continued to argue that TUSD's MAS program was operating unlawfully. On June 15, the newly elected state superintendent, John Huppenthal, formally threatened to withhold 10 percent of the district budget (amounting to $15 million) until the district dissolved the MAS program.

After receiving Huppenthal's ultimatum in June, TUSD appealed to the courts, and a hearing was held from August through December 2011. During the hearing, Stegeman testified that "he viewed the district's Mexican American Studies program as a cult and 'pure political proselytizing.'"[35] Also, during this hearing, two board members, Grijalva and Burns, coalesced with Cuevas in a 3–2 vote to depose Stegeman from the school board president position and elect Cuevas in his place.

Recalling these events, a district leader said that Stegeman was "manipulative" and "very hard to work with." He further described him as "the most twisted democrat I've ever met [and] he was more conservative along with Mike Hicks." On the other hand, he believed that Cuevas, who was only nineteen years old when elected to the board, wanted to be the "youngest board president in the state of Arizona." Concerned that the conservatives who were against MAS would be publicly upset at a change in the presidency, this district leader tried but failed to convince Cuevas to decline to serve as president.

Meanwhile, on October 27 of that year, Judy Burns, who had served since 2000, died suddenly of a heart attack. Two months later, the court affirmed Huppenthal's decision that TUSD violated HB 2281.

Appointment of a conservative board member

On January 4, 2011, Alexandre Sugiyama was sworn in as a board member to serve out the remainder of Burns's term.[36] During that same meeting, in a 3–2 vote, the board reappointed Stegeman as the board president, and the other conservative board member was voted in as the clerk. MAS supporters were upset at this shift in the board leadership.[37] One district leader claimed that Sugiyama later admitted that voting in Stegeman was a mistake.

In this highly political environment, fifty-four people submitted applications to fill the seat left vacant by Burns's death. On December 30, the Pima County school superintendent, a Republican, appointed Sugiyama, a registered Republican and a lecturer in the Department of Economics at the University of Arizona (UofA), the same department as the conservative-leaning board member Mark Stegeman. Technically, Stegeman outranked Sugiyama in his position at UofA, and his appointment may have been a conflict of interest that the district and the county superintendent ignored. Speculation among MAS supporters suggested that Sugiyama was appointed to align with Stegeman to vote against MAS.

Conversations with district leaders suggested that Stegeman, an econ-omist who studied game theory, was often very strategic in his thinking and actions. While his strategies were sometimes harmful to issues of equity, school board members should note, as emphasized in the School Board Governance for Equity (SBGE) framework, that engaging in coali-tion politics in the way he did requires strategy. They should consider how to adopt such strategies to advance equity. Equally important is to be aware when others are adopting such strategies that can hinder equity. In the latter case, board members might identify how they can disrupt coalitions before they cause harm. Perhaps if the other TUSD board members had disrupted the coalition between Sugiyama and Stegeman, then the vote to make Stegeman president would have failed, especially since it seemed that Sugiyama was not confident in his vote.

The vote that eliminated MAS

Six days later, on January 10, 2012, with hundreds of community mem-bers present, the TUSD school board voted 4–1 to eliminate MAS.[38] This vote aimed to move TUSD into compliance with Arizona's HB 2281. The two conservative board members, Hicks and Stegeman, swiftly (and not surprisingly) voted for the elimination of MAS. MAS supporters urged Sugiyama to recuse himself from the vote, arguing that since he had joined the board only days prior, he did not have a sufficient understand-ing of the issues surrounding MAS. But Sugiyama ignored them and decided to vote to dismantle the program.

Of the two Latinx school board members, only one, Adelita Grijalva, was adamantly against eliminating MAS. Deeply rooted in the commu-nity, Grijalva was the longest-standing board member and the mother of three children. She was also the daughter of Congressman Rául Gri-jalva, who had served on the TUSD school board from 1974 until 1986. She framed this vote as one of local control by noting that this decision should be made by the district, not the state. This framing was likely an attempt to convince her conservative board colleagues to side with her because their politics often prioritized local control. What Grijalva demonstrated is the importance of school board members identifying shared goals and values when attempting to push equity work forward. Board members committed to equity should identify shared goals and values, such as local control, to develop coalitions, even if short-lived, and even if this entails coalescing across political stances.

In addition to using the local control narrative, Grijalva presented this as a social justice issue by calling out this law's infringement on civil rights. In this way, she proclaimed that "this is an opportunity by this governing board to fight a bad law. It is unconstitutional. It is racist."

Her Latinx colleague, Cuevas, took a different stance. In the board meeting, he said, "While I may not agree with the law or the rulings, I have sworn to abide by them." He then noted, "My first responsibility as a governing board member is to provide a quality education to all students in this district." Finally, highlighting his racial background, he said, "As a member of the Latino community and as an individual of the governing board, I am committed [to the issue] for our students." Audience members replied to him angrily with comments such as "Shameful!" and "These are children that you are playing with!" As his comments illustrated, Cuevas took what one district leader called "a utilitarian approach" for the "greater good" to avoid the financial repercussions of the $15 million fine. Many people speculated that this approach also led to his failed election when he ran again for the school board in 2012.

Five years later, in 2017, an opinion by A. Wallace Tashima, a senior circuit judge on the US Court of Appeals for the Ninth Circuit, ruled that these Arizona state leaders had, in fact, violated the US Constitution. The judgment stated, "The court is convinced that decisions regarding the MAS program were motivated by a desire to advance a political agenda by capitalizing on race-based fears."[39] The court found that Tom Horne and other state leaders had racist and political intent in their targeting and eventual dismantling of TUSD's MAS program. As evidence of this, it later became known that on the *Daily Show*, a satirical comedy program broadcast on the Comedy Central cable channel, Hicks, one of the board members who voted against MAS, held several concerning and inaccurate ideas about history and civil rights. He also acknowledged that MAS, not any other ethnic studies program, was the target of HB 2281.[40]

Yet when the debate over MAS was at its height, only one school board member had used her elected position to call out the racism of this law and vote against it. The damage of the law cannot be undone: it targeted and eventually diminished one of TUSD's most successful and equity-focused academic programs. Although TUSD reinstated MAS as part of a culturally responsive curriculum program, many of the staff who were passionately committed to MAS and had built it from the ground up had left the district by that time. The reinstated program was much lower in terms of quality and impact, according to news reports.

These events remind us that school board members should stand courageously and steadfast with their communities and students to protect their civil rights. They must be willing to engage in civil disobedience and push back when navigating against inequitable policies that harm vulnerable students. If the board had voted against the elimination of MAS, the school district may have been responsible for the $15 million fine. But as Grijalva noted, TUSD could have appealed the constitutionality of HB 2281 at the federal level which, as the 2017 court decision showed, was in fact unconstitutional. If TUSD had appealed, the court would have likely paused the fine until after the issue was litigated, and perhaps it could have stopped the unconstitutional attack on MAS before the program was abolished.

Resisting: The Board Shifts in Power and Direction
Electing progressive board members
The vote to dismantle TUSD's MAS program prompted twelve candidates to vie for three at-large seats in the 2012 election.[41] Stegeman, Sugiyama, and Cuevas had filled these three seats. Stegeman was the only incumbent to win, carrying the second-largest percentage of votes behind

Kristel Foster, who had been an educator for more than twenty years and worked in the neighboring Sunnyside Unified School District as a specialist in the language acquisition department. Foster is also bilingual in Spanish and English. Cam Juarez, an urban planner and community organizer with close ties to Dolores Huerta, earned the third-largest percentage of votes.[42] Juarez also was a former volunteer for Congressman Grijalva. Given Juarez's experience and knowledge, as well as the fact that Juarez's child was about to begin kindergarten in TUSD, Congressman Grijalva had urged Juarez to run for school board. Juarez reflected on this, saying, "In retrospect, I think he just wanted me to get on the board to support his daughter who at this point had been in the minority for close to six years, and basically wasn't able to achieve too much because she had been in the minority with a fairly conservative board majority."

Congressman Grijalva's strategy worked

Following the 2012 elections, a clear shift happened on the school board. As one board member explained, "The vote to bring in Mr. Juarez and Ms. Foster as candidates who were known to be (1) more progressive and (2) really supportive of Mexican-American studies, that was the shift." These two, along with Grijalva, created a voting bloc that flipped the board to a more progressive philosophy. While some district leaders viewed this as a victory, others saw it as a defeat. For instance, one school board member expressed, "I have three board members who . . . it's really, the way I see it is if you're not Hispanic, you're not anything and I disagree with that. I disagree with that wholeheartedly." Nevertheless, this voting bloc ushered in several changes related to EL policies and practices, with the first being changes in leadership.

Leadership changes

The first leadership change was on the board. At the first meeting following the election, the board majority voted to make Grijalva president which, as one board member explained, "had enormous impact on how we were going to move forward."

The other leadership change was to district administration. Super-intendent Pedicone resigned because, according to district leaders, he wanted the newly elected board to appoint someone else who would be aligned with their vision. In April 2013, the board voted 4–1 to hire Superintendent Sanchez, with Stegeman issuing the sole no vote.

Of the new superintendent, one board member stated, "We have two board members now that are making our current superintendent's life pretty miserable because they don't have confidence in him." These were the two conservative-leaning board members, Hicks and Stegeman. Yet another board member highlighted the significance of hiring Sanchez, explaining, "You have a Latino superintendent that speaks Spanish. That attends meetings and speaks Spanish without translators. It's through pol-icy, through these decisions made by the board majority. We are commu-nicating effectively to our communities, 'You're not lost on us. We're going to make the changes necessary to help your child graduate and achieve.'"

This board member understood the impact of such leadership changes: they signify the importance of having school board members and leaders with personal ties and connections with the community they serve in schools, especially those who are often most marginalized. To achieve this, you must encourage your community to engage in the electoral process at the school board level. This includes getting people to vote and urging people to run for their local school board. Voter turnout for school board elections is notoriously low, and as one recent survey showed, nearly 40 percent of school board candidates run unopposed.[43] Building an equity-focused school board pipeline is essential, and as a school board member, identifying and supporting board candidates who are committed to equity, either to work with you or to replace you, is key to this pipeline.

Changes to curricula
During the first meeting following the elections, the school board voted 3–2 to reverse an objection from the formerly elected school board that

would allow for the development of Culturally Relevant Curriculum (CRC) courses. As part of the school desegregation Unitary Status Plan, CRC would become a revised version of MAS.

Then, about a month later, during the fourth meeting of the newly elected board on February 12, 2013, Foster requested a study/action to deliberately make dual-language programs part of the Advanced Learning Experience. A few months later, after staff reported on dual-language programs, the board voted 4–1 in support of them. This change meant that the district would recognize students' completion of dual-language programs on students' transcripts, similar to an honors program.

Among many items, the staff's report highlighted the substantial demand for dual-language programs: from 2005 to 2013, there was an increase from 132 to 2,408 students across twelve dual-language sites, not counting the students on the waiting list. Since the state policy related to the SEI requirement allowed only ELs who were age ten or older to opt out of SEI in favor of dual-language programs, very few ELs were enrolled. Still, those ELs in dual-language programs were reclassified to non-EL status at a higher rate than those in the SEI programs (46.4 percent versus 34.5 percent in 2012). Also, students in these programs in grades three through five attained higher scores on average on state exams than the district average.

The majority of the board demonstrated growing awareness of dual-language programs. However, some were concerned that dual-language teachers worked more than their counterparts and were not compensated fairly. Grijalva said, "What do we have to do internally to ensure that we can attract more endorsed teachers, ask more teachers to become endorsed, and how we figure it out? Because . . . ideally I would love for us to give some sort of stipend, compensation. . . . I know that the teachers that teach it love it, but it's extra work."

Despite the growing awareness and success of the district's dual-language programs, leaders supporting these programs still faced pushback. Hicks, the other relatively more conservative school board member, expressed misgivings, making it clear that his concerns were because these programs were only Spanish-focused and not in his area of town. At a board meeting, Hicks asked the staff why there were no dual-language programs in his area of residence, which was relatively affluent and white. In response, the staff explained that, as part of the desegregation plan, students on that side of town could opt to transfer to a school with a dual-language program as the staff explained. Hicks replied that he was concerned about them having to travel outside their community for these services. He also thought that the district prioritized Spanish-language programs, noting that "I want to make sure that we're not going to segregate French, we're not going to segregate Chinese or any other language and only focus, only going forward with Spanish." TUSD staff explained that although they planned to include other languages later, Spanish was currently the only available option. Hicks responded by saying, "Well I'd like to see expansion in *other* languages. I mean we have quite a bit; and I've met quite a bit of individuals who are a little distraught that we don't do anything with that." Even though the status of ELs was a different issue, Stegeman, concerned about the state law, asked if any of TUSD's EL services were noncompliant, and staff said that they were in corrective action from 2008 to 2011 and were determined to be compliant after that. These comments illustrate the pushback against dual language programs that might serve Spanish-speaking ELs and other Latinx students, and thus reflect an anti-Latinx sentiment.

It is important to note a couple of facts. First, very few ELs could access any dual-language program and therefore had little opportunity to participate in the official Advanced Learning Experience to earn recognition of their bilingual or multilingual skills on their high school diploma. Parents of ELs could opt in to dual-language programs if their children were age ten or older, but most ELs were under ten years old. In addition, the transition from SEI to dual-language programs after age ten presents challenges, such as having to navigate the district's choices and potentially move schools. Second, of the approximately $1.5 million spent on these programs, staff in this meeting indicated that all of it, except for $3,000, was funded by either Title III federal funding or desegregation funds. In other words, dual-language services and programs had relatively little financial support from local funding streams. TUSD's desegregation lawsuit provided only temporary funding. The funding would dissipate once the district is in post unitary status, and these programs would likely dissolve after that.

As board members, it is important to understand the barriers that can exclude minoritized students from educational opportunities so you can push back against these barriers to expand their opportunities. It is also important to understand how programs are being funded and what the future might hold because of these funding streams.

Strategic plan

While former superintendent Pedicone did not believe that a strategic plan was necessary outside of focusing on academic achievement, the newly elected board requested that the new superintendent develop TUSD's first strategic plan. During July 2014, the board voted unanimously to put a new five-year plan into effect. Notably, the plan included very little in terms of EL-related goals besides expanding world languages and analyzing staff diversity skills, including state-level bilingual endorsements.

Summary of the board shift

With a newly elected school board in place, the majority vote shifted. Board members used this opportunity to change the leadership of the board and district. They also decided to allow the district to develop culturally relevant courses and amplify the dual-language program. As emphasized in the SBGE framework, the power of knowing your community, being proactively responsive to the community, identifying leaders who connect with the community, and building a coalition to get important equity items on the agenda are crucial factors in moving equity forward. Still, when it came to ELs, their strategic plan included little that would specifically strengthen opportunities for ELs. Although most dual-language programs were in Spanish, many ELs could not participate because of state law. If a program or resource is failing to expand equity for the populations that need it most, we cannot call it "equity." In these cases, school board members should take an honest assessment of whom the district is serving and consider how to dismantle barriers to expand opportunities.

Not all TUSD board members supported these equity efforts. For instance, Hicks and Stegeman both voted against the development of CRC, Stegeman voted against amplifying dual-language programs, and Hicks expressed concerns about dual-language programs not serving students in relatively more white and affluent neighborhoods. When school board members push back against equity efforts, you should pay attention to their rationales and take note of their preferred language. You might consider calling out comments that support inequity and privilege (e.g., white privilege, economic privilege), either in a board meeting so it is public and documented, or in private if you think that that person is open to engaging in dialogue and shifting his or her perspective. By doing this, you might plant the seeds of change because either the public will take note of what is happening or the individual might change.

As we see in the next section, the lack of focus on ELs often reflected the beliefs and social constructions of ELs, particularly in relationship to the anti-immigrant environment in the United States during that time.

BELIEFS OF ELS IN THE DISTRICT

This section provides a brief overview of the beliefs of ELs in TUSD. Recall that the beliefs here are part of social constructions that, as the SBGE framework points out, are important for school board members to reflect on, examine, and consider as they make policy decisions that often have far-reaching impacts on minoritized communities.

ELs "Not on the Agenda" Despite the "Horrible" English Immersion Program

Although most district leaders conveyed their desire to provide more support to ELs, this group was often not prioritized at the district level. Many blamed state policies for the district's inability to support ELs adequately. Moreover, they said that the state-required SEI program was "not humane," "not good for students," "horrible," and "modern-day segregation." One school board member said that the SEI program contributed to ELs being "pushed out" of school because they were taken out of their academic classes for four hours a day. A different board member described these practices of "isolating your children for four-hour blocks in a classroom; no content, just language with a teacher who doesn't necessarily speak Spanish and is unable to communicate with a child in their native language" as "criminal." In addition to getting pulled from core classes, district leaders noted that ELs often experienced burdens of low expectations, bullying, and significant testing. During a school board meeting in 2011, board members questioned TUSD administrators about the SEI program. In response, administrators explained that SEI was a top-down practice, with no research supporting its effectiveness.

Despite most TUSD board members knowing the SEI program had adverse consequences for ELs, TUSD still implemented it. ELs were not a large part of discussions at the board level. As one board member recalled, EL-related items had not been on the agenda in TUSD for a couple of years. They explained, "If it's not on the agenda, the board doesn't discuss it." In comparison, some district leaders shared that TUSD's neighboring Sunnyside Unified School District in Tucson refused to implement the SEI program for about five years until they almost lost funding. Comparing the two school boards, these district leaders described Sunnyside school board members as more progressive and willing to resist SEI.

ELs as "Invisible," "Undocumented," "Fucking Migrants"

Many district leaders shared beliefs of ELs that aligned with the broader anti-immigrant sentiment in Arizona. As one community member emphasized, the situation with ELs was an "interesting paradox," in that they were "both an invisible population and they're very visible." She further explained that ELs were "visible in the sense that they are in every school." Yet "the general public doesn't know very much about that population, and there is a perception that all those kids are undocumented." This sentiment about the EL population in TUSD was reflected in many district leaders' comments. TUSD's EL population includes children who speak various languages and are from numerous countries of origin, including Indigenous children from the United States. Still, some district leaders conflated ELs with immigrants, refugees, undocumented, and Mexican/Latinx or other Spanish-speaking people.

These preconceived notions of ELs were embedded within existing deficit perspectives about these children and their families. As one board member said, the community often expressed a "real ugly anti-immigrant, anti-Mexican sentiment." This sentiment, they said, was reflected in such comments as "These kids don't speak English" and "We're in America. If they don't want to speak English, then let 'em go back to Mexico." Another district leader shared that many people in the Tucson community think that ELs are "all a bunch of fucking migrants" who come to the United States with "no language" and "no education." One board member noted, "We don't, as a state, acknowledge or value the contributions of immigrants with language/culture."

Connecting the anti-immigrant stance to racism, one community member said, "We're [TUSD] so close to the border and in some ways, we are a really racist state, there's no other way to say that. You know I've lived here twenty years and it pains me to have to say." Some district leaders used SB 1070 as a manifestation of such racism. The anti-immigrant state law sparked fear among some immigrant families, who were frightened that sending their children to school might risk them being deported. As one board member reflected, "ELLs, much like immigration, are seen as a Brown issue opposed to an issue of students and equity." As these comments suggest, people often lumped ELs into categories associated with deficit-oriented beliefs. When we group people together, such as assuming that all ELs are "undocumented" or that all Black students are poor, we embrace deficit-oriented views and fail to recognize any nuance of these groups. It's a dehumanizing approach. And this dehumanization results in either less support or misdirected support for those who need it most.

ELs as Valued

It was less common for district leaders to describe ELs as a valued group, but some did. These board members and leaders expressed the ways that they valued ELs from the standpoints of equity, cultural diversity, and linguistic representation. From an equity perspective, some shared their hope of reversing the inequities that ELs experience. For instance, one board member explained, "I didn't enter this board because I wanted to take anything away from white kids. I just wanted to make sure that all kids had equal access . . . you talk about equality versus equity and you're talking about a very different conversation because you can't provide the same thing to all students and expect them to perform exactly the same." This board member believed that ELs had unique needs and it was TUSD's responsibility to support these unique needs rather than taking a cookie-cutter approach.

Several district leaders reflected on the issue from a linguistic perspective, calling for support of bilingual and multilingual skills. When the school board voted for dual-language programs to be recognized as Advanced Learning Experiences on students' diplomas, similar to an honors diploma, one school board member described this move as partially designed to give "an elevated status to our ELL students." A different board member pointed out that three of the five members of the school board were "ideologically highly invested in dual language" for reasons that they believed were based "philosophically" and, in some cases, "politically." In other words, they likely thought that multilingualism was beneficial and saw the elevation of dual-language programs as a way to push back politically against English immersion.

From a cultural perspective, a few district leaders expressed wanting more community members to understand that ELs contribute diversity to both schools and the community. They explained that having ELs in schools created opportunities to use language to connect the community and strengthen the culture within the district. One school board member described wanting their own children to develop a strong foundation in both Spanish and English.

Summary of Beliefs

The beliefs of ELs within the TUSD community varied widely. While many expressed empathetic sentiments toward those ELs who participated in the SEI program, others described extreme anti-immigrant sentiments, and some shared that ELs were valued. Although state policy and politics presented challenges for ELs to force them to participate in a program that many district leaders believed was "criminal" and "inhumane," TUSD did not push back like their neighboring district or how the group of Navajo teachers did. ELs were very much part of TUSD (visible) and conflated with communities of immigrants and "Brown" people (hypervisible), but not often prioritized or deserving enough to be on the agenda of the school board (invisible). The community's general push for ELs to assimilate reflected an "English as a priority" belief. Unsurprisingly, many of the policies put forward aligned with this belief. Such policies and practices suggest that authentic differences in language and cultures are to be resented and pushed away rather than embraced, and ELs bore the brunt of such reactionary policies.

In hyperpolitical and polarizing places like Arizona, it is expected that social constructions and beliefs about groups vary in extreme ways. Even though in many states, school board members are charged with being bipartisan in their politics, that does not mean that they are apolitical. As established in chapter 1, education is political. And advancing equity is part of those politics. When it comes to beliefs, if you believe that *all* children deserve an equitable education, you must plant the seeds of change by calling out inequities, engaging in meaningful dialogue, and shifting people's beliefs.

SUMMARY

This story of TUSD is complicated by several social, political, economic, and legal factors. Although these factors merged to create a "perfect storm," which might have made TUSD unique, in many ways this story is actually not unique. Like TUSD, school boards in districts that serve large numbers of minoritized children, even those in rural and tribal communities, should anticipate becoming a target of disdain. Such consequences often depend on the political climate which, as the SBGE framework reveals, reflects the beliefs and social constructions that local and state communities have of various populations. In Arizona, the anti-immigrant climate was widespread. It took only a few key actors, some of whom came from other states, to completely dismantle equitable policies, practices, and programs in education.

This story is a cautionary tale to equity advocates on school boards. Deeply understanding your context, building strong coalitions, and mobilizing at all levels of government and the law are critical to moving equity forward. And sometimes school boards must be courageous and willing to engage in civil disobedience and resist inequitable policies that harm vulnerable students. Taking action is part of being proactively responsive when—not if—the storm hits.

5

The Case of Clark County School
District: Coalition Politics in Full Force

THE CASE IN this chapter is a story about profound contextual changes in
local and state growth and demographics and a school board that did not
reflect these changes. It is also a story of local leaders from Black and Latinx
communities who were committed to creating a responsive school board
and holding its members accountable for meeting the needs of the families
in their respective communities. This case reveals the messiness of democratic engagement and racialized coalition politics at the school board level,
including some failures and successes in advancing educational equity.

The story of Clark County School District (CCSD) emphasizes the important role of multiracial coalition politics presented within the School
Board Governance for Equity (SBGE) framework discussed in the previous chapters. Many school districts are experiencing demographic shifts,
including more students of color and English learners (ELs). From this
case, you will understand why some community leaders see these demographic shifts as a threat to their communities. You will also see how
many community leaders in this district failed to leverage their power to

substantially move equity forward for all groups because they engage in competition rather than coalition politics. In addition, you will learn how district leaders responded to this competition by supporting umbrella solutions that appeased both communities, as well as how these solutions failed to offer the unique resources and services that each community needed. This case shows why engaging in coalition politics, rather than competition or even just collaboration, is a key element toward achieving the most equitable conditions possible for minoritized children. Finally, despite these shortcomings, this case also highlights important lessons for successfully leveraging state policies to address district needs.

Using the SBGE framework to organize this story, I briefly describe some context and history to help you build an understanding of the board, district, community, and state. Then I explain the skills and strategies that stemmed from the coalition politics among the Black and Latinx communities and how they leveraged state policies. Following this, I highlight the district's shared beliefs about ELs in order to shed light on what types of knowledge the school board was operating from, which were largely deficit oriented. In conclusion, I offer an overview of changes in EL policies and practices that stemmed from these shared beliefs, skills, and strategies, as well as how the school board was part of these changes.

KNOWING AND UNDERSTANDING CCSD

District Context and History

As one of the fastest-growing states in the United States for the last few decades, Nevada's population soared 66 percent from 1990 to 2000 and 35 percent from 2000 to 2010.[1] CCSD, located in southern Nevada, is the fifth-largest school district in the United States, serving over 300,000 students.[2] Centered in the Las Vegas metropolitan area, the district spans urban, suburban, and rural areas.

CCSD grew rapidly, building 112 schools over a ten-year period (1998–2008) to accommodate almost 120,000 new students.[3] This growth,

coupled with its large, expansive demographic, presented many challenges to meeting the diverse needs of all its communities. Community
and political leaders representing heavily Republican areas of CCSD's
suburban and rural areas attempted to break away from this district.
These attempts have failed for economic reasons, but urban leaders,
mostly Democrats, also pushed back, arguing that a breakup would harm
minoritized children and contribute to increasing racial and economic
segregation.[4]

CCSD's history of school segregation is also notable. In 1972, the
NAACP sued the CCSD, forcing it to desegregate its schools. The school
board voted on the Sixth Grade Center Plan, which placed the burden
of busing on Black families. CCSD bused students out of the majority
Black neighborhood of "West Las Vegas" for eleven years. In contrast, the
district bused the majority white population into "West Las Vegas" for
only one year during sixth grade, to attend what they called "Sixth Grade
Centers." The plan remained for twenty years, until 1992.[5]

Soon after, with an influx of new residents, CCSD's demographics
shifted again. In the early 2000s, the Latinx student population soared
by 44 percent, and ELs increased more than 100 percent. CCSD became
what district leaders termed a "majority-minority" school district, which
meant that more students of color were enrolled there than white students.[6] Also, the once-majority Black schools shifted to almost 50 percent
Black, 50 percent Latinx, and 33 percent ELs by 2009.[7] Simultaneously, the
Great Recession in 2010 contributed to state and local budget cuts to education.[8] Consequently, the district faced the challenge of equitably serving a demographically different student population with less funding.

The state's funding system, established in 1967, failed to support
CCSD's growth and diverse student needs sufficiently. It did not provide
additional funding for capital outlay (i.e., buildings) or for unique needs
associated with student demographics, including income and language
ability. In comparison to other US states, Nevada ranked fourth lowest in
per-pupil annual expenditures, at $8,089.[9]

One costing-out study from 2006 determined that Nevada under-funded students by approximately $80 million, nearly 100 percent more than the state was providing.[10] Many areas were underfunded, including capital outlay (buildings) and services to students with unique needs, such as language ability. Soon after the study was completed, the Great Recession of 2010 hit Nevada especially hard because of the state's reliance on tourism, which declined rapidly. With close to 50 percent of the education budget coming from local sales taxes and 20 percent from property taxes, Nevada's economic downturn translated into large budget cuts to education.[11] Given the state's economic decline, state leaders essentially buried the study. Until 2013, Nevada was among one of only eight states that had not provided additional statewide funding for EL education, even though the 2006 study recommended allocation of around $132 million annually for ELs.[12]

The school board's governance changed along with the funding and growth challenges. In 2000, after a lawsuit over a school board member's unlawful involvement related to CCSD's human resources area, the board adopted a policy governance model.[13] This model requires boards to focus on setting policy and holding the superintendent accountable, while refraining from micromanaging district activities.[14] Although this model is supposed to usher in more efficiency and student achievement, the board had less authority to make positive changes, and student achievement did not increase.[15] In terms of equity, as one school board member stated, "The administrators loved it because you didn't have board members involved in anything." He also explained that the district reversed its equity work, including "not hiring outside administrators," canceling "diversity months," and "doing vanilla-type stuff."

The School Board and Superintendency

The CCSD school board is made up of seven members, each of whom represents a smaller district (also known as "at-ward") that ranges from approximately 38,000 to 50,000 students. Members are elected, in a staggered fashion, to four-year terms up to sixteen years and paid $750 per month.[16] During the four-year period that I monitored the school board, it had twelve members serving at different points in time. Of these members, eight were women and four were men. Racially, the majority were white (eight) and the rest were Latinx (three) and Black (one). Of the three Latinx members, two were appointed to fill vacancies. The longest-standing member had been on the board for fifteen years.

In addition, CCSD had three superintendents within these four years—two white men and one Black man. The first, hired within the district, worked as the superintendent for four years and previously in CCSD in other capacities for eight years. The second superintendent, the Black man, was an education reformer from Colorado and remained in the position for two years. The third worked at CCSD for nearly twenty-five years prior, including as a teacher, and worked as the superintendent for five years.

Summary of Context

CCSD experienced rapid growth, especially among Latinx and EL populations, inadequate state funding for education, a changing governance model, and leadership turnover. These changes, coupled with a majority white school board that had a history of inequitable treatment of Black students when the district was mandated to desegregate schools, were key factors in propelling advocacy toward a focus on equity issues.

COMMUNITY ADVOCACY, LEVERAGING STATE POLICY, AND COALITION POLITICS

Community advocacy, leveraging state policy, and coalition politics affected policies and practices in this district in prominent ways. Leaders representing the Black and Latinx communities spurred this advocacy and politics. Two leaders, one from each community, are central to this story. Pseudonyms are used in these descriptions of these women.

Norma was a Latina parent and CCSD resident who worked as a professor of law and helped to lead a Latinx community organization. Her involvement in education issues helped bring concerns about ELs to the forefront in CCSD. Between 2010 and 2013, she spoke at a minimum of seven school board meetings, and every person interviewed for this district described her involvement as critical in changing EL education in both CCSD and Nevada.

Deborah, another key leader, was a CCSD resident and a Black woman who led a political organization that advocated for issues on behalf of the Black community, including education. While other Black community leaders weighed in on educational issues in CCSD, Deborah participated on committees, met with school board members, testified in political spaces, and engaged with Latinx leaders on the issues affecting ELs and Black students.

In 2010, Norma and Deborah both served on a superintendent committee formed to examine the district's persistently underachieving elementary schools. Related to ELs, this committee recommended at least one bilingual staff member at each high-EL-populated school; more dual-language and bilingual programs targeting native Spanish speakers; an in-depth analysis to identify supports for ELs; and for the district to lobby the state for more EL-specific funding. For Norma, this committee work set the stage for her advocacy because she was exposed to data that showed ELs' lower performance on test scores. Norma believed that the district was "doing work with African American kids and . . . with special ed students," but she was "shock[ed]" that CCSD was "blow[ing] off ELL kids." In looking at this data, she said that "the numbers thing [was] crushing." Consequently, Norma started "asking questions and not getting answers." As she asked questions, Norma also cofounded a community organization focused on Latinx issues and cochaired this organization's education committee.

Norma used this newly formed Latinx community organization as a vehicle to legitimize and represent the Latinx position on several issues, including EL education. She also requested support for ELs from several other community organizations, within and outside the Latinx spectrum, including the Mexican American Legal Defense and Educational Fund, faculty and administration from the local university, and the American Civil Liberties Union of Nevada. Norma organized official meetings with these organizational representatives and other community members to highlight concerns about and discuss solutions for EL education issues in CCSD. Several media outlets characterized these meetings as the first step in a potential lawsuit against the state for providing inadequate funding for EL education. These organizational efforts offered her and others the leverage to advocate for ELs and other children in at least three areas: (1) shifting district leadership, including the board, and district committee development; (2) state-level advocacy; and (3) engaging in coalition politics with the Black community. Next, I detail these efforts.

Latinx Superintendent-Level Position and the EL Committee

First, community leaders pushed to increase Latinx representation among district administration and on the school board. When the CCSD deputy superintendent position opened in 2010, members of the Latinx organization made public comments about how important they thought having a Latinx leader in a high-level executive position was, and why this could usher in more cultural affinity within this majority-Latinx district. The Latinx organization pushed to hire one Latino applicant in particular, Pedro Martinez, and the board agreed.

With Pedro in this key position, he formed the EL committee that Norma had been "constantly nagging" him to create. The EL committee brought together educators and community leaders to develop EL-focused accountability measures for CCSD. Even though Pedro resigned from the district less than two years later and the EL committee was dissolved temporarily after he left, he planted the seeds of equity work that community leaders like Norma then cultivated. Prior to his departure to become the superintendent of a different district in Nevada, Pedro had proposed a $95,000 study on ELs by WestEd, a nonprofit research firm, as part of the EL committee recommendations, which the board approved.

In the early spring of 2012, WestEd examined ten high-EL-populated schools. Based on the WestEd report prepared by Aída Walqui in June of that year, six main findings emerged:

1. "Low expectations and perceptions of students as deficient are pervasive throughout schools visited" (p. 10).
2. "Observed classes indicated little evidence that teachers designed instruction to challenge and support English Language Learners" (p. 12).
3. "In observed classes, teachers focused on discrete disciplinary or linguistic elements" (p. 14).
4. "There is little sense of urgency, a general slow pace characterizes classes" (p. 17).
5. "When available, technology is used at its lowest potential, thus limiting ELs' opportunities to participate in a quality learning" (p. 20).
6. "Bilingual programs: A wasted opportunity."[17]

Overall, WestEd deemed EL education in CCSD insufficient, determining that ELs were missing out on the essential opportunities necessary for academic success. Furthermore, the report highlighted that teachers and principals often address EL education and EL students using a deficit framework. Following the report, WestEd proposed a contract for around $1 million that would include the implementation of professional development to improve EL education. However, the school board never even placed it on the agenda for a vote.

In 2014, Norma coordinated a follow-up meeting with Aída, the WestEd lead researcher, CCSD administrators, and school board members. Aída expressed her disappointment that the district had not responded to the report. As Norma recalled, Aída told the board members, "Listen, I wrote a report in 2010 and you guys haven't done a damn thing. You've made zero movement. My contract hasn't moved at all. . . . I'm coming here and I'm telling you these kids are not getting any education. That report is enough to make you like lose your hair."

These comments, according to Norma, "shocked" the board members. During the meeting, one board member acknowledged that the increasing community pressure was a key factor in forcing it to be more responsive to EL issues. Although some board members pushed the district to increase its support for EL issues, budget constraints and superintendent turnover made that difficult. Nonetheless, Norma and others relied on the findings of this study to advocate for more EL-related resources at the state level.

EL district-level position

In addition to using the WestEd study and the committee work as leverage, community leaders pushed to create a position at the executive level: someone who would have content expertise at the district level to oversee EL programs. CCSD hired Lucy Keaton, a CCSD principal who had excelled in increasing EL achievement at the school level, to be assistant superintendent of the EL program. Yet, when she resigned soon afterward (some said that she was pushed out because she was ineffective), the district downgraded this position from a superintendent-level to a director-level position and made plans to conduct an internal search to fill it.

The Latinx community pushed back on this decision. As Norma recalled of her conversations with district leaders, she said to them, "Someone needs to own it [ELL issues]. . . . I need to be able to call a person when something is effed up. Who is that person?" She further explained, "This person has to have clarity and also speak with authority, and executive directors do not speak with authority in the district."

Then, the Latinx community organization sent an official letter to the school board urging them to reinstate the position at the superintendent level and complete an outside search to attract more EL expertise. After the letter, Norma shared that it took several one-on-one follow-up conversations with district leaders to convince them to support their request. She said what "finally [got them] on board" was reminding them that "your constituencies, the Susie Lee, the Punam, the Mrs. Wynn, this elite group will not be impressed with a principal, and if Dwight [the superintendent] makes a second mistake by hiring a principal, he's done [i.e., fired or pushed out]." These are names of influential people in Nevada, including political leaders, casino owners (such as Elaine Wynn, the former spouse of casino mogul Steve Wynn), and executives, who were also invested in improving education in CCSD. Their voices mattered on education issues. And Latinx leaders employed the power of their voices to push forward their agenda in the district.

Convinced by the Latinx leaders' advocacy, the school board rescinded its original decision. Instead, it conducted an outside search to fill a superintendent-level position to oversee EL programs. They ended up hiring a Latino administrator who formerly oversaw EL services in the Tucson Unified School District for many years.

School board representation

Latinx and Black community leaders also pushed for more racially diverse school board representation. In the spring of 2011, the school board engaged in the process of redistricting election boundaries. During these school board meetings, Latinx leaders successfully urged the board to create zoning areas more populated by Latinx residents to increase the chances of electing a Latinx school board member. As Norma explained, "We [the community] needed authentic diversity on the school board . . . where real deliberation is happening." Yet she noted that the election boundaries were not the only challenge. It was difficult to encourage diverse school board representation because, as she noted, being a board member is "unaffordable," and the "lack of remuneration . . . is a real barrier." She shared that most of the school board members were "housewives who don't have to worry about being the main force of support" at home, and because most of them were "Mormon," the work of "serving in the community is a mission for them." This was pretty accurate. Four of the seven board members identified as Mormon; one was a retired teacher and the other two worked flexible jobs.

Although CCSD voters did not vote in a Latinx school board member right away, a board seat opened up in 2013 after one board member resigned. Latinx community leaders helped to identify Stavan Corbett, a Latino and former EL student who was born and raised in Las Vegas and was serving on the statewide board of education, as a potential appointee. During the meeting when the school board decided whom to appoint, eleven individuals, mostly representing various Latinx-based community organizations, pledged their support of Stavan in public comments. Some school board members publicly acknowledged the lack of diversity on the board relative to the community. The school board voted unanimously to appoint Stavan as the newest school board member.

Stavan, the only Latinx school board member in a district with a 44 percent Latinx student population, was a champion of equity issues. Everyone I spoke with named him as a key leader of pushing EL issues to the forefront. One of his first actions was to pressure the new superintendent to reinstate the CCSD EL review committee that had dissolved when Pedro resigned. He also helped fellow board members understand the inequities that ELs experienced in CCSD, or as one board member put it, Stavan "educated" them.

Stavan also had a deep understanding of the history and racialized context of Las Vegas. He made note of the importance of "recognizing the level of injustices that have happened for years, and to some extent, still yet hasn't been fully addressed." Because of this, he explained that there are "communities that feel like we have never really achieved what was promised to us because our students are underperforming, and all we want is for our children to know how to read, write, and do math so they can be successful."

Stavan observed that groups representing racialized communities were "engag[ing] in territorial" tactics to compete for "limited resources," which he attributed to the state's "funding mechanisms and structures" for education. When tensions between the Latinx and Black leadership emerged, he navigated these tensions to support both communities.

Even Deborah identified Stavan, alongside the only Black school board member, as one of two allies who advocated for issues affecting Black students in CCSD. She said that together, they "wanted to see things better for both our kids [Black and Latinx kids]," and then explained, "If it wasn't for Stavan, I probably would not work as closely with the Latino community as I do because he has given me hope that there are Latinos out there that really committed as much to our kids and . . . they're not gonna sell us down the river." She went on to share how he "resolved" and "saved" many relationships when she felt that Latino leaders "threw us [the Black community] under the bus."

This coalition went well beyond racial alliances. When Stavan was up for appointment by the board, a Black candidate competed against him. Still, Deborah spoke on Stavan's behalf at the board meeting because, as she described it, he had "proven to be an ally and a warrior right along with us on the front line." The Black candidate, however, showed up without much prior involvement in community efforts and appeared to be an "opportunist," as Deborah said.

After he served for about a year as an appointed board member, Stavan lost in the school board election. Several people blamed his loss on a lack of Latinx voters in the school board election and said that Stavan's Spanish surname deterred voters who did not want to elect a Latinx board member. The only other Latinx school board member who had been elected in the district had a last name that was not seemingly of Spanish descent.

State-level advocacy

The second area of community advocacy was at the state level.

Teacher evaluations

When Stavan served on the state board of education prior to his appointment as a CCSD school board member, he asked Norma to testify on EL issues at state board meetings. She recalled him saying, "I'm the only one there [speaking on EL issues], and people kind of ignore me, and I need you to come out and testify."

Norma testified on teacher evaluations: "It's impossible for you not to have an evaluation system in a school district where you have one in four ELL children, and not evaluate that teacher [on] whether they can adjust the needs of that child. I mean that has to be part of that skill set or else we will continue to be at the bottom [of the national education rankings]." Immediately after her testimony, the board voted to include cultural competency on teacher evaluations for the state. Norma noted that the state board "needed an advocate to make the point quite forcefully, and to make it sound ridiculous that they wouldn't even have that in there. I mean, how can you move the needle if you're not going to evaluate teachers in this area where we know they're so weak?" Norma and others continued this advocacy at the state legislature.

Zoom schools

After the school board did not put the contract with WestEd on the agenda to vote on it or even agree to discuss it, community leaders began lobbying the state. It was an ideal time to do so because the level of state support existed in ways that it had not in years prior. In 2010, Nevada voters elected Governor Brian Sandoval, the state's first Latino governor and a moderate Republican who appealed to a wider demographic. In addition, around 2013, eight Latinx legislators, which was a significantly higher number of Latinx legislators than Nevada had had up to that point, formed the Nevada Hispanic Legislative Caucus.[18]

Latinx community leaders from Las Vegas used the number and power of these Latinx political leaders to help pass Senate Bill 504 with bipartisan support. This bill had two components. First, it required the development of a committee to make recommendations regarding teaching standards for ELs that would be implemented at the district-level. The second component was the allocation of $50 million for two years toward what they named "Zoom schools" (no affiliation with the company Zoom). The idea was to accelerate ELs' learning (hence the term "Zoom"). The schools chosen to be Zoom schools were required to be elementary schools and highly populated by both ELs and low-income students. The bill also required school districts to use the money toward additional services such as early childhood education, reading support, and summer school.[19]

Although this was a huge step forward in policy and funding to support ELs, a few barriers stood in the way of Zoom schools making a large impact in CCSD. First, the bill was passed and signed by Governor Sandoval on June 12, 2013, with the requirement that it would be implemented in the fall of 2013. This left very little time for the district to prepare for the implementation, which would involve hiring qualified staff and developing programs. The criteria for Zoom schools included only those schools with over 35 percent ELs and rated as one or two out of five stars (based mostly on test score performance). Of the 357 elementary schools in CCSD, only 14 qualified as Zoom schools, which equated to approximately 12 percent of the EL population in the district.[20] Although the number of Zoom schools increased over the years, many ELs in CCSD still did not receive these specialized services. In addition, if Zoom schools increased their ratings, they would no longer meet the criteria for the extra funding to support programs and services that likely contributed to the increased performance in the first place—a win-lose situation.[21] And although the impact of these schools was beyond the results of this case study, external reports suggest that many Zoom schools did "well" at least as measured by academic test scores, particularly those that had this funding longer.[22]

Coalition Politics and Black Community Interests

Black community leaders had a long history of being highly engaged in educational issues affecting Black children in CCSD. Among other efforts, they advocated for having desegregation schools and returning to neighborhood schools, and they constantly pushed for equitable educational opportunities for the decades that followed. Yet their involvement shifted focus when some community leaders perceived that state and district funds allocated to EL education might be siphoned from Black students. Concerned about losing resources that might be shifted to ELs, some Black community leaders pursued certain goals to preserve and increase resources for Black students in CCSD.

Comparing resources of ELs and Black students
When it came to funding, these Black community leaders wanted to ensure that the Latinx community and other district and state leaders understood that EL-allocated resources were as much, if not more, than those allocated to Black students. Deborah explained that Latinx community leaders falsely believed that Black children had been provided sufficient funding through the additional support for Prime Six schools (which historically had been African American schools).

CCSD developed the Prime Six Plan in 1992 in response to Black advocates, mostly mothers, who advocated for a return to neighborhood schools for children in the majority Black community. As noted earlier in the chapter, the court forced CCSD to mandate desegregation in 1972. The plan required mostly white students to bus into the majority Black neighborhood for only one year to attend Sixth Grade Centers, while Black families bused their children for eleven years. In 1992, CCSD converted the Sixth Grade Centers to Prime Six schools and instituted Magnet programs to attract white families. The district allocated relatively more resources to support these schools and programs.

By 2009, these neighborhood schools, which were 80 percent Black in 2000, shifted to nearly 50 percent Black, 50 percent Latinx, and 33 percent ELs.[23] Deborah recalled telling Latinx community leaders, including Norma:

> I want you to please go back and make sure your community understands a few things about Prime Six. One, Prime Six has not been Black

for many, many years. Prime Six is very Hispanic; been for at least ten years. So, when we talk about all the resources that Prime Six has gotten, you guys should count your blessings because not only did you get those resources from Prime Six, you also got your ELL resources. So, you double dipped. So, let's keep it real.

Deborah's response to Latinx community leaders reflected these demographic changes, which meant that more educational resources were being used for an increasing number of Latinx and EL students who attended Prime Six schools.

Gathering the numbers

The percentage of Black students in CCSD had remained stable, but many Black families relocated to other neighborhoods in the district. While in the past, it was well known that the majority of Black students resided in "West Las Vegas" and attended Prime Six schools, as Black families dispersed to other local neighborhoods, community leaders shared that it was more difficult to know where they went and what schools they were populating. As Deborah noted, "When we talk about Black students and Black students getting resources . . . the district doesn't even know where those schools are, but they will." After she witnessed Norma's effective use of data to advocate for more EL funding during her testimony to the Nevada State Legislature, Deborah used the same tactic. Right before she gave her testimony, she said, "I got up and I ran out into the hallway with my calculator and a list of data that [district administrator] had given her and started crunching numbers." These numbers became the foundation of the Black community's platform. Deborah noted, "We were able to now put our hands on and feel 32,371 Black students that are on free and reduced lunch and make it about individual students. Rather than this vague, vague ghost that nobody sees and ever since we did that it's changed the dynamics, it's changed the perception and all of a sudden, these kids became a priority."

The Black community then connected demographic data to performance data and realized that Black students performed relatively low in terms of English proficiency on tests. They used this as an opportunity to collaborate with the Latinx community to improve EL education through a push to improve literacy support for all children, with an emphasis on low-income students.

The Black vote

In addition to collaborating with Latinx leaders, Black community members reminded school board members of their political obligations. Acknowledging the emergence of Latinx political power, Deborah explained, "One of the things I try to share with them is, 'Yes this [Latinx] community is a growing population but don't underestimate the power of the Black vote. Shelley Berkley is no longer congresswoman because she lost the Black vote, 30 percent of the base.'"

The Black community vote, in this case, was large enough to shift elections. She also explained that the Black community had the highest number of voters within any racial group in the most recent elections. Overall, many Black community members used various methods— committee involvement, community organizing, utilizing data, and political engagement—to help increase support for Black students and shift the focus to literacy for Black students.

Expanding EL services to literacy

Because of Deborah's and others' advocacy, school board members expanded their policies and resources to include Black children. They did this by shifting the focus from English-language acquisition for ELs to literacy for all students, which I later argue weakened the policy impact for both ELs and Black students. One board member explained their thinking as follows:

> If we change it from English-language learners to an issue of literacy
> for everybody, then you begin to also bring in the African American

population in the low-income population because that's where literacy is an issue, and not just ELL but African American and low-income and really the driving factor for literacy is low income. So, if you change the conversation from Latino, to let's address literacy across the board for this population for low-income families, now you bring in more diversity than just Latino.

Another board member said, "We've discovered through just talking a lot and hammering out difference of opinions, that these needs are . . . the same need." They also acknowledged that "the philosophical shift . . . has been beneficial to the school district since . . . there's no longer a need to navigate between one special needs population or high needs population, feeling like the other was drawing off limited resources from it."

Literacy became a key policy focus in the CCSD strategic plan developed in 2013 and published in 2014. Mentioned sixteen times in the sixteen-page document, literacy was one of the components among the "Strategies in Action," as follows: "Identify and implement research-based practices on English Language Acquisition (ELA) strategies that increase the proficiency of *ELL students and students with language difficulties* to ensure literacy for all by third grade."[24]

As written, not only does this strategy pertain to EL students, but the school board and the district also made it clear that practices and policies designed for EL students would expand to any student assumed to have language barriers impeding their literacy ability in English.

At the outset, this solution might appear positive. However, a couple of assumptions are embedded in the district's response to "address literacy across the board." One assumption is that the academic needs of Latinx, ELs, low-income, and Black children are the same. Yet research points to the unique needs of learning a new language.[25] Even within the same population, for instance, ELs differ in that some enter US schools with high literacy skills in their native language, requiring different instruction. The other assumption is that this approach, as the school board member stated, was "beneficial to the school district" because they did not need to "navigate" among these populations. By offering an umbrella solution that likely required less resources, district leaders appeased and reduced the tensions among these different communities. Although the district may have benefited from allocating fewer resources and not having to deal with competing interests, this did not likely extend to all students and their families because an umbrella solution does not necessarily account for their unique needs. Instead, this type of solution derives from an ideology that favors efficiency over effectiveness and pits groups against each other. It often leaves groups feeling as if they must compete for a small piece of the pie or settle for less, rather than ensuring that each group receives what they need and deserve as human beings.

Coalition politics reminds us of the importance of recognizing each community's differences as we move toward a shared goal. In this case, this would be identifying a shared goal—access to equitable educational opportunities for ELs and Black students in CCSD—and then defining what each community needs to meet the goal. This would have been more beneficial than an umbrella solution. This is a humanizing approach.

Victory schools
Deborah and others, including Latinx leaders, continued pushing at the state level. They advocated for a model similar to Zoom schools, but they focused on supporting Black students from low-income families. In the next legislative session, in 2015, the Nevada state legislature passed Senate Bill 432, which directed the creation of what it called "Victory schools." As with Zoom schools, the state allocated $50 million every two years to thirty-five low performing, one- and two-star schools in Nevada's highest poverty ZIP codes to support curricula, instruction, and social-emotional needs. Most of these schools served a higher-than-average Black student population. Although the impact of these schools was beyond the results of this case study, external reports suggest that some of these Victory schools improved greatly.[26]

CCSD SCHOOL BOARD–LEVEL POLICIES RELATED
TO CONTEXT AND SOCIAL CONSTRUCTIONS

As in chapter 4, this section provides a brief overview of the beliefs of ELs in CCSD. Although coalition politics played a significant role in EL education within CCSD, the economic context and the board's social constructions about ELs, who were heavily viewed in deficit ways, also affected how coalition politics influenced EL policies and practices. In addition to the "literacy for everybody" initiative, three other areas stood out—the budget, classroom support, and classroom instruction.

EL Budget

Economic downfalls will inevitably affect education, but it is important for school board members to closely examine where budget cuts are being made over a five- to ten-year period. In other words, you should look for trends in budget allocations. School board members vote on the budget and budgets reflect priorities.

In the case of CCSD, the budget for EL education was cut 56 percent within a five-year period, from $21.2 million in 2009 to $9.4 million in 2013. Although the economic downturn influenced the budget, CCSD's cuts to EL-specific resources were significantly more than the overall budget cuts, especially considering the increase in EL enrollment. From 2009 to 2012, EL enrollment grew 103 percent, compared to 0.5 percent of total enrollment. Meanwhile, the CCSD board approved a 52 percent decrease in allocation to the EL department, compared to a 14.5 percent decrease among total expenditures. Also, in 2013, for the first time ever, CCSD received state funding for Zoom schools amounting to $39.4 million for two academic years. Yet, because of the setup and criteria of Zoom schools, only fourteen elementary schools benefited from the additional funding. Funding from Zoom schools might have prompted the district to decrease its locally allocated funding. However, since this state funding was supposed to supplant, not supplement, the funding provided at the district level, any supplementation would signify a funding inequity. Moreover, the overall decrease in EL funding over time signified that this group was not prioritized.

Classroom Support for ELs

The policy governance structure tends to enforce territorial practices—school board members' role versus the superintendent's role. Consequently, when board members cross operational boundaries, the superintendent might feel validated in pushing back in an unprofessional manner. This type of conflict can prompt unhealthy dynamics between the board and the superintendent, which is what happened in this case.

Related to the budget, in 2011, CCSD removed all EL facilitators who provided direct classroom support to EL students in schools. Facing a significant budget shortfall, CCSD surveyed district employees on what they believe should be done to work within the budget. During a presentation at a school meeting, administrators highlighted that most respondents suggested that CCSD cut EL facilitators and literacy specialists. They also indicated that they planned to cut these positions by only 25 percent but ended up cutting all of them. Although hesitant, the school board approved the budget that included these decreases.

The superintendent agreed to redeploy funds that came specifically from these cuts to fund something more effective for ELs. However, this never happened. Instead, when asked for an update about his plan at a board meeting, one school board member recalled that the superintendent "snapped a little" and expressed "'you've [school board members] crossed the line into my territory.'" She noted that because of this, they "stopped following up out on the dais and started talking more intensively with him." The creation of the assistant superintendent for the ELL program position, she speculated, was in part to "get us off his back."

In this case, board members expressed that this territorial type of conflict became a barrier for them to ensure that all schools could provide

ELs with sufficient support. As school boards are pressured to develop a certain model of structure for governance, it is important to leave room for them to push district leaders to take responsibility for and prioritize areas of equity, especially since equity-related resources are often easily put aside in times of financial hardship.

English Immersion Focus

Another area of policy and practice for ELs was the district's narrow focus on English immersion programs. Although the superintendent committee related to Prime Six schools and the WestEd report made recommendations to the district to increase dual-language programs, CCSD programs decreased from seven in 2013 to three in 2016. Even the seven that were implemented lacked district support in terms of resources, requiring the principal to find outside funding to support these programs.

Research is clear that, on average, ELs perform better academically and socially in the long run when they engage in bilingual and dual-language programs compared to English immersion ones.[27] Although the budget cuts might have contributed to fewer dual-language programs, the lack of support for such programs that embrace bilingualism also might be connected to the social constructions (beliefs) that ELs were a commodity, a problem, and a threat, which I describe in the next section. When viewed in these ways, policy makers are less apt to invest in programs, such as bilingual ones, that are less about assimilation and more about embracing ELs' cultures, supporting multilingualism, and setting them up for a successful academic trajectory which would likely include outperforming their non-EL peers. The English immersion focus was evident in much of the literature and conversations about EL education. As one board member explained of EL students, "Until you learn the [English] language, you're really not going to be learning." This statement also reflects a narrow view that some board members have, equating English with the only avenue to learning.

This is why it is vital for school board members to identify and inter-rogate the beliefs and assumptions that they hold about the various groups of students in their school districts. These beliefs shape policy outcomes, which influence how and what children will learn.

BELIEFS OF ELS IN THE DISTRICT

The SBGE framework urges school board members to explore their beliefs about groups—which, we must remember, are socially constructed. When you think about different student groups and their families, what are your beliefs? What images and thoughts come to mind as you con-sider certain students (i.e., Black students, Asian-American students, stu-dents in general)?

The Commodification of the "EL Problem"

During this period, many district and community leaders talked about ELs in ways that framed them as a commodity. This was inherent in dis-trict leaders' expectations to seek a "return on investment" for resources allocated to support ELs. For some, the "return" equated to an economi-cal benefit to the broader community. As one board member explained, "If we [the district] educate them [ELs], they'll earn more money and pay more taxes and spend more money." For her, this was about making ELs "productive citizens and contributing members of our society." Similarly, other district leaders shared that ELs would likely become criminals if the district failed to invest in improving ELs.

For others, the "return" was about the district being ranked higher. One board member's comment reflected this sentiment when she said, "I think if we don't address that [EL] issue, we will never be successful as a district. The entire board understands that. They're not the only group, but they have the largest group, and so if we elevate our English-language learners, we will elevate the district."

Voicing related thinking from an asset-based perspective, one district leader mentioned research that pointed to the potential of ELs to score higher than non-ELs on tests after becoming bilingual. Consequently, they said many in the Latinx community saw ELs as a potential "gold mine" if they were provided sufficient resources.

In addition, district leaders repeatedly used language such as "attacking [the] ELL problem" and not ignoring the "ELL problem." This language demonstrated that the district thought of ELs not only as objects, but objects that they needed to fix. Community members posed questions like, "Why do we still have so many ELL kids? How come these immigrant people haven't moved away? When construction collapsed, I thought they would have been gone." One school board member explained, "There's an element of the community that thinks we should not be educating illegal immigrants, and I hear that all the time." This community's hostile comments suggesting that ELs were "taking our resources" often conflated ELs with undocumented immigrants, and as Latinx or Mexican. As one school board member said aloud, "Do those kids [ELLs] really want to learn English? Do they really want to become Americans?"

When ELs are framed as a commodity and thought of in terms of their productivity, their contribution, and/or even their connection to elevating the district or avoiding crime, they end up objectifying rather than humanizing this group. Even for those leaders who recognize the potential of ELs, the idea that they are a "gold mine" reinforces their commodification that reflects the "return on investment" ideals. Like any group of students, ELs are not an object to be bought or sold. These ideas have roots in slavery and colonialization where people became a commodity and were literally bought, sold, and killed for economic, political, and social gain.

ELs as a Threat

Other community leaders discussed ELs as a threat to Black students. As one community leader explained, "The problem with that [the increasing focus on ELs] is now we [Black people] take the chance of being left again at the back of the line." Although this leader supported bilingual education, she said Black children should also be given the opportunity to be bilingual. Then she noted, "You got immigrant kids that have now gone through EL and . . . qualified for that job because they're bilingual. Our kids, on the other hand, are not. Shoot, they can't even speak English well, or fill out the application for that matter. So how is that fair? These are taxpayer dollars we're talking about."

These comments reflect the zero-sum politics that is common among minoritized communities who are all fighting for a very small piece of the pie. When one group is perceived as taking resources from another group, the result is often competition. And sometimes this competition reaches the school board level. School boards often make decisions to fund, or not fund, educational resources that target groups of students. As *coalition politics* make clear, if school board members understand that minoritized groups are advocating for their respective resources, they can stop and listen to the unique needs of each group. In this way, you can navigate how to provide equitable, unique, and sufficient educational resources for *all*.

Summary of Beliefs

Beliefs about ELs in CCSD were mostly negative. The characterizations of this group implied that they were a problem, pulling the district downward and taking resources needed for Black students. While some believed that ELs could potentially benefit the school district and surrounding community, other comments showed concern that ELs would not sufficiently assimilate, even if they had citizenship or learned English. These social constructions translated into school board–supported policies and practices that arguably increased EL support but ultimately fell short of equitably and substantially supporting ELs in humanizing ways.

To avoid these pitfalls, school board members can engage in and facilitate coalition politics among minoritized groups, helping them to understand that advancing equity efforts should be a win-win for each community. Each group matters. Rather than competing for a small piece of pie, the goal should be to increase the size of the pie and support each group in receiving an equitable piece of pie—which includes the educational resources, services, and opportunities that every group in the community needs to experience an adequate education.

The SBGE framework reminds us that how we socially construct groups is consequential. As with this case, it is tempting for school boards to characterize students as needing "investment," with the "returns" being higher academic test scores or more economic gains for the community. Although school boards should monitor whether funding is being used as intended, we should not think about children in ways that commodify them. When we do this, our support will likely align with these social constructions, and we will seek outcomes that are about competition or protecting our own interests. Instead, when we think about students in humanizing ways, our support goes beyond these narrow goals; they should include helping children feel human and feel loved and valued in their journey toward learning and growth. For ELs, this might mean supporting them to preserve their culture and first language by providing services that help them be fully bilingual and bicultural. This might not pay off in higher test scores, at least not right away. But this type of support offers cultural affirmation and embraces the whole child and where they come from. When children feel seen, safe, and valued, they are more likely to thrive socially, emotionally, and academically.

SUMMARY

As you can see, the case of CCSD was driven by the combination of demographic shifts and community advocacy. As a rapidly growing community, district leaders were forced to reckon with meeting the demands of providing an adequate education for an increasingly diverse student population. The costing-out study showed that Nevada's education system was drastically underfunded, and the economic downturn from the Great Recession offered state leaders an excuse to ignore this reality. Meanwhile, community leaders noticed how the district was falling short of adequately supporting minoritized students. This prompted them to act. They advocated for more resources and services for Black students and ELs at both the district and state levels. While they successfully leveraged some resources and support to make important shifts, including increased representation in district leadership, an intense focus on issues of equity, and the opening of Zoom and Victory schools, they did not fully engage in coalition politics to use their collective power to gain more and better resources for their respective communities. However, the small coalition between Deborah and Stavan discussed in this chapter illustrated the power and potential of coalescing across racial boundaries, which required deep commitment, trust, and an understanding of the racialized history and context of that community. This story also highlighted how beliefs shape policies, and in this case how the belief that ELs are commodities and threats contributed to narrow and inconsistent policies and practices.

Overall, this case demonstrates how important it is for school board members to deeply understand their community context and histories. From this place of understanding, school board members can begin to engage in coalition politics with community leaders to move equity forward. This work is difficult and complex, but community advocacy is powerful. As the case of CCSD shows, it can shift a whole education system, increasing the resources and services for students statewide in a matter of only a couple of years. Given this potential, it is worth putting in the work to leverage the power necessary to move the system, especially if this move is in a humanizing direction.

6

The Case of Salt Lake City School District: "No Plan in Place"

THIS CHAPTER TELLS two insightful stories about the Salt Lake City School District (SLCSD). Each one reveals a different theme: the first provides lessons about the ability of one person to spark change by leveraging federal-level laws; the second tells us how social, economic, and religious contexts can shape policy decisions that contribute to educational inequities. Both stories paint a picture of how beliefs are at the heart of district-level decisions and policy actions.

In the first story, you will see the importance of understanding the district and employing federal policies as presented within the School Board Governance for Equity (SBGE) framework. As student demographics change, many school districts fail to shift with these demographics and fall short of providing equitable educational opportunities for new and emerging populations. In SLCSD, one person saw inequities among a growing student population of English learners (ELs), asked questions, and eventually went to the federal government with his concerns. This propelled significant changes to promote equity because district leaders enacted two other SBGE principles—being proactively responsive and imagining the possibilities.

The second story emphasizes the SBGE's principles about the role of state policies and understanding the community context. Unlike the previously highlighted cases in Arizona and Nevada, state leaders in Utah embraced bilingualism and created a policy to support and fund dual-language immersion (DLI) programs. However, because of the design of this policy, these programs largely excluded ELs. From this story, you will understand how policy roots and development, which in this case were driven by cultural and economic incentives, can contribute to educational inequities. You will also learn how district leaders navigated these policies to help support minoritized students.

These two stories have something important in common: both provide a window into the broader beliefs about ELs in this community. These beliefs reveal how school boards and community members viewed ELs as distinct from some groups but conflated with others. We will see how these beliefs reflect a desire to "melt" ELs into the community, while others showed a desire to support and respect these students. As you will learn, these stories and beliefs contributed to the implementation of some equity efforts instituted in the district's strategic plans and its organizational leadership. You will also understand how these efforts helped move the needle toward equity but sometimes fell short because of lack of resources and willingness to institute these equity policies and practices across all schools and classrooms in the district.

I begin this chapter by briefly describing the state and district context in SLCSD, including the school board and superintendency, and the social and legal context in the state of Utah. Then, I described the two stories that shaped equity in the district for ELs and other minoritized students. Finally, I discuss the social constructions of ELs in the SLCSD community and how these beliefs may have informed EL policies and practices.

KNOWING AND UNDERSTANDING SLCSD

The School Board and Superintendency

The SLCSD school board includes seven members, each representing smaller precincts (also known as "at-ward"). Precincts are determined by the number of voters rather than the number of students. School board members are elected to four-year terms in a staggered fashion and paid $3,000 per year. Since 1972, Utah has urged local school boards to appoint student board members as well.[1] The student school board members are nonvoting and are appointed rather than elected by board members.[2]

During the four years that I monitored the school board, there were twelve elected school board members and four student members. Of the nonstudent members, eight were females and four were males. Ten of these school board members were white, one was Latino, and one was Pacific Islander. Aside from the student board member, one school board member was appointed; the rest were elected. The two nonwhite elected members represented the same precinct on the west side of Salt Lake City. Two longest-standing members had been on the board for nearly twelve years. From 2003 to 2016, McKell Withers, who grew up in the SLCSD community, served as the superintendent for the district. Before being hired in SLCSD, he was a teacher, principal, and assistant superintendent in the neighboring school district of Granite.[3] After his departure, the district has had five superintendents between 2016 and 2023.[4]

District Context and History

Utah ranked third in the United States, behind Arizona, in population growth from 2000 to 2010.[5] Economically, Utah's experience with the Great Recession was relatively mild. In 2008, Utah's unemployment rate increased, but only slightly, while median housing prices grew.[6] Reports speculate that because of its economic diversity and the strong investment of the Church of Jesus Christ of Latter-day Saints (LDS), Utah remained largely insulated from the impacts of the recession.[7] Even though Utah fared well during the Great Recession, the state is traditionally among the lowest funders of schools in the nation. In 2011–2012, the state was second-lowest in the United States in per-pupil annual expenditures, at $6,672 per student.[8]

Approximately 40 percent of the state's population currently resides in Salt Lake City.[9] In 2004, after a demographic shift that occurred in the student population over the years, SLCSD became a "minority-majority" district.[10] White student enrollment shifted from over 62 percent to about 40 percent from 1997 to 2013. Latinx students made up SLCSD's largest racial demographic, which was close to 42 percent in 2013.[11]

With nearly 24,000 students between 2010 and 2013, SLCSD was the ninth-largest school district in the state of Utah's forty-one districts, including 54,900 charter schools. SLCSD shares the same boundaries as Salt Lake City.[12] In the 1990s, Utah implemented an open-enrollment policy that allows families to enroll their children in any school outside their residential school zone and school district. Since then, as of 2023, SLCSD has experienced a declining enrollment to approximately 19,700 students, including the phenomenon of "white flight." As a result, district leaders are currently considering closing seven schools.[13]

From 2009 to 2013, the SLCSD experienced budget reductions of approximately $26 million, which totaled more than 13 percent in per-pupil revenue.[14] Among revenue sources for the district, in 2013, the state provided about 45 percent, followed by local (42 percent) and federal sources (10 percent).[15]

The Social and Legal Context in the State
Church influence
Utah has the largest number of LDS members (also known as Mormons) in the United States, at more than 55 percent of the population. Members of the LDS church are encouraged to complete a mission, lasting about two years, that involves teaching and converting individuals to the LDS

faith.[16] Between 55,000 and 85,000 LDS members serve missions each year across over 4,000 mission sites around the world, with 60 percent of these being outside the United States.[17]

In my conversations with several district leaders, they told me that the LDS culture, which includes a desire to convert people and missionary endeavors to many non-English-speaking countries, contributes to a relatively welcoming culture toward immigrants and the desire to learn more than one language. These factors influenced schools by increasing the support and demand for dual-language programs targeting certain languages. For instance, in 2012, Utah added Portuguese to the list of dual-language programs because Brazil is among the most popular missionary sites.[18]

Copycat of Arizona's SB 1070 Bill

While some in Utah may have had a more welcoming attitude toward immigrants, others did not. In 2011, the Utah state legislature passed House Bill 497, the Utah Illegal Immigration Enforcement Act. This bill gave law enforcement officers the authority to require proof of citizenship during lawful stops, creating the possibility of racial profiling. Cosponsored by thirty-eight of the seventy-five representatives in the House, the bill passed by approximately 80 percent of the vote in both the State Senate and the House.[19] Soon after it was passed, a federal judge halted the law because two civil rights groups filed a lawsuit against the state.[20] In 2013, Utah's attorney general and the civil rights groups settled the lawsuit when the state agreed to amend HB 497 and remove the requirements regarding proof of citizenship.[21] Although this law does not directly affect individuals in terms of race or immigration status, it does speak to the climate around immigration in Utah.

School Community Councils

School Community Councils (SCCs) were legislatively approved by the state of Utah in 2000. Each public school is mandated to have an SCC represented by a minimum of five individuals from a combination of elected parents and school staff constituencies. The state provides SCCs with $20,000–$50,000 in annual funding from a School Learning and Nurturing Development (LAND) Trust program toward the implementation of school-level services outlined in an SSC-developed plan that is approved by the local school board.[22] Several district leaders said that the SCCs encouraged family involvement at the school level. In addition, most of the board members shared that SCCs were their first point of entry into school politics, which eventually led them to run for the school board.

No Child Left Behind Act

The federal government's No Child Left Behind (NCLB) Act of 2001 was enacted in the same year that the Office of Civil Rights (OCR) complaint was filed against SLCSD, which will be discussed in the next section. Many district leaders mentioned that NCLB's requirement to disaggregate academic performance data by subgroups helped the district make changes. As one school board member explained, "It's kind of interesting, No Child Left Behind, which was a crappy law overall, . . . was helpful in that it told school districts, 'Look. You have to stop just using aggregate data. We want you to parse your data and display it based on things like race and socioeconomic status.'" Overall, this type of data, presented in a disaggregated manner, helped SLCSD board members and staff better understand academic disparities between ELs and non-ELs, as well as other populations.

FORCED TO ACKNOWLEDGE AND SUPPORT ENGLISH LEARNERS

An official, federal-level complaint filed by a family member of a student in the district was one of the most significant factors that prompted SLCSD to change how it provided educational opportunities for ELs. As we will see in the next section, these complaints spurred years of changes and resulted in a very different set of policies and practices for ELs.

OCR Complaint

In 2012, Michael Clára ran and was elected to the school board in Salt Lake City, serving there for four years. Prior to this, in 2001, Clára filed a complaint with the US Department of Education's Office of Civil Rights (OCR) regarding the inadequacies of EL education in the district. This complaint launched massive changes for ELs in this district.

Clára made this complaint after visiting his nephew's junior high school and seeing that a group of Latinx students had been assigned to one area of the school all day. Meanwhile, all the other students were rotating between their core and elective classes. Curious, he asked the principal, "Hey, what's that one wing? How come nobody is switching there?" The principal said, "Those are the Mexicans . . . they don't speak English." For Clára, "that didn't sound right."

When Clára asked, "What do they do?" the principal told him, "They just stay in there and they don't pay taxes or anything." Afterward, Clára talked to some people in his home state of Texas about this strange response, and that was when he learned about *Lau v. Nichols* (1974), a court case that required schools to offer ELs the supplemental instruction needed to understand their curriculum.[23] After further conversations with the principal and later the superintendent, Clára confirmed that the district was not providing adequate resources and services to ELs at this school or other schools nearby. He made the connection that many of these EL students were dropping out by the time they were freshmen in high school.

After not receiving a sufficient response from school and district leaders, Clára filed the OCR complaint. He reflected on this process in the following statement:

Somebody told me about OCR, and being a cop for ten years, I know how to write a probable cause affidavit. So I did that. And OCR from Denver, they physically showed up in two weeks . . . then told the district. "Here are these allegations. Here is what you've got to start doing, or we kick this over to the Justice Department, and we'll take over the school district." You lose $50 million a year. And so the district had to change everything.

In 2009, after OCR completed five site visits and eight years of monitoring, the district was released from the investigation. The office's official letter stated that ELs now "have meaningful access to the district's education programs."[24]

Journey to OCR Compliance

Although SLCSD came into compliance, the journey to get there was not easy. When investigating the district, according to one district leader, OCR officials found that the district "didn't have a process for addressing the needs of our English learners. What they discovered was that we didn't have ESL-endorsed teachers, or at least they weren't assigned to teach our ELL population, which was small but growing."

This district leader further explained, "Teachers who were actually teaching English learners couldn't identify what they were doing to meet the needs of the English learners.... There was just *no plan in place*. Nothing." Instead, school leaders regularly segregated ELs in a combined class, away from non-ELs. In addition, they had not developed academic standards specific to ELs. The lack of standards contributed to inconsistent practices with no monitoring across schools or classrooms in the SLCSD.

When I spoke with district leaders in 2014, most of them said that this OCR complaint was critical to pressuring the district to recognize the need to serve ELs adequately. When I asked how the school board changed its approach to ELs, one Latino district leader reflected, "They've had to first because of that OCR review. And it's sad that not until people feel coerced, do they make changes." He also pointed to two other factors that pushed the board to change—the shift in the community and student demographics and the increase of Latinx elected officials. He added that "policy [has] been driven at a whole different level ... they are no longer in a place where they can negotiate that." Accordingly, these three factors—OCR regulations, demographic changes, and political leadership—merged to force meaningful changes in the level of support that the school board members provided ELs in the district.

Some district leaders cautioned against the overuse of OCR as a method to prompt change. One Latina educator explained, "Organizations like OCR . . . are there as a support for us," but she noted, "We need to be more careful about when we use them." She admitted that OCR "did make a big difference with how English learners were served in the Salt Lake School District, but there's been several other complaints that have been filed that don't go anywhere because there actually is work being done." Yet she maintained that the OCR complaint about ELs "obiligat[ed]" the district to implement changes, and she also noted that "people care about the kids," but "they don't always recognize that there's going to need to be a different kind of remedy to support English learners as opposed to other kids." In other words, according to her, the OCR complaint was critical to getting the ball rolling, but these necessary changes were supported by the fact that most of the educators cared about ELs.

Another school board member had no qualms about calling Clára a "rebel rouser." They explained that Clára's approach was different. By contrast, this board member's "philosophy" was, "Can't we just work together? Let's figure this out. Let's not waste hundreds of thousands of dollars on OCR complaints every time." For him, the OCR complaints represented needless conflict and funding.

From a different angle, one board member remembered how vast the OCR agreement was and how the "compliance talk" was a lot to digest. She said that the document was "very big . . . it included a lot of very specific things that the district was required to do around not only instruction but also translation services. . . . It was pretty unwieldy. There were so many different rules that people had to follow." She also highlighted that although most ELs were Spanish native speakers, "we have a wave of refugees . . . it could be Arabic . . . it could be Swahili." A different district leader echoed these comments, noting, "We're a refugee resettlement site . . . so there's over 100 different languages spoken here." When this district leader read "what was written and put in print [by the OCR], it was really undeliverable. It was trying to sound good but not practical in terms of serving." As the comments of these board members illustrate, sometimes compliance over small details becomes overwhelming for school and district leaders, but it's important to work toward ensuring that students have the necessary opportunities to access instruction regardless of how "practical" it is.

Overall, there was a consensus among district leaders that the OCR complaint was a necessary measure to move the district toward equity for ELs. Yet district leaders also expressed concerns that using OCR to address all equity issues became unnecessary. Instead, these leaders felt that additional complaints following the one filed in 2001 served as a distraction from "good" work going on inside schools. Plus, these complaints were costly and time-consuming. This illustrates the possibilities of leveraging federal involvement to help address inequities at the district level. It also, however, shows the limitations of overexhausting this tool to the point that it is ineffective. School board members and community advocates must find a balance between the two.

Leveraging federal involvement might be a useful option when local-level educators and leaders (teachers, school and district leaders, and school board members) do not respond to concerns about inequities by making meaningful changes. To reduce the overuse of federal involvement, we need to have systems in place that provide families, youth, and communities with opportunities to document their concerns in ways that are transparent for the district, including school board members. This system should include an ample review of every concern and a documented response to each concern.[25]

Changes After the OCR Complaint

After realizing that there "was just no plan in place" for ELs, the district created a committee to develop the ESL Master Plan. This plan was periodically revised by district leaders after learning what was working and what was not.

In addition, the school board hired a new superintendent, who developed a new position at the superintendent level to oversee a newly established equity department. Much of the OCR compliance work came under the umbrella of this equity department. Overall, because of the OCR complaint, the district made several changes during the eight years that they were monitored.

The EL teacher endorsement requirement

First, district leaders required newly hired teachers to become officially endorsed to teach ELs within less than three years of their hire date. To support the implementation of this requirement, the district partnered with a local university to develop a program and committed funds toward subsidizing tuition costs for teachers. This district requirement made a far-reaching impact throughout the state. As one district administrator noted, "We've also been able to influence all of the state institutions in Utah to make sure that you [teachers] don't leave your preservice [training] without an ESL endorsement because of our experiences in pushing for that across the state." The number of EL-endorsed teachers in the district soared from 97 in 2001 to 644 in 2009.

District leaders had mixed views of this requirement. On the one hand, the superintendent explained, "It has been frustrating at times, however, to work with OCR officials because they are 'mostly lawyers' focused on compliance and not on students' academic results."[26] He pointed out that some nonendorsed, more experienced teachers were effective EL instructors, but they were not allowed to teach ELs because of the OCR mandate. On the other hand, another district leader noted that those more experienced teachers, or "veteran teachers," needed the EL training the most—and resisted it the most.

Still, a different district leader posed a series of questions about this requirement, including this: "You're telling me that the endorsement will help you from here on out, and you'll understand the cultural biases, the assumptions that are happening within the classroom? . . . I would say no." He felt that this requirement gave the district an excuse to not address many areas where they were falling short. The false premise was, as he stated, "'we're OK because everybody in our district is ESL endorsed.' That's what the struggle I think Salt Lake has." In other words, he wanted the district not to just be satisfied with the EL endorsement requirement but to continue beyond this requirement in ways that ensured teachers and school leaders were offering many high-quality educational opportunities for all students, including ELs.

English-language development

Soon after the EL teaching endorsement was instituted, OCR reviewed the program. One district leader recalled that OCR "just went around the district and started interviewing teachers, and asking them, 'So can you tell me how you're serving your English learners?' The teachers couldn't." Together with OCR, district leaders noticed some ELs were what they called "lifers," which were "kids who don't get past a certain language proficiency level." She noted, "They showed us our data, and they said 'OK, you will do something about this. What you are doing is not enough. You're not providing English-language development.'" That was when the district realized that the EL endorsement program trained teachers about ELs, not about how to support ELs in their English-language development (ELD). OCR urged the district to create a daily forty-five-minute block focused on ELD for ELs.

This district leader recalled that there were "a lot of complaints, resistance in teachers. They were not understanding. There were several times I had to go before them and explain just what this is. What is ELD, and why do we have to do it?" She noted, "We spent a whole year just trying to get in compliance on that."

E.L. Achieve

After the district instituted the forty-five-minute block mandate for all ELs, one district leader explained that they told teachers, "OK, you got these forty-five minutes." And the teachers "were like, 'What do I do?' They didn't have . . . curriculum for it. They didn't know what to do in terms of just teaching" ELs in that time frame. After learning that teachers did not have quality curricula to support ELD for ELs, the district adopted a nationally known program called E.L. Achieve, which offered teachers curricula and training in this area. Although the program was costly, the school board approved it. Following these changes, district data reflected an increase in English proficiency among ELs.

State Support for Dual-Language Immersion (not for ELs)

In addition to these changes described above, Utah also experienced an increase in dual-language programs that could have benefited ELs, but given the roots of this policy initiative, mostly targeted non-EL students. In 2004, two schools in Farmington, Utah, implemented one of the state's first DLI programs. Impressed by the results in these schools, Gregg Roberts, a district leader of the Granite School District, a nearby district in Salt Lake City, adopted similar programs in two schools. Later, Roberts took a position at the Utah State Office of Education and helped launch a committee focused on world languages.[27]

In 2007, Roberts met with the state's former governor Jon Huntsman and State Senator Howard Stephenson, the chair of the Utah State Senate Education Committee, to discuss the expansion of dual-language programs. Huntsman was fluent in Mandarin, and after his tenure as governor ended in 2009, he went on to serve as an ambassador to China during Barack Obama's administration.[28] In addition, district leaders recalled that Huntsman would often refer to his children, whom he and his wife adopted from China and India, as an inspiration for his support of the DLI program. Also, inspired by his own experience outside the United States, Senator Stephenson experienced an "epiphany" on a trip to China, where he observed Chinese students fluently speaking English. Seeing China as a "rising nation," Stephenson was "worried about America's future," and he thought, "What could I do as a policymaker to assist in helping the United States connect to these rising nations?"[29]

The meeting between Roberts, Huntsman, and Stephenson prompted the development and passage of Utah Senate Bill (SB) 80 in 2007. SB 80 focused only on languages that the National Security Language Initiative deemed "critical," which included "Chinese, Arabic, Russian, Farsi, Hindi, and Korean."[30] Roberts later convinced Huntsman and Stephenson to expand the program to Spanish and French. Consequently, in 2008, after SB 80 was successful and well received, the Utah State Legislature passed SB 41. This new bill maintained the "critical languages" piece and added incentives for fifteen DLI pilot programs—six Chinese, six Spanish, two French, and one Navajo.[31] Starting in 2013, Utah permitted the expansion of DLI programs to add Portuguese, German, and Russian.[32] In addition, this bill ushered in $750,000 in state funding to support schools in developing new DLI programs.[33]

State policymakers argued that SB 80 and SB 41 would provide the state with economic and cultural benefits. Representative Greg Hughes, who introduced SB 80 to the House in 2007, said, "This is a good pilot program. It helps us remain and be even more competitive in the global market and is worthy of your support."[34] District leaders also highlighted that state policymakers supported DLI programs largely for economic reasons. One district leader explained, "It's so strong here [in Utah] because there's a lot of backing legislative-wise and money, people with money. And the reason they like those programs is because they have Chinese, right? Portuguese. These are all business related-duals." Another district leader explained,

> They were encouraging school districts to look at Chinese, Arabic. . . . So, everyone was looking at these "critical languages." The goal in the state, then, from whoever sponsored this legislation, was our kids needed to become global citizens and they need to learn these "critical languages" because that's who we're going to be doing business with.

That's who you know ... and trade, and we want our kids to be able to be successful in the global economy.

At the root of Utah's DLI initiative and support was the goal of building a population of Utah residents who could employ their linguistic skills and proficiency in "critical languages" to create more business opportunities, which would in turn spur the state's economy. Who was not included at the heart of this DLI initiative? ELs.

What about ELs?

Many dual-language programs in the United States are made up of students who are about half native English speakers and half native speakers of the target language (e.g., Spanish). This is called a "two-way DLI program," and it includes learning both languages and cultures from teachers and student peers. Yet most of Utah's DLI programs were not set up that way. Instead, the majority of students participated in one-way DLI programs, which included instruction in the target language from the teacher to the student for 50 percent of the day and in English the other 50 percent of the day. However, as one district leader recalled, "It wasn't even dual-language, in my opinion, and it wasn't bilingual. It was definitely dual immersion, and we tried to help people to understand the difference." This district leader further explained, "When you look at our dual immersion at the state [level], it was geared towards white middle-class kids whose parents ... want their kids to learn another language. It's not about supporting English learners. That's the difference. That's the crux of the problem. It's not about supporting English learners. It's about creating a language program."

Echoing this comment, another district leader said, "If you look at all the duals [DLI programs], the bulk of the kids in those duals are Caucasian, white, affluent kids." In fact, in 2013, among third graders, 89 percent of DLI students were white, 67 percent were relatively middle or upper class, 22 percent were Hispanic, and only 8 percent were ELs.[35]

With one of the highest numbers of ELs in Utah, making up nearly 17 percent of its total student population in 2013, SLCSD had some bilingual education programs prior to Utah's support for DLI programs.[36] Yet, as one district leader explained, "the district never put the funding into bilingual ed[ucation]," and "the state never really had a bilingual program." Funding for these bilingual programs came mostly from federal dollars, which are intended to supplement, not supplant, educational support for ELs. Upset about this, one district leader recalled being on a state-level subcommittee for ELs and challenging state leaders, "What are you doing at the basic level for English learners? What's your plan? Nada, right? . . . That's the problem." He further described that moment:

> I actually gave them a visual of a cake. . . . "This cake should be your Lau plan. . . . This frosting is some Title I resources, and then the Title III resources are the sprinkles on the cake. . . . A lot of districts have that cake upside down. That's the problem. . . . You think these sprinkles are going to cover what you need to cover at that level, but we don't have a Lau plan here."

The "Lau plan" is a requirement stemming from the *Lau v. Nicols* (1974) case, which made it unlawful not to provide ELs with ELD.[37] The plan should aim to identify ELs in each district and provide them with adequate educational resources and services.

With little state funding for ELs, district leaders requested resources to support their bilingual programs that were being offered through SB 41. One district leader remembered, "I was going to the state and saying, 'Can some of our bilingual teachers be included in your professional development?' And the answer was 'No' because these were not DLI programs." Since the state's DLI program had no ELD, as this district leader explained, "we actually held off for several years until just like the last four or five years." Eventually, she said, "Our schools felt that they had no other choice than to go with the state's model" because they needed funding. Still, as she noted, the district felt that they had to "battle" the state because "nowhere in there [DLI programs] did they build any English-language development. And they don't want to" because it would "skew their data . . . they [ELs] don't score as high on end-of-year testing until they get to that point where they are fluent in English, and then they outscore English-only kids."

Still, SLCSD worked toward incorporating DLI programs into its schools so that it could receive more funding to support its ELs. As it did this, district leaders tried to guide state officials in better supporting ELs by using other DLI approaches. Yet the reality, according to one district leader, was that "they've [the state] lost the focus of teaching native Spanish speakers English language and keeping them bilingual and bicultural. That's not their emphasis anymore. It's more about just the language now." This statement emphasized that the DLI programs focused mainly on whatever (non-English) language that schools built a program around, rather than focusing on ELD for ELs and embracing their native languages and cultures.

For school board members, knowing how state policy and funding intersect for district-level opportunities and barriers is important. In this case, the roots and goals of the state's DLI policy that funded language programs offered additional resources and services that benefited non-ELs over ELs. Yet many ELs in the district did not receive additional state funding to support the resources and services they needed to access a meaningful educational curriculum. These types of inequities must be understood within communities first. Then districts, including school board members, must examine, ask critical questions, challenge, and leverage state policies in ways that will support our most vulnerable students. Remember that it does not have to be a zero-sum game, but it should be an even playing field.

POLICIES AND PRACTICES AIMED AT EQUITY

Despite the battle with the state over dual-language programs for ELs, and perhaps thanks to the OCR monitoring, the district incorporated some solid equity-related policies and practices. I describe two of these in the following sections.

Student Achievement Plan

As described in chapter 3, strategic planning is a key component of governing toward educational equity. SLCSD had a very comprehensive and useful plan that they called the Student Achievement Plan. The plan includes goals for a five-year period based on the "eight essentials of a learning community."

As one district leader stated, this plan was not one that "sat on the shelf." Rather, it became the framework that reflected "eight essentials," grounded in research on effective schools. As this leader noted, it was about "making sure we have the right anchors" that were "centered around curriculum, instruction, and assessment, and what makes that successful for kids," and then getting the board and community to describe how the district will achieve those essentials. A different district leader who also distinguished this plan from one that "gets set on the shelf" said that the district works hard to "keep it a living document that really guides and directs the work." He further explained that the board discussed the plan every summer in-depth, and every month, they had a study session where someone from the team who was accountable for moving one of the eight essentials forward was invited to report on the team's progress toward the written goals within that essential.

One of the essentials on "Equity and Advocacy" was defined as follows: "District-wide practices, programs, policies, and procedures to provide all students with a rigorous curriculum, safe learning environments, differentiated educational opportunities, and the resources necessary to achieve comparably high outcomes. Equity requires that educators develop the skills, knowledge, and beliefs necessary to meet the needs of every student, with an emphasis on students of color, English learners, students in poverty, and students with disabilities."

The aim of this essential was to ensure that educators are equipped to improve academic disparities for marginalized students. ELs were included as a target population in this essential. The plan for 2010–2015 had two to three annual goals related to "Equity and Advocacy" that included concrete steps, responsible persons, and accountability measures. Each year, the responsible parties presented a report to the board about their progress.

For instance, in 2012–2013, essential goal number six was to increase achievement and close gaps through implementing World-Class Instructional Design and Assessment (WIDA) standards that target ELs. On January 22, 2013, six staff members from the Educational Equity Department presented the board with an update on their progress toward the 2012–2013 goals. The staff shared what they had accomplished and the difficulties that they encountered, such as finding time for professional development, so the district could make necessary changes. Overall, this plan outlined clear steps toward providing and improving educational equity, including steps to cultivate cultural relevancy and sensitivity and increase family engagement. This plan was both accessible online and available in Spanish.

Equity Leadership Team

As of 2015, district leaders operated a district-level Equity Leadership Team for about six years. In addition, equity teams also operated at some school sites. These teams conducted equity audits in schools, assessed disaggregated data (i.e., by race and income), such as student test scores and placement in special programs, and instituted training for staff, among other tasks. Often, these teams built a foundation by engaging in shared reading, including the books *Courageous Conversations About Race*, *Using Equity Audits to Create Equitable and Excellent Schools*, and *The Dreamkeepers*.[38] One district leader recalled her own experiences on this team, noting that this shared reading was to "try to get all of us having a more open and courageous conversation about what was going on in our schools," and then she said that they moved on to "equity audits . . . to figure out where there's inequity in our schools."

Not all board members were immediately in support of equity efforts. For instance, one board member had to see with his own eyes what this work resulted in for students. When the district funded the hiring of Edwin Lou Javius, an Ed Equity educational specialist, to complete equity audits of classrooms and schools, this board member expressed doubts when Javius's equity audits came up on the board agenda. This doubtful board member asked the district leadership who he was and whether he could observe Javius at work. After some pushback from the district leadership, the board member explained that he would vote no on this budget request and "make an issue of it" if he could not see what Javius was doing. The following day, he was invited to the school where Dr. Javius had videotaped a teacher during a lesson and then went through the video with the teacher and offered feedback. Recalling this experience, the board member recounted:

> Dr. Javis starts watching this video. I was moved to tears because he says, "You see this kid right here?" Now understand this is a teacher that cares, right? And he says, "See, you got five whites in your class-room of . . . 28/29 students." . . . He had these like circles where each time they raise their hands, they were getting picked on. This white male teacher was calling on them, and they answered the questions. . . . They did some statistical things on how all these other kids would raise their hands, and this teacher wasn't . . . and he was aware that this is what they were talking about with sensitivity, and this guy [the teacher] was devastated. I got up and left because I was embarrassed for this teacher. . . . Before I left . . . Dr. Javis is pointing out there's this Hispanic kid who keeps raising his hand and after about three or four times . . . [the kid] closes his book and gets out his notebook. The teacher looked and said, "What are you doing? Open up your book. You're not paying attention." . . . So Dr. Javis points that out.

This board member, in tears, expressed to the curriculum director how much he appreciated this equity audit work. However, he said, "I was livid the next day when I found out it's only happening in three schools, and only then by volunteers, and they could be gone at any time." Nonetheless, this experience prompted board members to dive deeper into equity work happening in the district.

Three school board members in this district volunteered to serve on the district-level equity leadership team. In many ways, the school board used this team to identify and work to remedy the inequities in the district. As one district leader noted, many of the board members "don't have the background to be able to advocate in the way that most of us would kind of see advocacy, and so that Equity Leadership Team . . . fulfills more of that role than does anyone on the board." They further explained that board members on that team have "seen the data . . . the achievement gaps. They see kids being pushed out of high school. They see some of the inequity in our schools, and so . . . they're the ones who will say help us know how to fix this."

Creating an official group of educators, leaders, and school board members at a district level offers a powerful opportunity to make structural changes. The development of this equity team, for instance, created the space and time for individuals who were committed to equity to coalesce toward advancing equity in meaningful ways from the level of the classroom, inside schools, and across the district. As one teacher on an equity team described in a board meeting, "I have never been to professional development that has meant more to my teaching. . . . It's totally changed the way I look at what I do in my classroom, the school practices, the children." He further explained how the equity team prepared him to talk about race and empathize with students' experiences. The downside, in this case, was that this work was not happening across several of the district's schools.

BELIEFS OF ELS IN THE DISTRICT

This section offers a brief description of some of the overall beliefs about ELs in SLCSD based on my conversations with district leaders. Many of these beliefs were deficit-based, but not in explicitly negative ways. Much of the district leaders' language was kind or neutral, but the implicit meanings behind the language often (but not always) positioned ELs as less than their non-EL counterparts. As this section shows, you will understand why it is important to examine the language closely to uncover any implicit messages about students in your community. In other words, what do people really mean when they talk about certain groups? What and whom do people associate groups with? What metaphors and comparisons do they use to describe groups? These implicit ways of talking about groups might sound neutral or nice on the surface, but a deeper examination might reveal otherwise.

Distinguishing and Conflating ELs

Many comments about ELs reflected ways to distinguish them from non-ELs and conflated ELs with other groups. When distinguishing between ELs and non-ELs, district leaders used geographical descriptions, highlighting that most ELs lived in the Westside of Salt Lake City, whereas most white, relatively more affluent students lived in the Eastside. In addition, some district leaders used language such as "normal" or "regular" to describe non-ELs in order to differentiate them from ELs.

Other district and school leaders' comments reveal how the community conflated ELs with Latinx, low-income, and immigrant groups. For instance, some district leaders pointed out that neighborhoods are experiencing "white flight" due to critical masses of "Brown kids" and anti-immigrant sentiment. Similarly, when asked about how the community feels about ELs, one board member said that some people "are very prejudiced" and then shared, "I remember one parent came up to me and said they pulled their kids out of [one school] because there's too many Brown kids down there." Then he explained, "If you go out to the white suburbs, where there are a lot of conservatives that are angry about taxes going up for these things, Title I monies and things like that, that are unfair for some schools to have, and their school doesn't have those extra resources, there's a little bit of angst, but still the attitudes are improving."

These descriptions illustrate how ELs were often differentiated from white, more affluent communities and also conflated with Latinx, immigrant, and low-income communities.

Push for the "Melting Pot"

Some SLCSD leaders spoke about ELs as a group that needed attention but also needed to assimilate. One school board member noted that, as a growing population in the district, "You can't ignore their [EL] needs." He went on to say, "There are obvious challenges . . . but it's our job . . . to get around those challenges. Get those kids speaking English." Similarly, two school board members spoke about ELs in the context of a "melting pot" and as a positive experience.

Although it was used over two centuries ago, the concept of the "melting pot" became more popular in the early 1900s when it was used in a play featuring immigrants in the United States. The origins of this metaphor are specific to migration to the United States, and it includes the idea of many cultures merging and dissolving to create a new, single culture. It disregards the fact that some groups might not want to merge and dissolve, such as those who were forced to come to the United States through slavery and/or were harmed by the colonizers' attempt to assimilate or "melt" them into a culture that was not theirs. On the other hand, the concept of the "salad bowl," which emerged in the 1960s in the Civil Rights era, is not perfect, but it is a more equitable and humanizing alternative to the "melting pot." The "salad bowl" refers to how different cultures can mix, but they still maintain their wholeness and identities.[39]

Some SLCSD leaders described ELs in the context of the LDS church, and specifically related to missionary experiences. One district leader told me, "I think the LDS church actually is a really good support in terms, again, of the culture and the beliefs, and attitude. We have lots of young men who go on missions to foreign countries and learn other languages, and so they're more open to it in a diminutive way, in a white privileged kind of way. In an 'I'm superior to you' kind of way, but regard-less, I think it's a little more humane than it could be."

While school board members and district leaders did not directly express patronizing and colonialist beliefs to me aside from the melt-ing pot idea, such comments about the community's beliefs of ELs are indicative of how this community's culture, which is closely tied to the LDS church, reflects a mix of benevolence and colonialism toward ELs. It is important to remember that beliefs of communities may affect how elected officials shape policies. And perhaps this community's missionary experiences might have motivated some in the community to embrace ELs but also seek to convert them and their families to the LDS church.

ELs' Economic and Academic Potential, but English as Supreme

Other comments illustrated a holistic understanding of ELs. Describ-ing what they thought the SLCSD should aim to do, one board member explained:

> The goal is to get students academically proficient in the English lan-guage, which is the language that they'll have to do future work in this country, by and large, without dishonoring their language, their home language, and the culture that surrounds that language. So that's the overarching philosophy is to try to get kids proficient as quickly as pos-sible in English so that they will have access to the curriculum that is in English so that they'll be able to graduate from high school and then go on to secondary education and work.

This board member's statement reflects mixed sentiments that are asset- and deficit-based. These are also common perspectives among many well-meaning school board members and educators. Concerns about protecting ELs' cultures come from an asset-based perspective because they assume that those cultures are worth protecting. However, stressing English as a priority comes from a deficit-based perspective that assumes that other languages are not important or do not deserve to be given priority. It might not always be easy to patiently support our students from a practical standpoint. However, research shows that it takes many ELs four to ten years to become academically fluent in both their native language and English, but once that foundation is built, they often thrive.[40] And yes, all children should be able to access the curriculum, but that curriculum should be culturally relevant and accessible, meeting children where they are and engaging and honoring their learning processes. This requires cultural competency, asset-based assumptions, patience, resources, and goals that are not rooted in the logic of capitalism but instead seek to humanize our children.

Some district leaders also acknowledged the contribution of ELs within their communities. For instance, one school board member explained that families appreciate the "richness of different cultures" within the district's schools. Another district leader described the potential advantage that ELs, as bilingual people, provide to employers in the community. Two district leaders highlighted ELs' ability to outperform non-ELs academically, with one saying, "The great thing that we see is that kids who do develop that English proficiency along with their home language proficiency, they do better overall than kids who are monolingual once they've gotten to that place."

These comments reflect the belief that ELs have the potential to be successful, which is asset-based, but only if they speak English, which is deficit-based. Again, the implication is that English is supreme and has an economic advantage, and those who do not speak English do not have the same potential. While these beliefs are not explicitly negative, the positive parts of these comments are qualified by prioritizing one difference over another. Some school board members might argue that speaking English is a practical necessity. And yes, while knowing English is helpful in the United States, those who speak a language that is not English also have potential. So, rather than holding implicit beliefs about narrow expectations, school board members and leaders should prioritize opportunities to create educational spaces that explicitly encourage and reflect diversity, whether that be racial, linguistic, or cultural diversity, as equally important, if not, more so.

Summary of Beliefs

From district leaders' and board members' words and actions, we see how they and others in the community portrayed ELs. ELs were distinguished from white, affluent communities while being conflated with Brown and immigrant communities. Some leaders and board members expressed the desire for ELs to assimilate, while others shared how the differences of ELs were embraced. Nonetheless, their comments emphasized how English was prioritized in the SLCSD.

The beliefs that the leaders and board members expressed aligned with the district's policies and practices, including the underfunding of resources and services for ELs, the lack of focus on ELs before the OCR complaint, and later the emphasis on ELD rather than supporting ELs to be academically fluent in both English and their native language. These beliefs also aligned with equity efforts via the equity departments, teams, and training. As presented in the SBGE framework in chapter 2, the beliefs of groups are socially constructed, and these beliefs shape the policies and practices that show up in our schools. When you and the community who elected or appointed you to your school board position hold beliefs that are humanizing and asset-based, the policies that you initiate and support also will be humanizing and asset-based, and vice versa. That is why it is essential to recognize these beliefs, examine them, and perhaps work to shift them if needed so you can advance equity in humanizing ways.

SUMMARY

The stories that have shaped equity in the SLCSD demonstrate how the power of federal enforcement and state policymaking affects the same group differently. This included federal enforcement bringing attention to how the district was inequitably serving ELs, and state policies developing dual-language programs that excluded many ELs. These stories also underscore the influence of outside forces and the possibilities when a district is strategic and responsive. Finally, when we also consider the beliefs of ELs in the community, these stories reveal the underlying social constructions that, on the one hand, show a commitment to minoritized communities and, on the other hand, show the desire to "melt" ELs into the dominant community.

For school board members, these stories and beliefs point to the importance of understanding a community's culture and its influence on district-level opportunities. School board members must learn to leverage federal involvement and advocate for political action that benefits all students, especially those students who are most vulnerable. When they are forced to act, as SLCSD was, school boards must use such opportunities to proactively respond to and imagine the possibilities through strategic plans that institute equity efforts as a priority. These strategic plans must have clear, measurable, and accountable goals toward advancing equity. School board members must also recognize and examine the implicit messages within themselves and their communities that hold particular biases. In SLCSD, for instance, the use of the "melting pot" metaphor seeks to mask differences, such as those that show up in students' homes, cultures, and languages. Instead of masking differences, school board members must seek to support practices and policies that embrace differences, allowing all students to bring their full selves into their classrooms. Believing in the assets of minoritized students will build a platform for imagining the possibilities *when* (not if) a district is forced to respond to inequities so that it can move closer to equity.

7

Conclusion: Connections, Implications,
and the Future of School Boards
in Planting the Seeds of Equity

MOVING TOWARD EQUITY as a school board member is not easy, but it is possible. As the three case studies in this book show, it can be hard and messy. Each case highlights principles of the School Board Governance for Equity (SBGE) framework. When adopted and enacted, these principles offer an opportunity to advance equity. In the next section, I sum up how the SBGE principles showed up in each case study. Then, I consider how these might be relevant in your school district. And finally, I conclude this chapter and this book with my heartfelt thoughts on the future of school boards in terms of research and practice when it comes to advancing educational equity in this dynamic context.

THE SBGE FRAMEWORK AND THESE CASE STUDIES

The case of Tucson Unified School District (TUSD) in chapter 4 showed us the power of using *skills* to *leverage federal policies and laws* to push back against the unlawful dismantling of Mexican American Studies (MAS) in TUSD and the inequities of misclassifying English learners (ELs). It also showed the importance of *knowing and understanding* the community context. In that district, the economic downturn and school choice environments contributed to closing schools, and the anti-immigrant environment and actors outside the state contributed to the development of state laws that were racist, harmful, and repressive. These factors significantly changed the context of TUSD, putting limits on how and what the district could offer ELs and other minoritized students in the classroom. District leaders missed some opportunities to be *proactively responsive* and engage in *coalition politics* toward gaining a majority vote on the school board that could have stopped the dismantling of MAS, among other potential future changes. Still, after this event, the *strategic response* from local community advocates and voters led to a shift in the school board that allowed them to *imagine possibilities* by hiring a new superintendent and electing a new school board president, approving culturally relevant curricula, and expanding dual-language programs. However, the mixed beliefs about ELs in the community—that they were hypervisible and valued but "invisible," "undocumented," and "not on the agenda"—also limited what *possibilities were imagined*. Although the board expanded and elevated dual-language programs, we can see that this *strategy* did not offer more equitable opportunities for most of the ELs in the district since their participation in these programs was limited by state law.

The case of Clark County School District (CCSD), from chapter 5, showed us the power of advocacy by community leaders who used their *skills* to *leverage state policy* to move equity forward. It also showed us the potential of *coalition politics* that could have moved equity even further ahead if done well. By *understanding* the community context of CCSD, including racialized histories, a shifting demographic, and the inequities that children and their families experienced, community leaders worked to expand the *knowledge* among the district's leadership by increasing racial representation at the district level and urging district and state leaders to acknowledge the existing educational inequities. Yet because community beliefs positioned ELs as commodities and threats, exacerbated by the chronic underfunding of education statewide, *strategies* to *imagine possibilities* and be *proactively responsive* lacked substance and hindered coalition politics that otherwise could have advanced equity. We also saw how the district's strategic plan was too broadly focused on literacy, how the programs overwhelmingly pushed English immersion, and how the state intervention of Zoom schools served only a fraction of the district's ELs.

The case of Salt Lake City School District (SLCSD), discussed in chapter 6, emphasized how the *skills* of *leveraging federal policies* by filing a complaint with the Office of Civil Rights (OCR) prompted immense changes for ELs. It also highlighted how the *strategies* of being *proactively responsive* to this complaint and *imagining possibilities* through developing a meaningful and highly used plan helped to advance equity for ELs and other minoritized students in this district. The district ushered in teacher training and curricula that would better support ELs. We can see how the school board used its Student Achievement Plan, which was detailed and accessible, to guide their governance *strategies* toward improvement in the area of "Equity and Advocacy." Yet the mixed beliefs that ELs should "melt" into the community and learn English, but still somehow have their native cultures honored, contributed to policies and practices that emphasized English immersion. *Knowing and understanding* these *beliefs*, along with the community context, which was influenced by economic and religious factors, help us to make sense of why state leaders spearheaded the expansion of dual-language programs that largely excluded ELs from participating. Although district leaders had some success in *using state policy* to better support ELs, as they acknowledged, the way that these state-sponsored dual-language programs were built did not account for ELs' needs for English-language development support and fell short of truly embracing their native cultures and languages.

Despite the differences in these individual cases, we can see the common thread that unites them: advancing equity efforts required the SBGE principles of school board members deeply knowing and understanding themselves and their communities, enacting skills to engage in coalition politics and to leverage state and federal policies, and adopting strategies to be proactively responsive and to imagine the possibilities.

Connecting to Your School District

If you think about your own school district, how have you seen these principles play out? Is there a history of school desegregation movements, as in CCSD, or legal cases that affect statewide policies, as in TUSD? Who are the key actors and community leaders that move policy in education? Are some of them from outside the state, as in the case of TUSD, or are they powerful voices from the business and academic communities, like those in CCSD, or from the political community, as in SLCSD? Do the overarching and deep-seated beliefs of minoritized students reflect the desire to melt away differences, as in SLCSD, or maybe commodify to benefit others, as in CCSD? With whom can you engage in coalition politics? Are there people across racial or economic boundaries who can help advance equity and with whom you can build collective power, like what Stavan and Deborah in CCSD found in each other? How might you leverage state and federal policies to disrupt inequities as the community activist did in SLCSD, community leaders did in CCSD, and district leaders did in TUSD? When you leverage these policies, are you ready to be proactively responsive and imagine possibilities that further equity in relatively substantial ways as school board members did in SLCSD with their Student Achievement Plan?

In each case, we saw how context, history, beliefs, and community advocacy matter in creating the momentum for issues of equity to surface as a priority for the school board. Once equity is prioritized, school board members must examine deficit-based beliefs and then enact skills and strategies to move equity in the right direction toward asset-based ways of providing humanizing opportunities for *all* children. Coming into a school district as a board member who is committed to advancing equity is a huge responsibility that requires guidance and insight to respond proactively to the issues that will arise along the way. And adopting the SBGE principles, along with other basic foundational skills that reflect the legal and political day-to-day duties needed to operate as a board member, takes time and effort. Remember that this journey is like following a recipe. While you must follow it one step at a time, you might need to prepare one item while the other item is "cooking." Similarly, as you get to know your community, you might also need to start leveraging state or federal policy to achieve your goals.

Thankfully, as a school board member you bring to the role your own knowledge and skills. You may already have a deep understanding of some aspects of their community. You might have already engaged in coalition politics or imagined some possibilities. Once you bring these principles together, movement to advance equity at a district level will happen. You will build a deep understanding of your context, see the inequities that exist in your district, and use your skills to advance equity strategically, either little by little or in a huge way.

THE FUTURE OF SCHOOL BOARD RESEARCH

Research on school boards is challenging, underdeveloped, and fascinating. Across all fifty US states, there are 13,000 elected school boards in districts that vary by type, structure, size, and demographics, each with their own set of statutes and laws, making it difficult to compare school boards and their members. The three case studies, from three different states, featured in this book are a small subsection of that heterogeneity. I spent more than two years watching school board meetings, reviewing meeting agendas and minutes, sifting through district archives, scrutinizing policies, and interviewing school board members and other district leaders. Then I spent another two years writing about and sharing what I found from all this information. After conducting that study, along with other similar research, for over a decade, I can attest that meaningful research on school boards and their role in education is not easy. And it is often even more difficult to explore the impact of school board governance on educational equity.

Political science scholars have paid some attention to school boards in recent years. Often, they are interested in quantifying the effectiveness of school boards by examining their ability to represent constituents, voter accountability, and the impacts of school board electoral structures and campaigning on who gets elected. Education scholars have also given some attention to school boards. In this academic discipline, scholars often examine the role of the school board in relationship to the superintendent and its role in controversial topics that are publicized at board meetings, and some scholars lump school boards with other district leaders.

Still, many scholars do not dive deeply into this research because school boards are often seen as operating on the periphery. Unlike other locally or state elected officials, school boards do not make policies that affect every aspect of public life. And unlike teachers or principals, school boards are not in schools on a day-to-day basis. But they play a critical role as leaders and policy makers in thousands of educational ecosystems (e.g., districts) throughout the United States.

School boards are part of an ecosystem that involves many players, including youth, families, educators, school and district leaders, staff, and community members, and their work is affected by state and federal laws. School boards are a fascinating part of this ecosystem because they connect the broader local community to our schools. They can bring the voices of the community into what is happening in schools, and vice versa. School boards can have a significant impact on education, and as a result, in the community. With one vote, they can pave the way for new programs or new curricula. With one vote, they can remove programs or curricula that had been in place for decades. With attention to detail, they can present the necessary questions and push back about inequitable budget allocations or inequitable treatment of students. They can hire the perfect superintendent to lead the district or fire one that has done a poor job. These are just a few examples of the power and authority that school board members can have. But their power is not all-encompassing. It is the voters in each local community who have the power and authority to determine who sits on the dais as a school board member.

When I began my research on school boards, I started with the book-shelves of my university's library. Almost every book that I found on school boards told an anecdotal story of a former school board member. While these stories are important, they do not transcend most school board members' experiences. Nor are these stories systemically collected and analyzed in ways that bring out the implications of how and why these stories matter to current and future board members. I finally found two edited books that were research-based. One, *Besieged: School Boards and the Future of Education Politics*, was filled mostly with chapters written by political scientists; and the other, *The Future of School Board Governance: Relevancy and Revelation*, had content from mostly education scholars.[1] These were helpful, but at that point, both books were nearly a decade old. It was clear then, as now, that we need more research in this area.

We need more studies that offer cross-case analyses of various types of school boards throughout the country. While recently some research-ers have examined the role of school boards in rural areas, and a handful of researchers have explored large-city politics in education that include school boards, we have limited research about school boards across urban and suburban areas, and even less research on school boards in tribal communities or youths' role on school boards.[2]

More significantly, until recently, we had very little knowledge of school boards and educational equity. In addition to myself, a few of my colleagues have explored equity through a district lens that takes school boards into account.[3] That said, we need more researchers who are interested in the role of school boards in educational equity and can use critical theories to ask critical research questions. These questions could further explore how school boards can advance equity for various minoritized groups of students, such as Black or Indigenous students, or students who identify as LGBTQIA+. Future research might explore how school board members make meaningful connections between minoritized families, voters, and the district. We know little about how school boards can make policies and support practices that can prevent school closures. Also, we need more research that transcends disciplinary boundaries, including exploring the role of school boards in lobbying state and federal policy makers to create or eliminate policies that advance educational equity. Finally, we need to build on research and practices to develop pipelines for school board members who are committed to advancing equity, including recruiting, campaigning, training, and supporting these individuals throughout their trajectory as school board members. Overall, our research needs to be solution oriented. It needs to be embedded in communities and answer questions that are important to those who live, work, and go to school in these communities.

Universities and colleges have a role to play in this work. We can make more efforts to share our research through creating training opportunities, continuing professional development, and disseminating studies in accessible and meaningful ways. We do this for teachers, school leaders, and district administrators. But most of us in these academic walls leave our school boards with nothing from our institutions. This is a disservice.

THE FUTURE OF SCHOOL BOARDS AND PLANTING THE SEEDS OF EQUITY

The democratic project of elected school boards as the governing bodies for our public schools has been under threat for nearly a century. Since the progressive era of the early 1900s, there have been many moves to critique, undermine, and completely dismantle elected school boards. However, these moves have succeeded in only a few places, such as New York City and Chicago, at least for now. There has been a lot of pushback from local communities. In fact, in November 2024, Chicago will return to having a locally elected school board after almost thirty years of having a state-mandated, mayor-appointed school board, which many community leaders advocated against for years after its implementation.[4] Despite all the efforts to get rid of locally elected school boards, they stand tall and resemble a cornerstone of American democracy.

Still, locally elected school boards, as entities by themselves, are not the panacea for advancing equity. As the case studies in this book show, other entities, including courts, federal policies, and community advocates, have often had to push school boards to advance educational equity. Also, not all locally elected school boards are representative of their communities. Advancing equity as a school board member requires the knowledge, understanding, skills, and strategies reflected in the SBGE framework.

Our public education system is uniquely designed with the hope of serving all students. Our governance model is uniquely designed to give each of us an opportunity to weigh in. As education historian David Tyack writes, "No other nation in the world has created such a decentralized system of public education, and no other nation has built such an inclusive and comprehensive system of public education. Local control and public support—the two characteristics are inextricably linked."[5]

Although inclusivity does not mean equity, we do have a public education system that serves one of the most diverse student populations in the world. And local control offers an avenue to allow every community member to take part in supporting public education. When all voices are included in this democratic project and have the power to elect a governing board that represents their desires and needs, and when participants are guided by principles such as those in the SBGE framework, equity has an opportunity to take root.

If we, as individuals committed to advancing an equitable education, fail to collectively take part in this democratic project, we will miss our opportunity to plant, water, and give light to the seeds of equity so that it *can* take root. If we tend to equity, it can grow in the right direction, toward a humanizing education for *all* our children—one that generations to come will be able to harvest and be nourished by. If we leave the responsibility of education to corporations and private companies, we risk leaving many children behind.

One of the biggest fallacies in this contemporary education system is the idea that private and even public charter schools, which are governed by appointed boards, provide a better education than traditional public schools. This notion is the foundation of school choice arguments. This notion suggests that by expanding school choice through policies, such as open enrollment and voucher systems, the competition between the private and public sectors of education will improve public schools. Yet this is far from the truth. What we know from research is that many private and charter schools are not the inclusive system that David Tyack praised. Instead, these schools often practice exclusivity, including not admitting or even pushing out students with greater needs (e.g., students with disabilities and ELs). These practices contribute to significant differences in the student populations that these schools serve. Studies that control for these differences show that, on average, students in public schools did better on the National Assessment of Educational Progress tests than their private school peers. However, since the most influential predictor of a student's academic success is socioeconomic status, followed by other factors such as access to health care and learning opportunities outside of school, these differences matter. To be clear, factors inside schools matter too, but such factors (e.g., teacher effectiveness) account for only about 30 percent of students' academic success. Since public schools are obligated to meet the needs of all students, no matter their background, when more students are lured away from public schools, especially those who are relatively affluent, and when funding follows them, what are left behind are many public schools with our highest-need students, but with much less funding to meet those needs. The result of this trend is likely an increasingly inequitable public system of education.[6]

But there is hope. In many local communities, moves to privatize education are not irreversible. As elected school board members, you are entrusted not only to govern this public institution, but also to protect it. You are protecting public schools so the most vulnerable of our children, alongside our children who are most advantaged, can *all* get the educational opportunities that they need in the most humanizing ways that they deserve. Public schools are the unique places where these very distinct populations of children can come together and learn what it means to walk in a world of differences and similarities, where they can be seen and heard in public spaces, and where they can become their own person outside their homes. These are transformative spaces where children grow not only academically, but also emotionally and socially. Public schools are worth protecting and cultivating into the most equitable places possible.

Planting the seeds of equity and helping those seeds to grow is a collective responsibility that requires many people and groups who are committed to the process. School boards can and should be one of those groups. The SBGE principles of knowledge, understanding, skills, and strategies provide a pathway to help you, at the governance level, get to the root of educational inequities and tend to the growth of something beautiful. You are the link between local communities and our public schools. In your multifaceted roles as a policy maker and elected official, and as a community and educational leader, you can help shape both the factors inside schools and factors outside of schools in ways that have lasting impacts on educational equity. My hope is that, by offering you a brief history of public schools and school boards and a new way to think about equity as educational opportunities, the SBGE framework, and case studies that feature the framework's principles, you will do the work needed to cultivate a new harvest full of equitable educational opportunities in your school district.

In the beginning of this book, I explained that elected school board members are tasked with representing their local community's concerns and desires, and they also are responsible for ensuring that all students have a humanizing and equitable opportunity to learn. Then I posed two questions: Can elected school boards accomplish this lofty undertaking, and do they want to? I wholeheartedly believe that school board members can, and many of them want to. With the right tools and support, they will.

NOTES

FOREWORD

1. See, for instance, Gabriella Borter, Joseph Ax, and Joseph Tanfani, "School Boards Get Threats over Race, Gender, Mask Policies," NewsNation, February 19, 2022, https://www.newsnationnow.com/us-news/education/school-boards-get-threats-over-race-gender-mask-policies/.
2. Stephen Sawchuk, "Why School Boards Are Now Hot Spots for Nasty Politics," EducationWeek, July 29, 2021, https://www.edweek.org/leadership/why-school-boards-are-now-hot-spots-for-nasty-politics/2021/07.
3. Sawchuk, "Why School Boards Are Now Hot Spots."

PREFACE

1. Ruy Teixeira, *America's New Swing Region: Changing Politics and Demographics in the Mountain West,* ed. Ruy Teixeira (Washington, DC: Brookings Institution Press, 2012).
2. Cheryl Harris, "Reflections on *Whiteness as Property,*" *Harvard Law Review* 133, no. 9 (2019–2020), 3–4.

CHAPTER 1

1. Michael Barbaro, "The School Board Wars, Part 1," *The Daily* (*New York Times,* November 16, 2021), https://www.nytimes.com/2021/11/16/podcasts/the-daily/school-boards-mask-mandates-crt-bucks-county.html.
2. Carrie Sampson, "(Im)Possibilities of Latinx School Board Members' Educational Leadership Toward Equity," *Educational Administration Quarterly* 55, no. 2 (2019): 296–327, https://doi.org/10.1177/0013161X18799482.
3. Jeremy Redford and Kathleen Mulvaney Hoyer, "First-Generation and Continuing-Generation College Students: A Comparison of High School and Postsecondary Experiences," *National Center for Education Statistics,* 2017,

https://doi.org/10.7326/0003-4819-90-5-795; National School Boards Association, "Today's School Boards & Their Priorities for Tomorrow," 2018, https://www.nsba.org/resource-library/surveys.

4. I use the term *minoritized* to describe an individual who is part of a group that has experienced systemic and institutional oppression because of their background, including their race, ethnicity, language, citizenship status, gender, socioeconomic status, and sexuality.

5. Richard R. Valencia, *The Evolution of Deficit Thinking: Educational Thought and Practice* (London: RoutledgeFalmer, 1997).

6. Prudence L. Carter and Kevin G. Welner, *Closing the Opportunity Gap: What America Must Do to Give Every Child an Even Chance* (New York: Oxford University Press, 2013).

7. Gloria Ladson-Billings, "From the Achievement Gap to the Education Debt: Understanding Achievement in U.S. Schools," *Educational Researcher* 35, no. 7 (2006): 3–12; Carter and Welner, *Closing the Opportunity Gap*.

8. Linda Darling-Hammond, "Inequality and School Resources: What It Will Take to Close the Opportunity Gap," in *Closing the Opportunity Gap: What America Must Do to Give Every Child an Even Chance*, ed. Prudence L. Carter and Kevin G. Welner (New York: Oxford University Press, 2013), 77–97, https://doi.org/10.1093/acprof:oso/9780199982981.001.0001.

9. Jason A. Grissom and James R. Harrington, "Local Legislative Professionalism," *American Politics Research* 41, no. 1 (August 8, 2012): 76–98, https://doi.org/10.1177/1532673X12448212; Michael A. Resnick and Anne L. Bryant, "School Boards: Why American Education Needs Them," *Phi Delta Kappan* 91, no. 6 (March 2010): 11–14, https://www.jstor.org/stable/27755659.

10. Hayes Mizell, "School Boards Should Focus on Learning for All," *Phi Delta Kappan* 91, no. 6 (March 2010): 20–23, https://www.jstor.org/stable/27755662.

11. Michael D. Usdan, "School Boards: A Neglected Institution in an Era of School Reform," *Phi Delta Kappan* 91, no. 6 (March 2010): 8–10, https://www.jstor.org/stable/27755659.

12. Usdan, "School Boards," 9.

13. Usdan, "School Boards," 9.

14. Mass Moments, "Massachusetts Passes First Education Law," n.d., https://www.massmoments.org/moment-details/massachusetts-passes-first-education-law.html.

15. PBS, "PBS Online: Only a Teacher: Schoolhouse Pioneers," n.d., https://www.pbs.org/onlyateacher/horace.html.

16. Ernest Cassara, "Reformer as Politician: Horace Mann and the Anti-Slavery Struggle in Congress, 1848–1853," *Journal of American Studies* 5, no. 3 (December 16, 1971): 247–63, https://doi.org/10.1017/S0021875800000931; James D. Anderson, *The Education of Blacks in the South 1860–1935* (Chapel Hill: University of North Carolina Press, 1988).

17. Anderson, *The Education of Blacks*.
18. History.com Editors, History, "Jim Crow Laws," January 22, 2024, https://www. history.com/topics/early-20th-century-us/jim-crow-laws.
19. Anderson, *The Education of Blacks*.
20. Zinn Education Project, "April 14, 1947: Mendez v. Westminster Court Ruling," n.d.
21. *Brown v. Board of Education of Topeka (2)*, Oyez, https://www.oyez.org/cases/1940-1955/349us294.
22. Halley Potter and Michelle Burris, "Here Is What School Integration in America Looks Like Today," December 2, 2020, https://tcf.org/content/report/school-integration-america-looks-like-today/#data.
23. Virginia Museum of History & Culture, "Civil Rights Movement in Virginia," n.d., https://virginiahistory.org/learn/civil-rights-movement-virginia/closing-prince-edward-countys-schools.
24. Carrie Sampson and Sonya Douglass Horsford, "Beyond Legal Remedies: Toward Funding Equity and Improved Educational Opportunities for English Language Learners," in *Law & Education Inequality: Removing Barriers to Educational Opportunities*, ed. Jeffrey C. Bon and Susan C. Sun (Charlotte, NC: Information Age, 2015), 35–48.
25. Richard Briffault, "The Local School District in American Law," in *Besieged: School Boards and the Future of Education Politics*, ed. William G. Howell (Washington, DC: Brookings Institution, 2005), 24–55, http://www.jstor.org/stable/10.7864/j.ctt127xjr.5.
26. Kenneth J. Meier, Eric Gonzalez Juenke, Robert D. Wrinkle, and J. L. Polinard, "Structural Choices and Representational Biases: The Post-Election Color of Representation," *American Journal of Political Science* 49, no. 4 (2005): 758–68, https://doi.org/10.2307/3647695.
27. Jacqueline P. Danzberger, "Governing the Nation's Schools: The Case for Restructuring Local School Boards," *Phi Delta Kappan* 75, no. 5 (1994): 367, https://www.jstor.org/stable/20405112; Sonya Douglass Horsford, "A Nation (of Students) at Risk: The Political Rhetoric of Equity and Achievement in US Education Reform," in *Advancing Equity and Achievement in America's Diverse Schools*, ed. Camille M. Wilson and Sonya Douglass Horsford (New York: Routledge, 2014), 9–24.
28. Christopher R. Berry, "School District Consolidation and Student Outcomes," in *Besieged: School Boards and the Future of Education Politics*, ed. William G. Howell (Washington, DC: Brookings Institution, 2005), 56–80, http://www.jstor.org/stable/10.7864/j.ctt127xjr.4.
29. Berry, "School District Consolidation," 8.
30. Eva Gold, Jeffery R. Henig, and Elaine Simon, "Calling the Shots in Public Education: Parents, Politicians, and Educators Clash," *Dissent* 58, no. 4 (2011): 34–39.

31. Kenneth K. Wong, Warren E. Langevin, and Francis X. Shen, "When School Districts Regain Control: The Political Economy of State Takeover of Local Schools and Its Withdrawal," The Annual Meeting of the American Political Science Association (Chicago, 2004).

32. Lorraine M. McDonnell, "Educational Accountability and Policy Feedback," Educational Policy 27, no. 2 (March 1, 2013): 170–89, https://doi.org/10.1177/0895904812465119; Wayne D. Lewis and Lance Fusarelli, "Leading Schools in an Era of Change: Toward a 'New' Cultural Accountability?," in New Perspectives in Educational Leadership, ed. Sonya Douglass Horsford (New York: Peter Lang, 2010), 111–25.

33. Thomas L. Alsbury, The Future of School Board Governance: Relevancy and Revelation (Lanham, MD: Rowman & Littlefield Education, 2008), xvi.

34. "H.R.1—No Child Left Behind Act of 2001," Congress.gov, 2001, https://www.congress.gov/bill/107th-congress/house-bill/1.

35. Julian Vasquez Heilig, James T. Brewer, and Jimmy O. Pedraza, "Examining the Myth of Accountability, High-Stakes Testing and the Achievement Gap," Journal of Family Strengths 18, no. 1 (2018): 1–14, https://doi.org/10.58464/2168-670X.1389.

36. Lewis and Fusarelli, "Leading Schools in an Era of Change"; McDonnell, "Educational Accountability and Policy Feedback," 170–89.

37. Andrea Boyle et al., "Title III Accountability: Behind the Numbers," US Department of Education, Office of Planning, Evaluation and Policy Development (Washington, DC, May 2008), https://www2.ed.gov/rschstat/eval/title-iii/behind-numbers.pdf.

38. Audrey Amrein-Beardsley, David C. Berliner, and Sharon Rideau, "Cheating in the First, Second, and Third Degree: Educators' Responses to High-Stakes Testing," Education Policy Analysis Archives 18, no. 14 (2010), https://doi.org/10.14507/epaa.v18n14.2010.

39. Thomas S. Dee and Brian A. Jacob, "The Impact of No Child Left Behind on Students, Teachers, and Schools," Brookings Papers on Economic Activity, Fall 2010, https://www.brookings.edu/wp-content/uploads/2010/09/2010b_bpea_dee.pdf; Craig Alan Mertler, "Teachers' Perceptions of the Influence of 'No Child Left Behind' on Classroom Practices," Current Issues in Education 13, no. 3 (2010), https://cie.asu.edu/ojs/index.php/cieatasu/article/view/392/105; Anna J. Markowitz, "Changes in School Engagement as a Function of No Child Left Behind: A Comparative Interrupted Time Series Analysis," American Educational Research Journal 55, no. 4 (August 1, 2018): 721–60, https://doi.org/10.3102/0002831218755668; Sean F. Reardon et al., "Left Behind? The Effect of No Child Left Behind on Academic Achievement Gaps" (Stanford, CA: Stanford Center for Education Policy Analysis, 2013), https://cepa.stanford.edu/content/left-behind-effect-no-child-left-behind-academic-achievement-gaps.

40. William G. Howell, "Results of President Obama's Race to the Top—Education Next," *Education Next* 15, no. 4 (2015): 58–66, https://www.educationnext.org/results-president-obama-race-to-the-top-reform/.

41. US Department of Education, "Awards: Race to the Top District," n.d., https://www2.ed.gov/programs/racetothetop-district/awards.html.

42. Alyson Klein, "Rules Proposed for District Race to Top Contest," *Education Weekly*, May 22, 2012, https://www.edweek.org/education/rules-proposed-for-district-race-to-top-contest/2012/05.

43. Every Student Succeeds Act, Pub. L. No. 1802 (2015).

44. Dustin Hornbeck, "Who Is Betsy DeVos?," *The Conversation*, 2017, https://theconversation.com/who-is-betsy-devos-70843.

45. Kenneth K. Wong, "Education Policy Trump Style: The Administrative Presidency and Deference to States in ESSA Implementation," *Publius: The Journal of Federalism* 50, no. 3 (July 1, 2020): 423–45, https://doi.org/10.1093/PUBLIUS/PJAA016.

46. Wong, "Education Policy Trump Style," 423–45.

47. The White House, "Fact Sheet: Back to School 2022: Giving Every School the Tools to Prevent COVID-19 Spread and Stay Safely Open All Year Long," August 16, 2022, https://www.whitehouse.gov/briefing-room/statements-releases/2022/08/16/fact-sheet-back-to-school-2022-giving-every-school-the-tools-to-prevent-covid-19-spread-and-stay-safely-open-all-year-long/.

48. US Department of Education, "Education Stabilization Fund," n.d., https://covid-relief-data.ed.gov/?utm_content=&utm_medium=email&utm_name=&utm_source=govdelivery&utm_term=.

49. Katherine Silberstein and Marguerite Roza, "The Massive ESSER Experiment: Here's What We're Learning," *Education Next* 24, no. 1 (2024), https://www.educationnext.org/the-massive-esser-experiment-heres-what-were-learning/.

50. William G. Howell, ed., *Besieged: School Boards and the Future of Education Politics* (Washington, DC: Brookings Institution, 2005), http://www.jstor.org/stable/10.7864/j.ctt127xjr.4.

51. David Tyack, "School Governance in the United States: Historical Puzzles and Anomalies," in *Decentralization and School Improvement*, ed. J. Hannaway and M. Carnoy (San Francisco: Jossey-Bass, 1993), 1–32; Danzberger, "Governing the Nation's Schools," 367–73.

52. Danzberger, "Governing the Nation's Schools"; Michael W. Kirst, "The Evolving Role of School Boards: Retrospect and Prospect," in *The Future of School Board Governance: Relevancy and Revelation*, ed. Thomas L. Alsbury (Lanham, MD: Rowman & Littlefield, 2008), 37–59.

53. Kirst, "The Evolving Role of School Boards"; Danzberger, "Governing the Nation's Schools"; Howell, *Besieged: School Boards*; Gary J. Miller and Jack H. Knott, *Reforming Bureaucracy: The Politics of Institutional Choice* (Upper Saddle River, NJ: Prentice Hall, 1987); Tyack, "School Governance in the United States."

54. Miller and Knott, *Reforming Bureaucracy*.
55. Miller and Knott, *Reforming Bureaucracy*; Howell, *Besieged: School Boards*.
56. Kirst, "The Evolving Role of School Boards."
57. Howell, *Besieged: School Boards*; Kirst, "The Evolving Role of School Boards"; Tyack, "School Governance in the United States."
58. Berry, "School District Consolidation."
59. Berry, "School District Consolidation"; William G. Howell, "Introduction," in *Besieged: School Boards and the Future of Education Politics* (Washington, DC: Brookings Institution, 2005), 1–23, http://www.jstor.org/stable/10.7864/j.ctt127xjr.4; US Department of Education, National Center for Education Statistics, "120 Years of American Education"; US Department of Education, Institute of Education Sciences, National Center for Education Statistics, "Public Charter School Enrollment," 2023, https://nces.ed.gov/programs/coe/indicator/cgb/public-charter-enrollment#suggested-citation; US Department of Education, National Center for Education Statistics, Institute of Education Sciences, "Digest of Education Statistics 2010."
60. US Department of Education, National Center for Education Statistics, Institute of Education Sciences, "Digest of Education Statistics 2010," 2011, http://nces.ed.gov/pubs2011/2011015.pdf; US Department of Education, National Center for Education Statistics, "120 Years of American Education: A Statistical Portrait," 1993, http://nces.ed.gov/pubs93/93442.pdf.
61. US Department of Education, "Digest of Educational Statistics 2010"; US Department of Education, National Center for Education Statistics, "120 Years of American Education."
62. Berry, "School District Consolidation"; Howell, *Besieged: School Boards*.
63. Berry, "School District Consolidation."
64. US Department of Education, Institute of Education Sciences, National Center for Education Statistics, "Public Charter School Enrollment."
65. US Department of Education, Institute of Education Sciences, National Center for Education Statistics, "Public Charter School Enrollment."
66. David Campbell, "Contextual Influences on Participation in School Governance," in *Besieged: School Boards and the Future of Education Politics*, ed. William Howell (Washington, DC: Brookings Institution, 2005), 288–307, http://www.jstor.org/stable/10.7864/j.ctt127xjr.15; Kendra Taylor, Erica Frankenberg, and Genevieve Siegel-Hawley, "Racial Segregation in the Southern Schools, School Districts, and Counties Where Districts Have Seceded," *AERA Open* 5, no. 3 (July 1, 2019), https://doi.org/10.1177/2332858419860152.
67. David B. Tyack, *Seeking Common Ground: Public Schools in a Diverse Society* (Cambridge, MA: Harvard University Press, 2003), 145.
68. Stephen Sawchuk et al., "Defunded, Removed, and Put in Check: School Police a Year After George Floyd," *Education Week*, June 4, 2021, https://www.edweek.

org/leadership/defunded-removed-and-put-in-check-school-police-a-year-after-george-floyd/2021/06.

69. Robert Chappell, "Madison School Board Unanimously Votes to Remove Police from Schools," Madison 365, June 30, 2020, https://madison365.com/madison-school-board-unanimously-votes-to-remove-police-from-schools/.

70. "AZ Doctors, School Board Members Discuss Reopening," Facebook Live, https://www.facebook.com/watch/live/?ref=watch_permalink&v=969515566836661.

71. Guilia Heyward, "Some School Districts Are Defying State Bans on Mask Mandates," New York Times, August 5, 2021, https://www.nytimes.com/2021/08/05/us/schools-mask-mandates-Arizona-Florida.html.

72. Billy Gates, Jaclyn Ramkissoon, and Christopher Adams, "LIST: Texas School Districts with Mask Mandates in Place," KXAN Austin, August 10, 2021, https://www.kxan.com/news/education/set-for-school/list-texas-school-districts-with-mask-mandates-in-place/.

73. Amanda Morris, "Children with Disabilities Sue the Texas Governor over His Ban on School Mask Mandates," New York Times, August 19, 2021, https://www.nytimes.com/2021/08/19/us/19virus-abbott-texas-lawsuit-mask-mandate-ban.html.

74. Tim Steller and Henry Brean, "Political Notebook: Crowd Claims 'Robert's Rules' Let Them Pick New Vail School Board," Tuscon.com, April 30, 2021, https://tucson.com/news/local/govt-and-politics/political-notebook-crowd-claims-roberts-rules-let-them-pick-new-vail-school-board/article_5433910c-a90d-11eb-82f1-d79eb36292c5.html.

75. Nicole Carr, "He Became Convinced the School Board Was Pushing 'Transgender Bullshit': He Ended up Arrested—and Emboldened," ProPublica, July 19, 2023, https://www.propublica.org/article/winston-salem-nc-school-board-arrests.

76. Carrie Sampson et al., "The Politicization of Education: A Critical Analysis of Recent Media Coverage of School District Governance" (Presentation, Presidential Program Session at the American Educational Research Association Annual Conference, Chicago, April 14, 2023).

77. Russell Vought, "Memorandum for the Heads of the Executive Departments and Agencies," Office of Management and Budget, September 4, 2020, https://www.whitehouse.gov/wp-content/uploads/2020/09/M-20-34.pdf.

78. Kyle Reinhard, "CRT Forward Releases New Report on Anti-CRT Measures and Trends," CRT Forward, April 6, 2023, https://crtforward.law.ucla.edu/new-crt-forward-report-highlights-trends-in-2021-2022-anti-crt-measures/.

79. "School Board Recalls," Ballotpedia, n.d., https://ballotpedia.org/School_board_recalls.

80. Sampson et al., "The Politicization of Education."

81. Ryan Mills, "Outraged San Francisco Parents Push to Recall 'Disaster' School Board," National Review, March 10, 2021, https://www.nationalreview.com/

news/faced-with-a-school-board-focused-on-renaming-instead-of-reopening-these-parents-pushed-back/; Tom Scanlon, "Masks Are Gone, but SUSD Lawsuit Remains," *Scottsdale Progress*, April 10, 2023, https://www.scottsdale.org/city_news/masks-are-gone-but-susd-lawsuit-remains/article_f4d3185c-d7ce-11ed-897f-632b2fa3b81c.html.

82. Ali Swenson, "Moms for Liberty Removes Two Kentucky Chapter Leaders Who Posed with Far-Right Proud Boys," Associated Press, November, 15, 2023, https://apnews.com/article/moms-for-liberty-proud-boys-kentucky-d0 73732a6bbf2a65e08dcc76bc53cf06; Sana Sinha et al., "Moms for Liberty: Where Are They, and Are They Winning?," Brookings, October 10, 2023, https://www.brookings.edu/articles/moms-for-liberty-where-are-they-and-are-they-winning/; Sheera Frenkel, "Proud Boys Regroup, Focusing on School Boards and Town Councils," *New York Times*, December 14, 2021, https://www.nytimes.com/2021/12/14/us/proud-boys-local-issues.html.

83. Frenkel, "Proud Boys Regroup," 3.

84. Ben Chapman, "School Board Candidates Who Pushed 'Parental Rights' See Mixed Results," *Wall Street Journal*, November 13, 2022, https://www.wsj.com/articles/school-board-candidates-who-pushed-parental-rights-see-mixed-results-11668249004; Isabel Soisson, "Moms for Liberty's Far-Right Agenda Rejected by Voters," *UpNorthNews*, November 13, 2023, https://upnorthnewswi.com/2023/11/13/moms-for-libertys-far-right-agenda-rejected-by-voters/.

85. Brittany Shepherd, "Progressives Launch Their Own Campaign to Flip School Board Seats Nationwide," ABC News, June 23, 2023, https://abcnews.go.com/Politics/progressives-launch-campaign-flip-school-board-seats-nationwide/story?id=100246945.

86. TaRhonda Thomas, "Democrats Flip School Board Majority in 3 Pennsylvania Districts," ABC News, WPVI-TV Philadelphia, November 8, 2023, https://6abc.com/central-bucks-school-district-election-day-2023-democratic-majority-board-elections/14028806/.

87. Brooke Schultz and Geoff Mulvihill, "Liberal and Moderate Candidates Take Control of School Boards in Contentious Races Across US," Associated Press, November 8, 2023, https://apnews.com/article/school-board-elections-moms-liberty-progressives-1e439de49b0e8498537484fb031f66a6.

88. Linda Jacobson, "Chiefs Out in Half of Districts Where Moms for Liberty Flipped Boards Last Year," *The 74*, October 5, 2023, https://www.the74million.org/article/chiefs-out-in-half-of-districts-where-moms-for-liberty-flipped-boards-last-year/; Thomas, "Democrats Flip School Board Majority."

89. Sawchuk et al., "Defunded, Removed, and Put," 2021.

90. Turning Point USA, "School Board Watchlist," 2024, https://www.schoolboard-watchlist.org/.

91. Parents Defending Education, "IndoctriNation Map," 2024, https://defendinged.org/map/.

92. Antony Farag, "The CRT Culture War in the Suburbs," *Phi Delta Kappan* 104, no. 5 (February 1, 2023): 18–23, https://doi.org/10.1177/00317217231156225; William H. Frey, "Todays Suburbs Are Symbolic of Americas Rising Diversity: A 2020 Census Portrait," June 15, 2022, https://policycommons.net/artifacts/4140963/todays-suburbs-are-symbolic-of-americas-rising-diversity/4949253/.

93. Carol Anderson, *White Rage: The Unspoken Truth of Our Racial Divide* (London: Bloomsbury, 2016).

94. Milton Friedman, *Capitalism and Freedom* (Chicago: University of Chicago Press, 1962), 117.

95. Chris Ford, Stephanie Johnson, and Lisette Partelow, "The Racist Origins of Private School Vouchers," Center for American Progress, July 12, 2017, https://www.americanprogress.org/article/racist-origins-private-school-vouchers/.

96. William J. Mathis and Kevin G. Welner, "Research-Based Options for Education Policymaking: Do Choice Policies Segregate Schools?," National Education Policy Center (Boulder, CO, March 2016), https://nepc.colorado.edu/sites/default/files/publications/Mathis%20RBOPM-3%20Choice%20Segregation.pdf.

97. Casey Cobb, "Do School Choice Programs Contribute to the Resegregation of American Schools?," National Coalition on School Diversity, March 2022, https://files.eric.ed.gov/fulltext/ED623576.pdf.

98. Erica Frankenberg and Gary Orfield, eds., *Lessons in Integration: Realizing the Promise of Racial Diversity in American Schools* (Charlottesville: University of Virginia Press, 2007); Jack Schneider et al., "Student Experience Outcomes in Racially Integrated Schools: Looking Beyond Test Scores in Six Districts," *Education and Urban Society* 54, no. 3 (March 12, 2022): 330–60, https://doi.org/10.1177/00131245211004569.

99. Carrie Sampson et al., "Open Enrollment and Disrupting the Political Ecology of U.S. Public Education," *Peabody Journal of Education* 97, no. 1 (January 21, 2022): 62–73, https://doi.org/10.1080/0161956X.2022.2026721.

100. Katrina Bulkley, Jeffrey Henig, and Henry Levin, *Between Public and Private: Politics, Governance, and the New Portfolio Models for Urban School Reform* (Cambridge, MA: Harvard Education Press, 2010); Mathis and Welner, "Research-Based Options for Education Policymaking"; Kenneth J. Saltman, "Urban School Decentralization and the Growth of 'Portfolio Districts,'" Great Lakes Center for Education Research and Practice, no. June (2010): 23; Carrie Sampson and Sarah Diem, "NEPC Review: The Third Way: A Guide to Implementing Innovation Schools (Progressive Policy Institute, October 2020)," January 21, 2021, https://nepc.colorado.edu/thinktank/innovation-schools.

101. Council of the Great City Schools and Airick Journey Crabill, "Student Outcomes Focused Governance," 2014–2021, https://files.eric.ed.gov/fulltext/ED622543.pdf.

102. Angela Valenzuela, *Leaving Children Behind: How "Texas-Style" Accountability Fails Latino Youth* (New York: SUNY Press, 2004), 4.

103. José Vilson, *This Is Not a Test: A New Narrative on Race, Class, and Education* (Chicago: Haymarket, 2014), 20.

CHAPTER 2

1. Michael Omi and Howard Winant, *Racial Formation in the United States*, 3rd ed. (New York: Routledge, 2014); Judith Lorber and Susan A. Farrell, eds., *The Social Construction of Gender* (Newbury Park, CA: SAGE, 1990).
2. Helen M. Ingram, Anne L. Schneider, and Peter DeLeon, "Social Construction and Policy Design," in *Theories of the Policy Process*, 2nd ed., ed. Paul Sabatier (Bellevue, TN: Westview, 2007), 93–126.
3. Claude M. Steele, "A Threat in the Air: How Stereotypes Shape Intellectual Identity and Performance," *American Psychologist* 52, no. 6 (June 1997): 613–29, https://doi.org/10.1037/0003-066X.52.6.613.
4. US Census Bureau, "2010 Census Questionnaire," 2010, https://www.census.gov/history/pdf/2010questionnaire.pdf; US Census Bureau, "1960 Census of Population and Housing Questionnaire," 1960, https://www.census.gov/history/www/through_the_decades/questionnaires/1960_1.html.
5. Indian Country Today, "PBS Documentary Explores Navajo Belief in Four Genders," November 5, 2013, https://ictnews.org/archive/pbs-documentary-explores-navajo-belief-in-four-genders.
6. Ian Hacking, *The Social Construction of What?* (Cambridge, MA: Harvard University Press, 1999), 58.
7. Oscar Jimenez-Castellanos and Amelia M. Topper, "The Cost of Providing an Adequate Education to English Language Learners: A Review of the Literature," *Review of Educational Research* 82, no. 2 (2012): 179–232, https://doi.org/10.3102/0034654312449872; Sonya Horsford, Carrie Sampson, and Felicia Forletta, "School Resegregation in the Mississippi of the West: Community Counternarratives on the Return to Neighborhood Schools in Las Vegas, 1968–1994," *Teachers College Record* 115, no. 11 (2013): 1–28, https://doi.org/10.1177/016146811311501105; Jeannie Oakes, Amy Stuart Wells, and Makeba Jones, "Detracking: The Social Construction of Ability, Cultural Politics, and Resistance," *Teachers College Record* 98, no. 3 (1997): 482–510, https://doi.org/10.1177/016146819709800305; Russell J. Skiba et al., "The Color of Discipline: Sources of Racial and Gender Disproportionality in School Punishment," *Urban Review* 34, no. 4 (2002): 317–42, https://doi.org/10.1023/A:1021320817372; Ee-Seul Yoon and Christopher Lubienski, "How Do Marginalized Families Engage in School Choice in Inequitable Urban Landscapes? A Critical Geographic Approach," *Education Policy Analysis Archives* 25, no. 42 (2017), https://doi.org/10.14507/epaa.25.2655.
8. Luis Moll et al., "Funds of Knowledge for Teaching: Using a Qualitative Approach to Connect Homes and Classrooms," *Theory into Practice* 32, no. 2 (1992): 132–41, https://education.ucsc.edu/ellisa/pdfs/Moll_Amanti_1992_Funds_of_

Knowledge.pdf; Tara J. Yosso, "Whose Culture Has Capital? A Critical Race Theory Discussion of Community Cultural Wealth," *Race Ethnicity and Education* 8, no. 1 (2005): 69–91, https://doi.org/10.1080/1361332052000341006; Gloria Ladson-Billings, "Culturally Relevant Pedagogy 2.0: a.k.a the Remix," *Harvard Educational Review* 84, no. 1 (2014): 74–85, https://doi.org/10.1016/j.tifs.2007.02.003; Django Paris and H. Samy Alim, "What Are We Seeking to Sustain Through Culturally Sustaining Pedagogy? A Loving Critique Forward," *Harvard Educational Review* 84, no. 1 (2014): 85–100, https://doi.org/10.17763/haer.84.1.982l873k2ht16m77; Francesca A. López, "Altering the Trajectory of the Self-Fulfilling Prophecy: Asset-Based Pedagogy and Classroom Dynamics," *Journal of Teacher Education* 68, no. 2 (2017): 193–212, https://doi.org/10.1177/0022487116685751.

9. Tyrone C. Howard, *Why Race and Culture Matter in Schools: Closing the Achievement Gap in America's Classrooms* (New York: Teachers College Press, 2010), 13.

10. Sonya Douglass Horsford, "Whose Vision Will Guide Racial Equity in Schools?," *Education Week* (March 17, 2021).

11. Decoteau J. Irby, Terrance Green, and Ann M. Ishimaru, "PK–12 District Leadership for Equity: An Exploration of Director Role Configurations and Vulnerabilities," *American Journal of Education* 128, no. 3 (May 1, 2022): 417–53, https://doi.org/10.1086/719120.

12. Ann M. Ishimaru, Decoteau J. Irby, and Terrance Green, "The Paradox of Organizational Double Jeopardy: PK–12 Equity Directors in Racialized and Gendered Educational Systems," *Urban Review*, 2022, https://doi.org/10.1007/s11256-022-00653-2.

13. Gholdy Muhammad, *Cultivating Genius: An Equity Framework for Culturally and Historically Responsive Literacy* (New York: Scholastic Teaching Resources, 2020); Anna Maier et al., "Using Performance Assessments to Support Student Learning: How District Initiatives Can Make a Difference," Learning Policy Institute, October 13, 2020, https://doi.org/10.54300/213.365.

14. Associated Press, "Schools Debate: Gifted and Talented, or Racist and Elitist?," *New York Post*, October 28, 2021, https://nypost.com/2021/10/28/schools-debate-gifted-and-talented-programs-racist/.

15. Ann M. Ishimaru, *Just Schools: Building Equitable Collaborations with Families and Communities* (New York: Teachers College Press, 2019); Melanie Bertrand and Katherine C. Rodela, "A Framework for Rethinking Educational Leadership in the Margins: Implications for Social Justice Leadership Preparation," *Journal of Research on Leadership Education* 13, no. 1 (March 1, 2018): 10–37, https://doi.org/10.1177/1942775117739414.

16. Nathan Burroughs et al., "A Review of the Literature on Teacher Effectiveness and Student Outcomes," *Teaching for Excellence and Equity: Analyzing Teacher Characteristics, Behaviors and Student Outcomes with TIMSS*, 2019, 7–17, https://link.springer.com/chapter/10.1007/978-3-030-16151-4_2.

17. Anne Podolsky, Tara Kini, and Linda Darling-Hammond, "Does Teaching Experience Increase Teacher Effectiveness? A Review of US Research," *Journal of Professional Capital and Community* 4, no. 4 (January 1, 2019): 286–308, https://doi.org/10.1108/JPCC-12-2018-0032.

18. Rita Kohli, *Teachers of Color: Resisting Racism and Reclaiming Education* (Cambridge, MA: Harvard Education Press, 2021); Travis J. Bristol and Javier Martin-Fernandez, "The Added Value of Latinx and Black Teachers for Latinx and Black Students: Implications for Policy," *Policy Insights from the Behavioral and Brain Sciences* 6, no. 2 (2019): 147–53, https://doi.org/10.1177/2372732219862573.

19. Amaya Garcia, Jenny Muñiz, and Roxanne Garza, "Plugging the Leaks: Washington's Policy Approach to Strengthening the Latinx Teacher Pipeline," in *Handbook of Research on Teachers of Color and Indigenous Teachers*, ed. Gist D. Conra and Travis J. Bristol (Washington, DC: American Educational Research Association, 2023), 1021–38, https://www.jstor.org/stable/j.ctv2xqngb9.76.

20. Shawn A. Ginwright, *Black Youth Rising: Activism and Radical Healing in Urban America* (New York: Teachers College Press, 2009); Melanie Bertrand, "Reciprocal Dialogue Between Educational Decision Makers and Students of Color: Opportunities and Obstacles," *Educational Administration Quarterly* 50, no. 5 (December 12, 2014): 812–43, https://doi.org/10.1177/0013161X14542582; Carlos R. Casanova and Ashley D. Domínguez, "Countering Racist Nativism Through a Liberating Pedagogy of Praxis," *Anthropology & Education Quarterly* (2023), https://doi.org/10.1111/AEQ.12476.

21. Bertrand, "Reciprocal Dialogue Between Educational Decision Makers and Students of Color."

22. Bertrand, "Reciprocal Dialogue Between Educational Decision Makers and Students of Color," 816.

23. Carrie Sampson et al., "Open Enrollment and Disrupting the Political Ecology of U.S. Public Education," *Peabody Journal of Education* 97, no. 1 (2022): 62–73, https://doi.org/10.1080/0161956X.2022.2026721.

24. Terrance L. Green, "Enriching Educational Leadership Through Community Equity Literacy: A Conceptual Foundation," *Leadership and Policy in Schools* 17, no. 4 (2018): 487–515, https://doi.org/10.1080/15700763.2017.1326148; Terrance L. Green, "From Positivism to Critical Theory: School-Community Relations Toward Community Equity Literacy," *International Journal of Qualitative Studies in Education* 30, no. 4 (2017): 370–87, https://doi.org/10.1080/09518398.2016.1253892.

25. Carrie Sampson and Sonya Horsford, "Putting the Public Back in Public Education: Community Advocacy and Every Student Succeeds Act," *Journal of School Leadership* 27 (September 2017): 725–54.

CHAPTER 3

1. Carrie Sampson, Dawn Demps, and Sara Rodriguez-Martinez, "Engaging (or Not) in Coalition Politics: A Case Study of Black and Latinx Community

Advocacy Toward Educational Equity," *Race Ethnicity and Education* 26, no. 7 (2020): 851–71, https://doi.org/10.1080/13613324.2020.1842346.

2. Shirley Chisholm, "Source: The Black Scholar," vol. 4 (1972): 31–32.

3. Sampson et al., "Engaging (or Not)."

4. I use the term "coalesce" to reflect the outcome of coalition building. In the context of this chapter, it means unification around specific issues.

5. Angela Davis, "Coalition Building Among People of Color: A Discussion with Angela Y. Davis and Elizabeth Martinez," in *The Angela Y. Davis Reader*, ed. Joy James (Hoboken, NJ: Wiley, 1998), 297–306.

6. Chandra Mohanty, *Feminism Without Borders: Decolonizing Theory, Practicing Solidarity* (Durham, NC: Duke University Press, 2003), 7.

7. Audre Lorde, "The Master's Tools Will Never Dismantle the Master's House: Comments at the Personal and Political Panel," in *This Bridge Called My Back: Radical Writings by Women of Color*, ed. Cherríe L Moraga and Gloria E. Anzaldúa (New York: Kitchen Table, 1981), 96 (emphasis added).

8. Bernice J. Reagon, "Coalition Politics: Turning the Century," *Home Girls*, 1983, 343–57.

9. Sampson, "Engaging (or Not)," 5.

10. Christin Alexandra Mujica, "'All Skinfolk Ain't Kinfolk': Attributions of Race-Based Discrimination When an Ingroup Member Is the Perpetrator" (masters thesis, University of Arkansas, 2022), https://scholarworks.uark.edu/etd/4397.

11. Jonathan J. B. Mijs, "The Unfulfillable Promise of Meritocracy: Three Lessons and Their Implications for Justice in Education," *Social Justice Research* 29 (2016): 14–34, https://doi.org/10.1007/s11211-014-0228-0; Stephen J. McNamee and Robert K. Miller Jr., *The Meritocracy Myth* (Lanham, MD: Rowman & Littlefield, 2009).

12. For more about this, read Derrick A. Bell, "Brown v. Board of Education and the Interest-Convergence Dilemma," *Harvard Law Review* (1980), https://doi.org/10.2307/1340546; bell hooks, *Feminist Theory: From Margin to Center* (Cambridge, MA: South End, 1984).

13. Carrie Sampson, "(Im)Possibilities of Latinx School Board Members' Educational Leadership Toward Equity," *Educational Administration Quarterly* 55, no. 2 (2019): 296–327, https://doi.org/10.1177/0013161X18799482.

14. Subini Ancy Annamma, Darrell D. Jackson, and Deb Morrison, "Conceptualizing Color-Evasiveness: Using Dis/Ability Critical Race Theory to Expand a Color-Blind Racial Ideology in Education and Society," *Race Ethnicity and Education* 20, no. 2 (March 4, 2017): 147–62, https://doi.org/10.1080/13613324.2016.1248837.

15. Melanie Bertrand and Carrie Sampson, "Exposing the White Innocence Playbook of School District Leaders," *Equity and Excellence in Education*, 2022, https://doi.org/10.1080/10665684.2021.2021669.

16. Bettina L. Love, *We Want to Do More Than Survive: Abolitionist Teaching and the Pursuit of Educational Freedom* (Boston: Beacon, 2019), 117; Rangita de Silva de

Alwis, "Addressing Allyship in a Time of a 'Thousand Papercuts,'" *Hastings Race and Poverty Law Journal* 19, no. 1 (2021), Scholarship at Penn Carey Law, 2798, https://scholarship.law.upenn.edu/faculty_scholarship/2798.

17. Love, *We Want to Do More*, 117–18.

18. Dani Birzer, "Superintendent Fired from Casa Grande Union High School District; Reasons Unclear," *Arizona's Family*, CBS, February 1, 2023, https://www.azfamily.com/2023/02/01/superintendent-fired-casa-grande-union-high-school-district-reasons-unclear/.

19. Meredith Mountford, "Historical and Current Tensions Among Board-Superintendent Teams: Symptoms or Cause?," in *The Future of School Board Governance: Relevancy and Revelation*, ed. Thomas Alsbury (Lanham, MD: Rowman & Littlefield Education, 2008), 81–114.

20. Carl A. Cohn, "Public Schools as Contested Places," *School Administrator*, February 2023, 21.

21. Cohn, "Public Schools as Contested Places," 21.

22. Benjamin Herold, "Suburban Public Schools Are Now Majority-Nonwhite: The Backlash Has Already Begun," *EducationWeek*, March 17, 2021, https://www.edweek.org/leadership/suburban-public-schools-are-now-majority-nonwhite-the-backlash-has-already-begun/2021/03.

23. Jeremy Duda, "Supreme Court Unanimously Strikes Down Mask Mandate, 'Critical Race Theory' Bans," *AZ Mirror*, November 2, 2021, https://azmirror.com/2021/11/02/supreme-court-unanimously-strikes-down-mask-mandate-critical-race-theory-bans/; Ben Giles, "Just Before Taking Effect, Arizona's School Mask Mandate Ban Ruled Unconstitutional," National Public Radio, September 27, 2021, https://www.npr.org/2021/09/27/1041044436/just-before-taking-effect-arizonas-school-mask-mandate-ban-ruled-unconstitutiona.

24. Joe Dana, "Phoenix Union Superintendent Defends Mask Mandate," *12 News*, August 10, 2021, https://www.12news.com/article/news/education/phoenix-union-superintendent-defends-mask-mandate/75-054774fa-236a-46e3-8eef-b181332d31c3.

25. Carrie Sampson and Sonya Horsford, "Putting the Public Back in Public Education: Community Advocacy and Every Student Succeeds Act," *Journal of School Leadership* 27 (September 2017): 725–54, https://doi.org/10.1177/10526846170270050.

26. Domingo Morel, *Takeover: Race, Education, and American Democracy* (New York: Oxford University Press, 2018); Holly Yan, Theresa Waldrop, and Nicquel Terry Ellis, "Texas Officials Will Take over the State's Biggest School District, Raising Questions About Who Controls America's Classrooms," CNN, March 17, 2023, https://www.cnn.com/2023/03/17/us/houston-texas-school-takeover/index.html.

27. Mike Morath, "Appointment of Board of Managers," Texas Education Agency, Austin, TX (March 15, 2023), https://tea.texas.gov/texas-schools/school-boards/hisd-coe-correspondence.pdf.

28. Alejandro Serrano, "Houston ISD Students and Parents Protest TEA Takeover," *The Texas Tribune*, April 6, 2023, https://www.texastribune.org/2023/04/06/houston-school-state-takeover-protest/.

29. Kenneth Wong, "Education Mayors and Big-City School Boards: New Directions, New Evidence," in *The Future of School Board Governance: Relevancy and Revelation*, ed. Thomas L Alsbury (Lanham, MD: Rowman & Littlefield, 2008), 319–56.

30. Yan et al., "Texas Officials Will Take Over the State's Biggest School District."

31. Yan et al., "Texas Officials Will Take Over the State's Biggest School District."

32. Arthur Jones II, "Texas Announces Takeover of Houston's School District, Sparking Concerns from Educators," ABC News, March 18, 2023, https://abcnews.go.com/US/texas-announces-takeover-houstons-school-district-sparking-concerns/story?id=97906502.

33. Carrie Sampson, "'The State Pulled a Fast One on Us': A Critical Policy Analysis of State-Level Policies Affecting English Learners from District-Level Perspectives," *Educational Policy* 33, no. 1 (2019): 3–15, https://doi.org/10.1177/0895904818807324.

34. Kevin P. Brady, "State Power and Equity," in *The Rising State: How State Power Is Transforming Our Nation's Schools*, ed. Bonnie C. Fusarelli and Bruce S. Cooper (Albany, NY: SUNY Press, 2009), 186.

35. Sampson, "The State Pulled a Fast One."

36. Christine E. Sleeter and Miguel Zavala, "What the Research Says About Ethnic Studies: Chapter 3 from Transformative Ethnic Studies in Schools: Curriculum, Pedagogy, and Research," Center for Enterprise Strategy, National Education Association, 2020, https://www.nea.org/sites/default/files/2020-10/What%20the%20Research%20Says%20About%20Ethnic%20Studies.pdf.

37. M. L. Delagardelle, "The Lighthouse Inquiry: Examining the Role of School Board Leadership in the Improvement of Student Achievement," in *The Future of School Board Governance: Relevancy and Revelation*, ed. T. L. Alsbury (Lanham, MD: Rowman & Littlefield, 2008), 191–223.

38. Carrie Sampson, "From a Lighthouse to a Foghorn: A School Board's Navigation Toward Equity for English Learners," *American Journal of Education* 125, no. 4 (2019): 521–46.

39. Robin D. Kelly, *Freedom Dreams: The Black Radical Imagination* (Boston: Beacon, 2000), n.p., xii.

CHAPTER 4

1. This study was conducted between 2014 to 2016. I studied four years (2010 to 2013) of data related to these local school boards, including 519 school board meeting agendas and minutes, many archival documents (e.g., policies and presentations, media articles, legislative archives), and thirty semi-structured interviews with fifteen school board members, eight district-level

administrators (e.g., superintendents, directors), and seven community members.

2. Arizona School Boards Association, "Election of Governing Board Members," Pub. L. No. 15–424 (2015), https://www.azleg.gov/ars/15/00424.htm.

3. Fernanda Echavarri, "Pedicone Resigns as TUSD Supt.," Arizona Public Media, March 20, 2013, https://news.azpm.org/p/news-splash/2013/3/20/23261-pedicone-resigning-from-tusd-website-reports/.

4. Alexis Huicochea, "TUSD Hires Sanchez as Superintendent," *Arizona Daily Star*, July 19, 2013, http://tucson.com/news/local/education/precollegiate/tusd-hires-sanchez-as-superintendent/article_fefa25c3-c515-5e22-b201-da035bdaf5a4.html; Tucson Unified School District, "District History—Superintendents: 1867–Now," 2013, https://www.tusd1.org/article-20221212-superintendents-1867-now.

5. David Safier, "A Multi-Factored Look at TUSD's Enrollment Decline," *Tucson Weekly*, June 20, 2019, https://www.tucsonweekly.com/TheRange/archives/2019/06/20/a-multi-factored-look-at-tusds-enrollment-decline.

6. National Education Association, "Rankings & Estimates: Rankings of the States 2011 and Estimates of School Statistics 2012," 2015, https://files.eric.ed.gov/fulltext/ED583098.pdf.

7. Elizabeth Walton, "WalletHub: AZ Cities Rank Low on List of 'Most Recession Recovered,'" *Tucson News Now*, September 14, 2015, https://www.kold.com/story/30024867/wallethub-arizona-cities-rank-low-on-list-of-most-recession-recovered/; Curtis Spicer, "Arizona's Economy Continues to Recover, Just Very Slowly," *Cronkite News*, September 2, 2015, https://cronkitenews.azpbs.org/2015/09/02/biz-economy/.

8. Alexis Huicochea, "TUSD to Close 11 Schools to Chip Away at $17 Million Shortfall," *Arizona Daily Star*, 2012, https://tucson.com/news/local/tusd-to-close-11-schools-to-chip-away-at-17-million-shortfall/article_92b790de-99a9-55af-a066-7c18fbaf2b29.html; Tucson Unified School District, "Operations," retrieved from P. Takahashi (March 5, 2013); Dwight Jones, "Reform-Minded Superintendent to Leave School District," *Las Vegas Sun*, 2016, https://lasvegassun.com/news/2013/mar/05/dwight-jones-resign-ccsd-superintendent-job/.

9. Tucson Unified School District, "Gov. Ducey's Budget Includes Deep Cuts to Public Education; TUSD Superintendent Sánchez Says Students Will Suffer," Facebook, January 21, 2015, https://www.facebook.com/tucsonunified/posts/news-releasefor-immediate-releasegov-duceys-budget-includes-deep-cuts-to-public-/793453824025921/.

10. William H. Frey and Ruy A. Teixeira, "America's New Swing Region: The Political Demography and Geography of the Mountain West," in *America's New Swing Region: The Political Demography and Geography of the Mountain West*, ed. Ruy A. Teixeira (Washington, DC: Brookings Institution, 2012), 11–68.

11. For more about the influence of this lawsuit in TUSD, refer to Francesca López, "When Desegregation Limits Opportunities to Latino Youth: The Strange Case of the Tucson Unified School District," *Chicanx-Latinx Law Review* 34, no.1 (2016): 1–34, https://www.jstor.org/stable/48648092.

12. Alexis Huicochea, "Bill to Cut TUSD Desegregation Fund Advances," *Arizona Daily Star*, February 11, 2015, https://tucson.com/news/local/education/bill-to-cut-tusd-desegregation-fund-advancesarticle_f052113a-2b54-5ce3-ba03-a1df2 e0e8e66.html.

13. Georgia Cole Brousseau, "Bridging Three Centuries: The History of Tucson School District, 1867–1993," Tucson Unified School District History, 1993, https://www.tusd1.org/_theme/files/stories/22-23/article-20230209-bridging-three-centuries.pdf.

14. Arizona State Senate Issue Brief, *Flores v. Arizona* (August 3, 2013), https://www.azleg.gov/Briefs/Senate/FLORES%20V.%20ARIZONA%202018.pdf.

15. Susan Carroll, "For Student Miriam Flores, Fines Worthwhile If They Help," *Arizona Republic*, February 26, 2006, http://web1.nusd.k12.az.us/schools/nhs/gthomson.class/articles/education/florez/Flores.fines.worthwhile.help.pdf.

16. Arizona Secretary of State, "Proposition 203," para. 1 (2000), https://apps.azsos.gov/election/2000/Info/pubpamphlet/english/prop203.htm#:~:text=Proposition%20203%20requires%20pupils%20who,without%20a%20specific%20time%20limit.

17. Wayne E. Wright, "English Language Learners Left Behind in Arizona: The Nullification of Accommodations in the Intersection of Federal and State Policies," *Bilingual Research Journal* 29, no. 1 (2005): 1–29, https://doi.org/10.1080/1 5235882.2005.10162821.

18. Mary Carol Combs, "Everything on Its Head: How Arizona's Structured English Immersion Policy Re-Invents Theory and Practice," in *Implementing Educational Language Policy in Arizona: Legal, Historical and Current Practices in SIE*, ed. M. Beatriz Arias and Christian J. Faltis (Bristol, UK: Multilingual Matters, 2012), 59–85.

19. Mary Carol Combs and Sheilah E. Nicholas, "The Effect of Arizona Language Policies on Arizona Indigenous Students," *Language Policy* 11, no. 1 (February 1, 2012): 101–18, https://doi.org/10.1007/s10993-011-9230-7; Wright, "English Language Learners Left Behind."

20. Amy J. Heineke, *Restrictive Language Policy in Practice: English Learners in Arizona* (Bristol, UK: Multilingual Matters, 2017).

21. Sonya Douglass Horsford and Carrie Sampson, "Beyond Legal Remedies: Toward Funding Equity and Improved Educational Opportunities for English Language Learners," in *Law and Education Inequality: Removing Barriers to Educational Opportunities*, ed. Jeffrey C. Bon and Susan C. Sun (Charlotte, NC: Information Age, 2015), 35–48.

22. Stephen Krashen, Kellie Rolstad, and Jeff MacSwan, *Review of "Research Summary and Bibliography for Structured English Immersion Programs" of the Arizona English Language Learners Task Force* (Takoma Park, MD, 2007), https://www.researchgate.net/publication/253707030_Review_of_Research_Summary_and_Bibliography_for_Structured_English_Immersion_Programs_of_the_Arizona_English_Language_Learners_Task_Force; Karen E. Lillie et al., "Separate and Not Equal: The Implementation of Structured English Immersion in Arizona's Classrooms," *Teachers College Record* 114, no. 9 (2012): 1–33, https://doi-org.ezproxy1.lib.asu.edu/10.1177/016146811211400; Francesca López, Elizabeth McEneaney, and Martina Nieswandt, "Language Instruction Educational Programs and Academic Achievement of Latino English Learners: Considerations for States with Changing Demographics," *American Journal of Education* 121, no. 3 (2015): 417–50, https://www.journals.uchicago.edu/doi/abs/10.1086/680410; Patricia Gándara and Gary Orfield, "Why Arizona Matters: The Historical, Legal, and Political Contexts of Arizona's Instructional Policies and US Linguistic Hegemony," *Language Policy* 11, no. 1 (2012): 7–19, https://doi.org/10.1007/s10993-016-9418-y; Elena B. Parra et al., "The Psychological Impact of English Language Immersion on Elementary Age English Language Learners," *Journal of Multilingual Education Research* 5, no. 1 (2014): 4, http://fordham.bepress.com/jmer/vol5/iss1/4.
23. Hipolito R. Corella, "English-Only Backers Ready to Sue," *Arizona Daily Star*, November 19, 2001, quoted in Wayne E. Wright, "The Political Spectacle of Arizona's Proposition 203," *Educational Policy* 19, no. 5 (2005): 662–700, https://doi.org/10.1177/0895904805278066, 1.
24. Flora Ida Ortiz, "Using Social Capital in Interpreting the Careers of Three Latina Superintendents," *Educational Administration Quarterly* 37, no. 1 (2001): 58–85, https://doi.org/10.1177/00131610121969244; Wright, "The Political Spectacle of Arizona's Proposition 203."
25. US Department of Education, National Center for Education Statistics, Common Core of Data (CCD), "Local Education Agency (School District) Universe Survey," 2004-05 v.1c, 2010-11 v.2a, 2022-23 v.1a, https://nces.ed.gov/ccd/pubagency.asp.
26. US Department of Education (2012), "Resolution Agreement: Among the ADE, USDOE, OCR, and USDOJ," OCR Case Number 08-06-4006, DOJ Case Number 169-8-81; available from https://www2.ed.gov.
27. Augustine F. Romero and Martin Sean Arce, "Culture as a Resource: Critically Compassionate Intellectualism and Its Struggle Against Racism, Fascism, and Intellectual Apartheid in Arizona," *Journal of Public Law & Policy* 31 (2009): 179.
28. Nolan L. Cabrera et al., "Missing the (Student Achievement) Forest for All the (Political) Trees: Empiricism and the Mexican American Studies Controversy in Tucson," *American Educational Research Journal* 51, no. 6 (December 24, 2014): 1084–1118, https://doi.org/10.3102/0002831214553705.

29. Ernesto Portillo Jr., "Neto's Tucson: The Vindication of Dolores Huerta," Tucson.com, September 30, 2017, https://tucson.com/news/local/netos-tucson-the-vindication-of-dolores-huerta/article_feb39962-9157-57cc-8a27-941e0130fe57.html.

30. Ann Morse, "Arizona's Immigration Enforcement Laws," National Conference of State Legislatures, July 28, 2011, https://www.ncsl.org/research/immigration/analysis-of-arizonas-immigration-law; Southern Poverty Law Center, "When Mr. Kobach Comes to Town: Nativist Laws and the Community They Damage," Special Report, January 30, 2011, https://www.splcenter.org/sites/default/files/Kobach_Comes_to_Town_final_web.pdf.

31. James E. Rogers College of Law, University of Arizona, "The Impact of SB 1070 on Arizona's Youth," 2024, https://law.arizona.edu/impact-sb-1070-arizonas-youth; Jeffrey S. Passel and D'Vera Cohn, "Unauthorized Immigrant Totals Rise in 7 States, Fall in 14," November 18, 2014, https://www.pewresearch.org/hispanic/2014/11/18/unauthorized-immigrant-totals-rise-in-7-states-fall-in-14/; Naureen Khan, "Five Years After SB 1070, Arizona Immigrants Defy Climate of Intimidation," *Aljazeera America*, March 23, 2015, http://america.aljazeera.com.

32. Arizona House Bill 2281 (2010), Arizona House of Representatives, Forty-Ninth Legislature, Second Regular Session, https://www.azleg.gov/legtext/49leg/2r/summary/h.hb2281_05-03-10_astransmittedtogovernor.doc.htm, 1.

33. Alexis Huicochea, "Ethnic Studies Supporters Overtake TUSD Meeting: Youths Protest Changes to Mexican American Studies Courses," *Arizona Daily Star*, April 27, 2011, https://tucson.com/news/local/education/ethnic-studies-supporters-overtake-tusd-meeting/article_176f8aed-4b95-53fc-9b49-0959cd5a26e5.html#:~:text=The%20board%20was%20scheduled%20to,President%20Mark%20Stegeman%2C%20be%20withdrawn.

34. Cambium Learning, "Curriculum Audit of the Mexican American Studies Department, Tucson Unified School District," May 2, 2011, https://www.tucsonweekly.com/images/blogimages/2011/06/16/1308282079-az_masd_audit_final_1_.pdf, 49.

35. Gary Grado, "Judge Upholds Ethnic Studies Decision, Orders Money Withheld from TUSD," *Arizona Capitol Times*, December 27, 2011, https://azcapitoltimes.com/news/2011/12/27/judge-upholds-ethnic-studies-decision-orders-money-withheld-from-tusd/.

36. Mari Herreras, "County Supe Appoints New TUSD Board Member: UA Econ Lecturer Alexandre Sugiyama," *Tucson Weekly*, December 30, 2011, https://www.tucsonweekly.com/TheRange/archives/2011/12/30/county-supe-appoints-new-tusd-board-member-ua-econ-lecturer-alexandre-sugiyama.

37. Dylan Smith, "Stegeman Ousted as TUSD Board President," *Tucson Sentinel*, August 23, 2011, https://www.tucsonsentinel.com/local/report/082311_tusd_stegeman/stegeman-ousted-as-tusd-board-president/.

38. Dylan Smith, "TUSD Axes Ethnic Studies," *Tucson Sentinel,* July 10, 2012, https://www.tucsonsentinel.com/local/report/011012_tusd_ethnic_studies/tusd-axes-ethnic-studies/.

39. Maggie Astor, "Tucson's Mexican Studies Program Was a Victim of 'Racial Animus,' Judge Says," *New York Times,* August 23, 2017, https://www.nytimes.com/2017/08/23/us/arizona-mexican-american-ruling.html#:~:text=Douglas-,Judge%20A.,program%20in%20Tucson%27s%20public%20schools.

40. KUGN9, "Daily Show's Satirical Take on the Mexican-American Studies Controversy," YouTube, April 3, 2012, https://www.youtube.com/watch?v=y1miLXqpcGs.

41. Mari Herreras, "The District's Dozen," *Tucson Weekly,* September 20, 2012, https://www.tucsonweekly.com/tucson/the-districts-dozen/Content?oid=3531061.

42. Fernada Echavarri, "1 TUSD Incumbent, 2 Newcomers Claim Seats," Arizona Public Media, November 9, 2012, https://www.azpm.org.

43. Kenneth Blackwell, "On-Cycle School Board Elections Make It Easier to Vote," July 25, 2022, https://americafirstpolicy.com/issues/20220725-on-cycle-school-board-elections-make-it-easier-to-vote.

CHAPTER 5

1. William H. Frey and Ruy A. Teixeira, "America's New Swing Region: The Political Demography and Geography of the Mountain West," in *Changing Politics and Demographics in the Mountain West,* ed. Ruy A. Teixeira (Washington, DC: Brookings Institution, 2012), 11–68.

2. National Center for Educational Statistics, "Digest of Educational Statistics: Table 215.30," 2017, https://nces.ed.gov/programs/digest/d19/tables/dt19_215.30.asp.

3. Trevon Milliard, "County Schools Struggle with Growing Enrollment," *Las Vegas Review-Journal,* August 24, 2014, www.reviewjournal.com.

4. Carrie Sampson and Sarah Diem, "NEPC Review—The Third Way: A Guide to Implementing Innovation Schools (Progressive Policy Institute, October 2020)," National Education Policy Center, January 21, 2021, https://nepc.colorado.edu/thinktank/innovation-schools.

5. Sonya Douglass Horsford, Carrie Sampson, and Felicia Forletta, "School Resegregation in the Mississippi of the West: Community Counternarratives on the Return to Neighborhood Schools in Las Vegas, 1968–1994," *Teachers College Record* 115, no. 11 (2013), https://eric.ed.gov/?id=EJ1020155.

6. Horsford et al., "School Resegregation in the Mississippi of the West."

7. Veronica Terriquez et al., "Expanding Student Opportunities: Prime 6 Program Review, Clark County School District, Las Vegas, Nevada," Civil Rights Project at the University of California, Los Angeles (UCLA), June 1, 2009, https://civilrightsproject.ucla.edu/research/k-12-education/integration-and-diversity/expanding-student-opportunities-prime-6-program-review-clark-county-school-district-las-vegas-nevada/?searchterm=Expanding%20student%20

opportunities:%20Prime%206%20Program%20review,%20Clark%20County%20School%20District,%20Las%20Vegas,%20Nevada.

8. Jay Chambers et al., *Study of a New Method of Funding for Public Schools in Nevada* (San Mateo, CA: American Institutes for Research, 2012), https://www.air.org/sites/default/files/downloads/report/AIR_NV_Funding_Study_Sept2012_0.pdf.

9. National Education Association, "Rankings of the States 2011 and Estimates of School Statistics 2012," 2015, https://files.eric.ed.gov/fulltext/ED583098.pdf.

10. John Augenblick et al., "Estimating the Cost of an Adequate Education in Nevada," Augenblick, Palaich, & Associates, Denver, August 2006, https://nevadahomeschoolnetwork.com/WP/wp-content/uploads/2015/10/Estimating_the_Cost_of_an_Adequate_Education_in_Nevada.pdf.

11. Chambers et al., *Study of a New Method.*

12. Carrie Sampson, "Task Force on K–12 Public Education Funding Technical Advisory Committee Exhibit," May 21, 2014, https://www.leg.state.nv.us/App/InterimCommittee/REL/Document/6250?rewrote=1.

13. Clark County School District, *Board of Trustees Brochure,* 2011–2012, http://ccsd.net/trustees/pdf/misc/board-brochure11.pdf.

14. John Carver and Miriam Carver, "Carver's Policy Governance Model," 2016, The Governance Coach, https://www.governancecoach.com/policy-governance/.

15. Marybeth Scow, "Nevada Legislative Counsel Bureau Research Library," Exhibit F, Senate Committee on Human Resources/Ed, February 19, 2007, https://www.leg.state.nv.us/74th/Exhibits/Senate/HR/SHR273F.pdf, 7.

16. Nevada Revised Statutes, "Chapter 386—System of Public Instruction: NRS 386.320," n.d., https://www.leg.state.nv.us/nrs/NRS-386.html#NRS386Sec320.

17. Aída Walqui, "Clark County Public Schools, Nevada Report on Instruction for English Language Learners," June 2012, 10–22, https://www.boarddocs.com/nv/ccsdlv/Board.nsf/files/A8SPW25BA2AB/$file/04.14.16%20Ref.%207.01.pdf.

18. Tovin Lapan, "Nevada's Hispanics Come of Age Politically," *Las Vegas Sun News,* February 17, 2013, https://lasvegassun.com/news/2013/feb/17/nevadas-hispanics-come-age-politically/.

19. Nevada Department of Education, "Annual Summary Report: SB 504 Implementation Report School Year 2013–14 and Fall 2014 Update," February 1, 2015, https://www.leg.state.nv.us/Division/Research/Library/Documents/Reports-ToLeg/2013-2015/198-15.pdf.

20. Carrie Sampson, "'The State Pulled a Fast One on Us': A Critical Policy Analysis of State-Level Policies Affecting English Learners from District-Level Perspectives," *Educational Policy* 33, no. 1 (2019): 3–15, https://doi.org/10.1177/0895904818807324.

21. Sampson, "The State Pulled a Fast One."

22. Chad W. Buckendahl et al., "Nevada External Outcomes Evaluation," January 7, 2019, https://www.acsventures.com/wp-content/uploads/2019/01/2018-

Nevada-External-Outcomes-Evaluation-Report-20190113-REVISED.pdf; Kenny Guinn Center for Policy Priorities, "Zoom and Victory Programs in Nevada," 2019, https://guinncenter.org/wp-content/uploads/2019/02/Guinn-Center-Zoom-Victory-Report-2019.pdf.

23. Sonya Douglass Horsford, Carrie Sampson, and Felicia Forletta, "School Reseg-regation in the Mississippi of the West: Community Counternarratives on the Return to Neighborhood Schools in Las Vegas, 1968–1994," *Teachers College Record* 115, no. 11 (2013).

24. Clark County School District, "Pledge of Achievement Strategic," 10 (emphasis added).

25. Council of the Great City Schools, "A Framework for Foundational Literacy Skills Instruction for English Learners: Instructional Practice and Materials Considerations," Spring 2023, https://www.cgcs.org/cms/lib/DC00001581/Centricity/domain/35/publication%20docs/CGCS_Foundational%20Literacy%20Skills_Pub_v11.pdf; Jennifer O'Day, "Good Instruction Is Good for Everyone—Or Is It? English Language Learners in a Balanced Literacy Approach," *Journal of Education for Students Placed at Risk* 14 (2009): 97–119, https://doi.org/10.1080/10824660802715502.

26. Buckendahl et al., "Nevada External Outcomes Evaluation"; Kenny Guinn Center for Policy Priorities, "Zoom and Victory Programs."

27. I. M. Umansky and S. F. Reardon, "Reclassification Patterns Among Latino English Learner Students in Bilingual, Dual Immersion, and English Immersion Classrooms," *American Educational Research Journal* 51, no. 5 (2014): 879–912, https://doi.org/10.3102/0002831214545110; Ofelia García and Joanne Kleifgen, *Educating Emergent Bilinguals: Policies, Programs, and Practices for English Language Learners*, ed. Ofelia García and Joanne Kleifgen (New York: Teachers College Press, 2010); Virginia P. Collier and Wayne P. Thomas, "Validating the Power of Bilingual Schooling: Thirty-Two Years of Large-Scale, Longitudinal Research," *Annual Review of Applied Linguistics* 37, no. 2017 (2017): 203–17, https://doi.org/10.1017/S0267190517000034.

CHAPTER 6

1. SoundOut, "Students on School Boards in Utah," April 6, 2015, https://soundout.org/2015/04/06/students-on-school-boards-in-utah/.

2. Student school board members were passive in their level of engagement in board meetings, and since they were nonvoting members, they were not interviewed as part of this study. Salt Lake City School District, "Board Policy B-1: Board of Education Legal Status, Responsibilities, and Ethics," 2015, https://resources.finalsite.net/images/v1696539086/slcschoolsorg/qc7eoubtv suu5cjsj6oc/b-1-policy-english.pdf.

3. Morgan Jacobsen, "Salt Lake School District Superintendent McKell Withers Announces Retirement," *Deseret News*, August 31, 2015, https://www.deseret.

com/2015/8/31/20571300/salt-lake-school-district-superintendent-mckell-withers-announces-retirement.

4. Sanders Connor, "A Revolving Superintendent's Door, Board Member Squabbling and a Blistering Audit Mark Three Tumultuous Years for the Salt Lake City School District," *Salt Lake City Weekly*, February 1, 2023, https://www.cityweekly.net/utah/a-revolving-superintendents-door-board-member-squabbling-and-a-blistering-audit-mark-three-tumultuous-years-for-the-salt-lake-city-school-di/Content?oid=19520526; Michael Lee, "Here's What SLC's New Superintendent Has Planned for the School District," *Salt Lake Tribune*, July 7, 2023, https://www.sltrib.com/news/education/2023/07/07/where-magic-happens-salt-lake-city/.

5. William H. Frey and Ruy A. Teixeira, "America's New Swing Region: The Political Demography and Geography of the Mountain West," in *America's New Swing Region: Changing Politics and Demographics in the Mountain West*, ed. Ruy A. Teixeira (Washington, DC: Brookings Institution, 2012), 11–68.

6. Josh Zumbrun, "In Depth: America's Recession-Proof Cities," *Forbes*, April 29, 2008, https://www.forbes.com/2008/04/29/cities-recession-places-forbeslife-cx_jz_0429realestate.html?sh=5e88eab179ac.

7. Terry Greene Sterling, "Utah: An Economy Powered by Multilingual Missionaries," *The Atlantic*, July 23, 2012, https://www.theatlantic.com/politics/archive/2012/07/utah-an-economy-powered-by-multilingual-missionaries/428250/.

8. National Education Association, "Rankings & Estimates: Rankings of the States 2011 and Estimates of School Statistics 2012," 2015, https://files.eric.ed.gov/fulltext/ED583098.pdf.

9. Cubit Planning, "Utah Counties by Population," Utah Demographics, 2024, https://www.utah-demographics.com/counties_by_population.

10. US Department of Education, National Center for Education Statistics, Common Core of Data, "Public Elementary/Secondary School Universe Survey," 2009-10 v.2a, 2010-11 v.2a, 2011-12 v.1a, 2012-13 v.1a, 2013-14 v.1a, 2014, http://nces.ed.gov/ccd/elsi/; US Department of Education, National Center for Education Statistics, Common Core of Data, "Survey of Local Government Finances, School Systems (F-33)," 2009-10 (FY 2010) v.1a, 2010-11 (FY 2011) v.1a, 2011-12 (FY 2012) v.1a, 2014, http://nces.ed.gov/ccd/elsi/; US Department of Education, National Center for Education Statistics, Common Core of Data, "Local Education Agency (School District) Universe Survey," 2009-10 v.2a, 2010-11 v.2a, 2011-12 v.1a, 2012-13 v.1a, 2013-14 v.1a, 2014, http://nces.ed.gov/ccd/elsi/.

11. US Department of Education, "Public Elementary/Secondary School"; US Department of Education, "Survey of Local Government"; US Department of Education, "Local Education Agency."

12. National Alliance for Public Charter Schools, "Utah Charter Schools," 2022, https://publiccharters.org/charter-school-state-resources/utah/#:~:text=

Charter%20schools%20account%20for%20137,specified%20institution%20of %20higher%20education; Jordan School District, "Jordan School District Maps," n.d., https://jordandistrict.maps.arcgis.com/home/index.html.

13. Logan Stefanich, "Where Have All the Children Gone? Utah School Enroll- ment Shows Recent Decline," KSL.com, August 16, 2023, https://www.ksl.com/ article/50710277/where-have-all-the-children-gone-utah-school-enrollment- shows-recent-decline#:~:text=According%20to%20the%20data%2C%20the, Utah%20charter%20schools%20at%201.3%25; National School Choice Week, "Utah State Guide," 2024, https://schoolchoiceweek.com/guide-school- choice-utah/#:~:text=Utah%20is%20one%20of%20just,where%20the%20 school%20is%20located;Benjamin Wood,"Utah'sOpen-EnrollmentLawAllows for 'White Flight' from Troubled Schools, Some Parents Say," *Salt Lake Tribune*, September 13, 2015, https://www.sltrib.com/; Marjorie Cortez, "Salt Lake City School District's Enrollment Is Half of What It Was in the 1960s," *Deseret News*, September 12, 2023, https://www.deseret.com/utah/2023/9/12/23870261/ salt-lake-city-school-district-closures-enrollment-decline.

14. Benjamin Wood, "Salt Lake City School Board Considering Property Tax Increase," *Deseret News*, May 17, 2013, https://www.deseret.com/2013/5/17/ 20519793/salt-lake-city-school-board-considering-property-tax-increase; US Department of Education, "Public Elementary/Secondary School"; US Depart- ment of Education, "Survey of Local Government"; US Department of Educa- tion, "Local Education Agency."

15. Salt Lake City School District, "Annual Budget: Fiscal Year 2013–14," 2013, https://resources.finalsite.net/images/v1602764601/slcschoolsorg/jyna sj4s8n98rdem4chk/2013-14-annual-budget-english.pdf.

16. Church of Jesus Christ of Latter-day Saints, "Missionary Program," Newsroom, 2024, https://newsroom.churchofjesuschrist.org/topic/missionary-program.

17. Tad Walch, "LDS Missionary Numbers to Peak at 88,000; More to Use and Pay for Digital Devices," *Deseret News*, July 2, 2014, https://www.deseret. com/2014/7/3/20544282/lds-missionary-numbers-to-peak-at-88-000-more- to-use-and-pay-for-digital-devices; Helen Whitney and Jane Barnes, "The Mormons: The Mission," WGBH Educational Foundation, 2007, https://www. pbs.org/mormons/faqs/mission.html; Church of Jesus Christ of Latter-day Saints, "Facts and Statistics," Newsroom, 2024, https://newsroom.churchofje- suschrist.org/facts-and-statistics; Church of Jesus Christ of Latter-day Saints, "Missionary Program."

18. Melinda Rogers, "Demand High for Dual Immersion Programs in Utah," *Salt Lake Tribune*, August 4, 2012, https://archive.sltrib.com/article.php?id=545918 46&itype=CMSID.

19. Vote Smart, "HB 497, Immigration Enforcement Act—Utah Key Vote," 2021, https://justfacts.votesmart.org/bill/13006/34286/immigration-enforcement-

act; "Utah Illegal Immigration Enforcement Act" (2011), HB 497, Utah State Legislature, https://le.utah.gov/~2011/bills/hbillamd/hb0497s01.pdf.

20. David Montero, "Federal Judge Blocks Utah Law Targeting Illegal Immigration," *Salt Lake Tribune*, May 11, 2011, https://archive.sltrib.com/article.php?id=51788264&itype=CMSID.

21. Brittany Felder, "Utah Reaches Settlement over Immigration Law," *Jurist*, November 26, 2014, https://www.jurist.org/news/2014/11/utah-reaches-settlement-over-immigration-law/.

22. Utah State Board of Education, "Councils," 2024, https://schools.utah.gov/schoollandtrust/councils.

23. *Lau v. Nichols*, 414 US 563 (1974).

24. Cited in Mary Ann Zehr, "Under Federal Pressure, District Addresses Ells," *EducationWeek*, June 10, 2009, https://www.edweek.org/policy-politics/under-federal-pressure-district-addresses-ells/2009/06.

25. Carrie Sampson and Sonya Horsford, "Putting the Public Back in Public Education: Community Advocacy and Every Student Succeeds Act," *Journal of School Leadership* 27 (September 2017): 725–54.

26. Zehr, "Under Federal Pressure," 12.

27. Jamie Leite and Raquel Cook, "Utah: Making Immersion Mainstream," in *Building Bilingual Education Systems: Forces, Mechanisms and Counterweights*, ed. Fred Genesee and Peeter Mehisto (Cambridge, MA: Cambridge University Press, 2015), 83–96.

28. Nina Porzucki, "Utah Bets Big on Foreign Language Learning, but Not Everyone Is on Board," *The World*, March 18, 2015, https://theworld.org/stories/2015-03-18/utah-bets-big-foreign-language-learning-not-everyone-board.

29. Cited in Porzucki, "Utah: Making Immersion Mainstream," paras. 5–6.

30. Howard A. Stephenson, "Education Reform: Critical Languages Program" (2007), SB 80, Utah State Legislature, https://le.utah.gov/~2007/bills/static/SB0080.html.

31. Howard A. Stephenson, "International Education Initiative: Critical Languages Program" (2008), SB 41, Utah State Legislature, https://le.utah.gov/~2008/bills/sbillenr/SB0041.htm.

32. Utah Dual Language Immersion, "History of Utah DLI," 2023, https://www.utahdli.org/history-of-utah-dli/.

33. Leite and Cook, "Utah: Making Immersion Mainstream."

34. Stephenson, "Education Reform: Critical Languages Program."

35. Utah Education Policy Center, University of Utah, "Dual Language Immersion Program Participation," accessed February 17, 2024, https://www.uepc.utah.edu/wp-content/uploads/sites/103/2019/02/Program-Participation-Brief.pdf.

36. Council of the Great City Schools, "English Language Learners in America's Great City Schools: Demographics, Achievement, and Staffing," April 2019,

https://www.cgcs.org/cms/lib/DC00001581/Centricity/domain/35/publication%20docs/CGCS_ELL%20Survey%20Report.pdf.

37. *Lau v. Nichols.*

38. Gloria Ladson-Billings, *The Dreamkeepers: Successful Teachers of African American Children*, 3rd ed. (Hoboken, NJ: John Wiley, 2022); Linda Skrla, Kathryn Bell McKenzie, and James Joseph Scheurich, *Using Equity Audits to Create Equitable and Excellent Schools* (Thousand Oaks, CA: Corwin, 2009); Glenn E. Singleton, *Courageous Conversations About Race: A Field Guide for Achieving Equity in Schools and Beyond*, 3rd ed. (Thousand Oaks, CA: SAGE, 2021).

39. Mohamed Berray, "A Critical Literary Review of the Melting Pot and Salad Bowl Assimilation and Integration Theories," *Journal of Ethnic and Cultural Studies* 6, no. 1 (June 2019): 142–51, https://doi.org/10.29333/ejecs/217.

40. Ilana M. Umansky and Sean F. Reardon, "Reclassification Patterns Among Latino English Learner Students in Bilingual, Dual Immersion, and English Immersion Classrooms," *American Educational Research Journal* 51, no. 5 (2014): 879–912, https://doi.org/10.3102/0002831214545110.

CHAPTER 7

1. Thomas L. Alsbury, *The Future of School Board Governance: Relevancy and Revelation* (Lanham, MD: Rowman & Littlefield Education, 2008); William G. Howell, *Besieged School Boards and the Future of Education Politics* (Washington, DC: Brookings Institution, 2005).

2. Allison Mattheis, Yanin Adila, and Sivan Levaton, "'We Think Differently': Student Representation and Voice at the Los Angeles Unified School District Board of Education," *Journal of Ethical Educational Leadership* (2018): 155–79; Daniella Hall Sutherland, "'Tell Them Local Control Is Important': A Case Study of Democratic, Community-Centered School Boards," *Education Policy Analysis Archives* 30, no. 178 (December 13, 2022), https://doi.org/10.14507/epaa.30.7439; George E. Burns, "Factors and Themes in Native Education and School Boards/First Nations Tuition Negotiations and Tuition Agreement Schooling," *Canadian Journal of Native Education* 22, no. 1 (1998): 53–66, https://eric.ed.gov/?id=EJ570807; Katherine Cumings Mansfield and Marina Lambrinou, "'This Is Not Who We Are': Students Leading for Anti-Racist Policy Changes in Alexandria City Public Schools, Virginia," *Educational Policy* 36, no. 1 (2022): 19–56, https://doi.org/10.1177/08959048211059214; Shaneé Adrienne Washington, "Sustaining Indigenous Students' and Families' Well-Being and Culture in an Ontario School Board," *Journal of Professional Capital and Community* (2020), https://doi.org/10.1108/JPCC-06-2020-0049.

3. Carrie Sampson, "(Im)Possibilities of Latinx School Board Members' Educational Leadership Toward Equity," *Educational Administration Quarterly* 55, no. 2 (2019): 296–327, https://doi.org/10.1177/0013161X18799482; Carrie Sampson, "From a Lighthouse to a Foghorn: A School Board' s Navigation

Toward Equity for English Learners," *American Journal of Education* 125, no. 4 (2019): 521–46; Carrie Sampson, "'The State Pulled a Fast One on Us': A Critical Policy Analysis of State-Level Policies Affecting English Learners from District-Level Perspectives," *Educational Policy* 33, no. 1 (2019): 3–15, https://doi.org/10.1177/0895904818807324; Carrie Sampson et al., "Open Enrollment and Disrupting the Political Ecology of U.S. Public Education," *Peabody Journal of Education* 97, no. 1 (January 21, 2022): 62–73, https://doi.org/10.108 0/0161956X.2022.2026721; Carrie Sampson and Melanie Bertrand, "'This Is Civil Disobedience. I'll Continue': The Racialization of School Board Meeting Rules," *Journal of Education Policy*, 2020, https://doi.org/10.1080/02680939.20 20.1778795; Carrie Sampson and Sonya Douglass Horsford, "Putting the Public Back in Public Education: Community Advocacy and Education Leadership Under the Every Student Succeeds Act," *Journal of School Leadership* 27 (2017): 725–75, https://doi.org/10.1177/10526846170270050; E. O. Turner, *Suddenly Diverse: How School Districts Manage Race and Inequality* (Chicago: University of Chicago Press, 2020); James Wright et al., "The Color of Neoliberal Reform: A Critical Race Policy Analysis of School District Takeovers in Michigan," *Urban Education* 55, no. 3 (November 25, 2018): 424–47, https://doi. org/10.1177/0042085918806943; Julie A. Marsh et al., "The Process and Politics of Educational Governance Change in New Orleans, Los Angeles, and Denver," *American Educational Research Journal* 58, no. 1 (February 1, 2021): 107–59, https://doi.org/10.3102/0002831220921475; Melanie Bertrand and Carrie Sampson, "Challenging Systemic Racism in School Board Meetings Through Intertextual Co-optation," *Critical Studies in Education* 63, no. 3 (2020): 1–17, https://doi.org/10.1080/17508487.2020.1765823; Melanie Bertrand and Carrie Sampson, "Exposing the White Innocence Playbook of School District Leaders," *Equity and Excellence in Education*, 2022, https://doi.org/10.1080/106656 84.2021.2021669; Muhammad A. Khalifa et al., "Racism? Administrative and Community Perspectives in Data-Driven Decision-Making: Systemic Perspectives Versus Technical-Rational Perspectives," *Urban Education* 49, no. 2 (2014): 147–81; Richard S. L. Blissett and Thomas L. Alsbury, "Disentangling the Personal Agenda: Identity and School Board Members' Perceptions of Problems and Solutions," *Leadership and Policy in Schools* 17, no. 4 (October 2, 2018): 454–86, https://doi.org/10.1080/15700763.2017.1326142; Sarah Diem, Erica Frankenberg, and Colleen Cleary, "Factors That Influence School Board Policy Making," *Educational Administration Quarterly* 51, no. 5 (December 2, 2015): 712–52, https://doi.org/10.1177/0013161X15589367; Tina M. Trujillo, "The Disproportionate Erosion of Local Control: Urban School Boards, High-Stakes Accountability, and Democracy," *Educational Policy* 27, no. 2 (2013): 334–59, https://doi.org/10.1177/0895904812465118.

4. Becky Vevea, "Chicago's Elected School Board Is Coming Soon. Here's What You Need to Know," *Chalkbeat*, May 4, 2023, https://www.

chalkbeat.org/chicago/2023/5/4/23711633/chicago-school-board-of-education-elections-faq-guide/.

5. David Tyack, *Seeking Common Ground: Public Schools in a Diverse Society* (Cambridge, MA: Harvard University Press, 2017), 130.

6. David C. Berliner and Gene V. Glass, *50 Myths & Lies That Threaten America's Public Schools: The Real Crisis in Education* (New York: Teachers College Press, 2014).

ACKNOWLEDGMENTS

I NEVER THOUGHT I would write a book, especially a book about school boards. But here I am, and here it is. It is interesting how, when you are open to the possibilities, life will take you in directions that you never could even have imagined. To make this book possible, many people opened the doors, provided support, offered guidance, and inspired me. To each and every one of you, thank you so much!

I will start by thanking the two most precious souls in my life—my children, Rose and Oliver. Being a mother-scholar is no joke—it's beautiful, difficult, and insightful. In this role, I have learned more than I have in any classroom. Some believe that children choose their parents, and if that is true, I am incredibly lucky and very grateful that they chose me to be their mother. They have made me an even fiercer advocate for educational equity. Because of them, I have taken what I have learned in my own research to push and support educational leaders, policy makers, and school board members in advancing equity. They, along with Isaac— who came along later but is now the oldest kiddo in our family—are brilliant, witty, funny, know that "Mom is writing a book" (which I'm sure they are tired of hearing), and motivate me every day to stay on this path. And to my partner, Chris, thank you for your love, patience, and support, for cooking my favorite foods, helping care for my babies, and even reviewing parts of this book. I am also incredibly grateful to my mother, who passed away before I began this book project, but helped me take care of my babies while I did so much of the research that shows up in this book. Thank you to the other parts of the village that support me and my babies: Mea (my cousin-sista in this life, who has been there for me through every milestone—I love you!), my father (the first to call me *doctor* and plant that seed for my future), my big brothers Tommy and Mike (your love and support is a beautiful gift), all the aunties, uncles, cousins, nieces, and nephews, Roslyn, Ruth, Salina, and Ms. Barb.

Thank you to my academic mentors and womyntors. Sonya Douglass, your guidance and support in the academy and in life from the day I stepped foot in your class helped make this book possible and are something that I will never forget and will forever be grateful for. Anita Revilla, you showed me what it meant to speak my truth and show up authentically in the academy—inspiring me to be fierce in the writing of this book. And thank you to other amazing mentors/womyntors who poured into me, lifted me up, and paved the way for this book: Doris Watson, Janelle Scott, Linda Tillman, Rich Milner, Sarah Diem, Ericka Turner, David Stovall, Tyrone Howard, Anna Lukemeyer, Angela Valenzuela, Terah Venzant Chambers, Ann Ishimura, Anjalé Welton, Michelle Young, Sherman Dorn, Jill Koyoma, Alfredo Artiles, Audrey Beardsely, Lee Bernick, Gustavo Fischman (encouraging me to write a book when I first got to Arizona State University), Anjala Krishen, Sheneka Williams, and many more.

To my sister and brother scholars and friends who have held me up, shared their work, reviewed my work, encouraged me, and listened to me vent about this book, thank you—starting with the #fiercepeloscholars, who support my academic work and my wellness: Claudia Cervantes-Soon, Amanda Tachine, Ruth López, Subini Annamma, Omaris Zamora; and the #badasspeolomoms, whose empathy as mammas, accountability, and friendship on and off the bike helped to keep me grounded and healthy while writing: Cristina Hernandez, Sinitra DeHaven-Harvey, Jennifer Chin, Tiana Hill, Mallory Cyr, Jasmine Rubalcava, and

Alicia Vink. To my other academic homies who have supported me throughout this chapter of life in so many ways that helped to make the book happen, thank you: Laura Chávez-Moreno (so grateful for our weekly check-ins!), Claudia García-Louis and Decoteau Irby (I appreciate your support in the proposal stage), Lok-Sze Wong, Melanie Bertrand, Keon McGuire, Daniel Liou, Lauren Katzman, Ersula Ore, Vanessa Fonseca-Chávez, Monica De La Torre, Antonio Duran, Dawn Demps, Emily Hodge, Steven Nelson, Sybil Durand, Terrance Green, Michelle Renée Valladares, Meseret Hailu, Yalda Kaveh, Tolani Britton, Ericka Weathers, and Nicole Marquez. To my beautiful research team that I colead with Ruth and who make this academic work fun, thank you for working on other aspects of school board–related research with me while I also wrote this book: Jasmine Pham, Alfonso Ayala, Justine Parnell, Christina Bustos, and a special shout-out to Jami Carmichael and Emily Nunez-Eddy, who also helped me with the nitty-gritty to wrap this book up. To my other friends who have supported and inspired me in this part of my journey, thank you: Chandeni Sendall, Catherine Bons, and Hillary Walsh. And thank you to my editor, Karen Adler, whose words of encouragement, detailed feedback, and gentle nudges helped carry me to the finish line. I'm sure I forgot to name many other folks who showed me their support, but please know I appreciate you.

Finally, this book would not be possible without those school board members, school district leaders, and community members who shared their stories with me and all the beautiful children we serve. Many of them showed me what it looks like to govern our public schools in a way that advances educational equity. The work is hard and often thankless. I see you. THANK YOU!

ABOUT THE AUTHOR

CARRIE R. SAMPSON, PHD, is an associate professor in the Division of Educational Leadership and Innovation at Arizona State University. Her scholarship explores how educational leadership and policy making at the K–12 level influence equity and social justice for minoritized communities. Dr. Sampson's research is centered at the school district level with an emphasis on governance (particularly the role of school boards, community advocacy, and district leadership). She has received various awards and recognition for her scholarship, including the National Academy of Education/Spencer Postdoctoral Fellowship, Ford Foundation Postdoctoral Fellowship, American Educational Research Division A (Administration, Organization, and Leadership) Early Career Award, and the UCEA William J. Davis Award for her article published in *Educational Administration Quarterly*, entitled "(Im)Possibilities of Latinx School Board Members' Educational Leadership Toward Equity." Dr. Sampson also serves as a fellow for the National Education Policy Center. Her degrees include a PhD in Public Affairs and a Graduate Certificate in Women's Studies from University of Nevada, Las Vegas, a MS in Cultural Foundations of Education from Syracuse University, and a BS in Economics from University of Nevada, Reno. Finally, Dr. Sampson is a proud and active mother of two school-aged children who attend public schools.

INDEX